PatternReview.com

# 1,000

## CLEVER SEWING
## SHORTCUTS & TIPS

**Creative Publishing international**

Copyright © 2010 Creative Publishing international, Inc.

Every effort was made to contact members for their permission to print their tips, and to credit tips to the appropriate members. We greatly appreciate all the tips sent in by members of PatternReview.com, and regret that we are unable to use all of them in the book.

First published in the United States of America by
Creative Publishing international, Inc., a member of
Quayside Publishing Group
400 First Avenue North
Suite 300
Minneapolis, MN 55401
1-800-328-3895
www.creativepub.com

ISBN-13: 978-1-58923-502-1
ISBN-10: 1-58923-502-9

10 9 8 7 6 5 4

**Library of Congress Cataloging-in-Publication Data**

Prakash, Deepika.
  Patternreview.com 1,000 clever sewing shortcuts & tips : top-rated favorites from sewing fans and master teachers / Deepika Prakash ; foreword by Sandra Betzina.
      p. cm.
  Summary: "One thousand sewing tips compiled from members of the popular sewing website: www.PatternReview.com plus five classes on specific sewing techniques taught by leading sewing specialists"--Provided by publisher.
  ISBN-13: 978-1-58923-502-1 (soft cover)
  ISBN-10: 1-58923-502-9 (soft cover)
  1. Machine sewing. 2. Machine sewing--Technique. I. Title.

  TT713.P73 2010
  646.2--dc22

                                                                2010016770

Developmental editor: Carol Spier
Cover Design: Dutton & Serman Design
Book Design: Dutton & Serman Design
Illustrations: Heather Lambert
Photographs:
      Glenn Scott Photography: 37, 77, 99, 150, 162
      Michael DePhilippi: 38, 39, 40, 78, 79, 80
      Courtesy of Kenneth D. King: 100-104
      Courtesy of Shannon Gifford: 151-153
      Courtesy of Anna Mazur: 163-165

Printed in China

PatternReview.com

# 1,000
## CLEVER SEWING
## SHORTCUTS
## & TIPS

**Top-Rated Favorites from Sewing Fans and Master Teachers**

**Deepika Prakash**

Foreword by Sandra Betzina

# CONTENTS

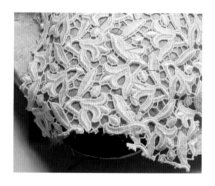

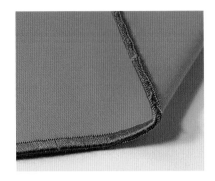

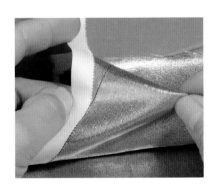

# Dedication

To Shannon Gifford, beloved teacher, mentor, and above all, a Friend.

From FBA to Stitch and Flip Jacket construction to her Beginner 101 sewing classes, Shannon de-mystified the sewing process for everyone. While teaching, she went above and beyond to help students achieve the perfect fit. Whether it was a small dart or a princess seam, she never gave up. She always had a solution for every sewing dilemma.

On Monday, April 19th, 2010, we said goodbye to Shannon for the last time. However, her legacy still remains on PatternReview.com, in her teachings, her students, and her kindness, which spread far and beyond. Even in her last days, she was giving sewing tips.

To all my sewing friends around the world: You've supported me in this journey and continue to inspire me each day with your creativity. And to women everywhere: This book stems from a simple idea I had a number of years ago that evolved into PatternReview.com, and I am very passionate about it. I have run this online sewing community since 2001 and during that time, seen so many of my members afflicted with breast cancer. They have inspired me to donate all royalties from this book to breast cancer research in their honor. So here's another reason to feel good about your purchase of this collection of sewing tips—you are helping millions of people out there you don't even know.

–Deepika Prakash
Founder, PatternReview.com

# Acknowledgments

The coming together of this book was truly a team effort under the expert guidance of Carol Spier, my editor, and Deborah Cannarella, who commissioned it and with whom I spent weeks brainstorming the concept. I'd like to thank Shannon Gifford, Susan Khalje, Kenneth King, Anna Mazur, and Sarah Veblen for generously contributing their expertise despite their busy schedule. Special thanks go to the lovely Sandra Betzina, who wrote the foreword. I also thank, from the bottom of my heart, all the PatternReview.com members whose participation on the site provided the content. After all, without you, PatternReview.com would just be me writing reviews and commenting on them! And how lonely would I be then? The unsung heroes of this story are the volunteers who help out on the site, keeping it fun and organized for everyone else. You guys ROCK!

I wish to express my gratitude to all the independent fabric and pattern storeowners who pour their passion for sewing into their business and provide us with inspiration every day. Also to the pattern companies who listen to PatternReview.com members and design patterns we want so we too can be runway ready!

And last, but not the least, I thank Creative Publishing international for helping me to bring this wonderful collection of sewing tips to you.

–Deepika

# FOREWORD

PatternReview.com is something garment sewers needed for a long time. Maybe we didn't know we needed it, but visionary Deepika Prakash did, and she created this wonderful online service and community. Finally we have a forum where we can share the good news about our sewing endeavors as well as the bad, where we can write about our experience with a specific pattern and even post photos of the way it turned out. Deepika has given sewing enthusiasts all over the world a way to benefit from each other's experience. Who wants to waste time making a pattern that is just so-so, not to mention spoiling a beautiful piece of fabric? And how wonderful to see that that pattern we've been yearning to try worked out beautifully for someone else—now we can happily make it too. Kudos for PatternReview.com! There are many good things on PatternReview.com in addition to the reviews, and among my favorites are the clever and useful tips so generously posted by many of the users. I'm excited that Deepika has collected the best of them here. You will so enjoy and treasure this wonderful book, which epitomizes the spirit and value of PatternReview.com.

Sandra Betzina

# INTRODUCTION

## Murphy's laws of sewing

- When you are two inches away from the end of the last seam in your project, you will run out of bobbin thread.
- You will break your last needle five minutes after the local fabric store closes.
- Buttonholes on your practice piece will go like a dream. The first one you do on the real thing will be a mess!

You've experienced this haven't you? I have, and so have many others who continue to share and inspire each other every day through their wonderful projects and tips posted on PatternReview.com.

Let's face it, how many of us have friends and family members who really understand how exciting it is to make that first bound buttonhole or perfectly match a plaid? They don't understand why it is so important that the inside of the garment look as nice as the outside. Oh, and how much fun it is to insert your first zipper–it's like magic. But they don't get it. They can't; they don't sew. We do! All 200,000-plus of us. When you flip the pages of this book, you'll see how fun sewing can be when you learn from others like you, who share their knowledge and discoveries. But before we get started, and because everyone loves a good story, let me tell you mine.

## The story of PatternReview.com

When I decided I wanted to try my hand at sewing, back in 2001, I had no idea what I was getting myself into. So I did what I do when I need help with something: I searched online for help. I made friends and got advice through Internet message boards. But it was only after I bought and returned two sewing machines that I realized I needed more than that. I needed to do more research, to find out what works and what doesn't. After a couple of successful attempts at making simple elastic-waist skirts, I made a fitted blouse–not realizing there is a lot more to a pattern than what is indicated on the envelope. So I started thinking: what if there was a Web site where people like me could share their experiences on specific patterns and sewing machines? After discussing this with a few friends,

I decided to put my plan into motion, and a few weeks later, on November 28, 2001, PatternReview.com was born. As the name suggests, the site is primarily a place for sewers to review and share their experiences with sewing patterns. As the word spread, I started getting requests to add reviews for books, sewing shops, and expos, for fitting help, tips and techniques, message boards, online classes and so much more. The Web site today is a true global community of sewers who share a passion: Sewing and Creativity! It's a place where you'll find everything you need to be successful at creating your own fashions, in your own style.

When I travel, members of PatternReview.com tell me their story, bits and pieces of which you'll read in this book. They tell me how much their sewing has improved since they joined the site, how easy it was finding their dream sewing machine after reading honest, unbiased reviews from the members. They tell me about the friends they've made—and the mistakes they've avoided too. If you are a PatternReview.com member, this is YOUR book. You made this happen! And if you're unfamiliar with the Web site and wondering whether or not this book will help you, let me tell you a little bit about it.

## 1,000 sewing tips

Hanging out online at PatternReview.com is fun, but sometimes you just need to curl up in bed with a good book—this book. The tips and techniques gathered here are unique and come from sewers with many different skill sets. From time- and money-saving tips to finding notions in your kitchen (did you know you could use Glad Press 'n Seal for making patterns and stabilizing garments as well as wrapping food?) to making foolproof welt pockets, you'll find a lot of useful information that will not only help your sewing,

but make you say "Why didn't I think of that?" You might even make some new sewing friends—all the members contributing to this book can be found online on PatternReview.com.

As you can imagine, categorizing one thousand tips is not an easy task, but I've tried my best to organize them in a useful, accessible way. Since sewing is so much more than just pushing fabric through a machine, the tips have been arranged in chapters that cover a number of different aspects of our craft, ranging from advice for using and choosing gear, through organizing your workspace, tracing off patterns, and info about fabric, thread, and notions, to great tips for the sewing process itself—cutting, fitting, sewing, finishing, and embellishing. Some tips could have been appropriately placed in more than one chapter, so you may find the index really helpful—especially if you're looking for something specific and don't find it right off.

Not only does this book have sewing tips and techniques contributed by members of PatternReview.com, there are also five special features created by master teachers who give online classes on PatternReview.com. These features bring professional expertise right into your sewing room—or take you right into the masters' sewing rooms—they are the icing on the cake in this book. Each piece focuses on techniques for which its author is well known; I know you'll enjoy seeing their work and learning how they do it.

Here's what I recommend: Sit back with a drink of your choice and enjoy the different voices in this book. Not only will you discover things you weren't even looking for, you'll find your horizons expanded, and besides, it's more fun this way. And hey, keep a paper towel handy in case you spill the drink when you laugh out loud at some of the tips. Ask me how I know ☺.

*Deepika*

# CHAPTER ONE

# Sewing Gear

> " *I talked my husband into agreeing that we spend our little money on a sewing machine for me as a "cost saving device" when we bought our first home. Boy, did I trick him on the "cost saving idea!"* "
>
> —drsue

# Machines, feet & needles

*Your machines do most of the stitching for you, so it's smart to take good care of them, master their abilities, and overcome their quirks. We'd all rather sew than be stymied by threading difficulties!*

## TAKE IT ALONG

**1** An insulated, soft-side 54-can cooler is perfect for transporting a sewing machine. Look for one with adjustable shoulder straps, straps on each end in case you need help lifting, telescoping handles, and wheels. These coolers are nicely padded, with pockets to hold all your sewing notions, and, best of all—pretty inexpensive. Check the measurements of your machine case before you go shopping.

—*Deborah L*

## USE IT RIGHT OR LOSE IT

**2** I love the basting stitch on my Bernina 180. I don't use that function very often and, when I do, my machine can get stuck in basting mode, which means a trip to the dealer. The repairman said that I need to use the stitch, even if it's just for a few seconds once a week. He also told me it sometimes works to run the machine at full speed for a minute or so when it's stuck in basting mode. You don't need a needle or even a foot on the machine to do this.

—*Irene Q*

**3** I just had my Huskylock 936 serger serviced for a loud squeaking noise. Turns out it needed a new bearing in the area above the needle, which cost me $79 in parts and labor. The tech said it was full of junk because I had never cleaned and oiled it there. (I didn't even know you should!) My model has a screw on the left side so I can remove the cover. He instructed me to open this area and clean and oil every moving part each time I do the rest of the machine.

—*jhansby*

## CLEAN OUT THE LINT WITH

**4** **Scrap of stretch velvet.** These make great wipes for the serger when you're in a hurry and can't bother with the vacuum attachments or lint brush. The nap catches the dust and lint inside the machine. I just toss the scraps in the wash when they get dirty, and they're ready to go again.

—*Jackie M*

**5** **Swiffer dusters.** I use them to clean the mechanical parts of my sewing machine. By wrapping one around the end of a chopstick, I get buildup out of tiny corners because the lint clings to the cloth and leaves no fibers behind. Expanding on this idea, I now "dust" the outside of my serger to keep debris from collecting.

—*Joni2*

**6** **Sable paintbrush.** During the process of making nylon tricot panties, my presser foot and other parts of the machine get covered in dust bunnies. With a small sable paintbrush (the type used by watercolor artists), I clean the foot and all other parts that I can reach. It takes only a few seconds, and when the project is finished I clean the shuttle, feed dogs, and all else.

—*Mary Stiefer*

**7** **Soft makeup brush.** My teacher at a class for new sewing machine users showed us how to clean in and around the bobbin area with a soft makeup brush. The soft bristles really pick up the fluff without forcing, and the difference in results compared to the typical, rather stiff little brushes is amazing!

—*Mufffet*

**8** **Rubbing alcohol.** After a lot of serging on polar fleece, my serger blades got coated with a light film of who-knows-what and weren't cutting as well as before the marathon. A sewing list member suggested cleaning the blades with a cotton swab and alcohol. Magic!

—*Patti B*

**9** **Silicone basting brush.** One of those little kitchen synthetic basting brushes snaps up all those horrible little threads and snippets that collect on me and my appliqué and embroidery work. Then I simply vacuum the bits off the bristles.

—*Pecan*

**10** **Stencil brush.** I clean my serger with a painter's stencil brush. The bristles are long enough to get into the inner workings of the serger and stiff enough to get the job done well.

—*SandraB*

**11** **The machine's whisk.** I know I shouldn't, but I use thread on wooden spools because I have so much from second-hand sources, and it seems a shame to toss them. The thread is usually dusty and the fibers tend to shed, getting that dread enemy, dust, into my new machine. So every time I change the bobbin or make up a new one, I sweep the bobbin area with the miniature whisk-broom that came with the machine. While I'm at it, I also clean the throat plate and feed dogs.

—*Shinobu*

## RUBBER PADS PREVENT TRAVELS

**12** I use a computer mouse pad underneath my serger. It cuts down the vibrations and noise, and it protects my table from the serger's feet marks.

—*katharin*

**13** When working on heavy fabrics, I put rubber jar grippers under my serger so it won't walk off the table. I put one under each front foot.

—*SewTwin*

**14** With Ultra-grip liner material under them, my serger and sewing machine foot pedals no longer go traveling. Plus, this stuff can be cut to size and is so inexpensive.

—*newlywedws*

**15** Sandpaper keeps my foot control pedal from slipping away. I traced the bottom of the pedal onto a piece of adhesive sandpaper, cut it out with curved corners, then peeled off the adhesive backing and stuck it on. Thanks to my woodworker husband.

—*SewTwin*

## NEEDLES & THREADING

**16** When you sew without thread, snip and remove the thread just as you would if you were changing thread. Don't just unthread the needle and start sewing, as I did! When I went to thread it again, thread was wrapped and knotted around the take-up lever. Ick.

—*Barbara R*

**17** To check whether the upper or lower tension on your sewing machine needs adjusting, thread the machine with two different colors. Be sure to use the same brand for each thread.

—*els*

**18** If you feel like a fumble-fingers when replacing a needle in your machine, try a dental tool called the interdental brush (available at most drug stores). It's a slender wand with a hole at one end for a tiny brush that fits in gaps between teeth. This hole is just the right size for a sewing machine needle, but too small for the needle shaft to drop through. Just drop the needle into the hole and use the wand to position it in place.

—*kkkkaty*

## SEAM GUIDE SOLUTIONS

**19** My European-made sewing machine has the seam allowance markings in metric units on the throat plate. I had been eyeballing the ⅝" and ½" (1.6 and 1.3 cm) seam allowances until I found this simple solution. If your machine has the capability to move the needle to the right or left, move the needle until the distance from the needle to one of the lines is the measurement you need. Put the needle down and check the measurement. This also works great to get a ¼" (6 mm) seam without needing a special quilting foot. Just move the needle to the right until the distance from needle to the right edge of your presser foot is ¼" (6 mm).

—*LoriB*

**20** The seam allowance guidelines on my machine are measured in centimeters, so I color-coded the guide in inches using electrical tape from my husband's workbench. The tape is about ½" (1.3 cm) wide and smooth as vinyl on top. I placed a short strip of red on my machine at ⅝" (1.6 cm), yellow at ½" (1.3 cm), and blue at ⅜" (1 cm). As you overlap each piece, it's important to place the edge of the tape parallel to the edge of the first strip to be sure the guideline is perfect.

—*jbrewer*

**21** The small Post-It pad is a good seam guide. The pad's thickness helps you control the fabric, and the sticky surface does not leave a gummy residue. Remove the brown backing from the bottom of the pad and stick it on the needle plate; you can easily re-position it. When it eventually loses some of its stickiness, just peel off the bottom sheet, and you have a fresh new adhesive surface.

—*Everyday Sewist*

**22** I find that a rubber band placed on the free arm of my machine creates a good seam allowance guideline. The raised edge helps guide the fabric, especially if it's wiggly, and I can adjust the band to whatever seam allowance width I prefer.

—*Jennifer shaw*

## FIVE TRICKS FOR SERGER SETUP

**23** I purchased my first serger the other day. During introductory class, the instructor told us to push the pedal way out of the way while threading so you don't step on it by mistake and then break something. When working with my machine at home, I also moved the cutter slightly so I could get the needle out easily.

—NanJones

**24** To make it easier to remember the threading order for my serger, I put a label next to each spool with a permanent marker. I used numbers to list the order of threading and also indicated which was the upper looper, lower looper, right needle, and left needle.

—BJ1400

**25** To learn which thread does what in serging, thread your machine with different colors. Most brands come with a color-coded threading chart. If you thread with the coded colors and do some practice sewing, you'll easily be able to see what each cone is doing. It's also easier to figure out which particular tension needs adjusting. One method to end off serging is to pull the needle threads out of the chain and then tie them with the looper threads. With color coding, you can get used to how the needle threads look in the chain (they are the straight ones). Try this for a rolled hem too, and see where it differs from regular serging.

—Shazza B

**26** I use dental floss threaders to thread the loopers on my serger. They are stiff enough to thread through the holes and loops, but flexible, and look like fishing line with a loop on the end. I just poke the thread through the loop on the threader, then pull it through the needle and looper eyes.

—MaryLynn in Long Beach

**27** The tiny screw-drivers for eye glasses are the perfect size for those itsy-bitsy screws on sergers!

—Christianne

## AN OUNCE OF PREVENTION

**28** I've broken needles by accidentally hitting the zigzag stitch selector on the front of my machine when I was using the straight stitch foot, which has a small hole and not a wide slot. To fix this, I covered the zigzag button with a very small, fluorescent adhesive label. I now have a visual reminder, and the button also feels totally different.

—Aless

**29** When lofty batting gets boggled up in the toes of your presser foot, remove the presser foot. Carefully wrap a piece of transparent tape around the toe area of your presser foot, but don't cover the area where your needle goes in and out. This creates an upward curving sort of ski that will glide nicely over the batting.

—anetjay

## BANISH SEWER'S ACHE

**30** I tilt my portable sewing machine to reduce neck and shoulder fatigue by placing a three-ring, loose-leaf office binder (mine is about 2" (5.1 cm) wide at the spine) under it. The front of the machine sits on the thin part of the wedge, and the back is on or near the spine of the binder. It doesn't slip or move, and the wedge raises the machine bed at an angle, increasing visibility so I don't need to crane my neck or hunch over my work.

—tweedcurtain

**Deepika adds:** Be sure to use a heavy-duty binder.

**31** My fold-up sewing machine table is too low, and a day of sewing hunched over the machine would leave me with some nasty upper back strain. To get more height, I put two, inch-thick books under the machine; with a gripper cloth under them for security, there is no wobbling or vibration.

—Joni2

### Narrow zigzag feet: no and yes

*Two PatternReview.com members had very different experiences zigzagging with a narrow presser foot—both worth noting.*

**32** **Rhonda in Montreal's booboo.** I thought you could zigzag with any presser foot, so I tried a zigzag stitch with my new (expensive) Teflon foot. Guess what!? I drilled a hole right into the side of it! The foot is pierced, but it still works fine.

**33** **Pocket Venus' ingenuity.** Sheer, slippery, and stretch fabrics may need a narrow zigzag stitch with all the control of a straight-stitch foot. I bought a spare straight-stitch foot for my machine and a round file that fits the hole of the foot, and filed the hole 1 mm wider. When I want to sew a narrow zigzag, I test the stitch width beforehand by turning the hand wheel and making sure that the needle goes cleanly into the hole.

## PUTTING THOSE SPECIAL FEET TO WORK

**34** To use a blind-hem foot as a guide for topstitching, move the needle position where you want the topstitching to be, and sew. The bar in the middle of the foot fits nicely in the seam if you are topstitching near the seam. For edge stitching, put the bar next to the garment edge.
—*Meggie LuLu*

**35** A narrow hemming foot that has a wide slot to accommodate a zigzag stitch may be used to apply 2 mm- to 6 mm-thick cording. Elastic cording can be stretched and helped into the foot, but only if you can manipulate the elastic and control the fabric at the same time.
—*newlywedws*

**36** The Hump Jumper is an invaluable tool when altering jeans. I slip it under the presser foot when ready to stitch over the super thick parts of cuffs, the crotch, and back part of the pants.
—*Jennifer.Huber*

**37** I finally learned how to use the binding foot that came with my machine. 1) Trim the allowance on the piece to be bound, fold the seam binding over the raw edge, and then push it through the slot on the side of the foot. 2) With the fabric in the foot, slide it forward and back until the seam binding settles into the little channels in the foot. Lower the presser foot and take a couple of stitches. 3) With the needle down, adjust the setscrew on the side so that the opening is just large enough for fabric and binding to fit through. This helps the binding fold over the edge of the fabric as you guide it with your fingers.
—*Nancywin*

**38** I had been looking high and low for a piping foot and a narrow hem foot for my Kenmore, which uses low-shank presser feet. My old White machine with snap-on hemmer and piping feet has a foot adapter (the piece that the snap-on foot is attached to), so I screwed it onto my Kenmore. It fits!
—*SexiSadi*

### Edge-joining extras

*Jbsew* offers two favorite ways to use an edge-joining foot.

**39** **Stitch-in-the-ditch.** I place the blade of the foot, which is directly in front of the needle, on the seam I am sewing in the ditch. I slightly pull the fabric apart so the blade tracks on the seam. The needle follows behind to sew a perfectly invisible stitch-in-the-ditch.

**40** **Topstitch.** With the blade at the edge of a pocket, I set the needle either to the left or to the right of center and edge-stitch a scant 1/8" (3 mm). When edge/top stitching a seam allowance, the blade runs in the seam; by positioning the needle I can choose how close to stitch. Give it a try.

## THE COVER STITCH ADVANTAGE

**41** If you are a new owner of a cover stitch machine, you're probably caught up in the excitement of using binders. There are two types, A and B, and here's how to remember which is which. The A binder has a double fold on top of the fabric and no fold on the bottom. B has a double fold on top and a double fold on the bottom. In other words, the B binder produces sort of a B look (rounded top and rounded bottom).
—*JEF*

**42** I bought a cover stitch machine for the look of its stitch; I had no clue that it would make my sewing MUCH quicker. Combined with large Kai scissors that speed cutting out, I'm making clothes faster than I ever did before. The machine is also simple to thread.
—*ryansmum*

## UNIVERSAL NEEDLES ARE NOT UNIVERSALLY BEST

**43** For really straight stitches, use a sharp or topstitch point needle. The universal point needle will allow the fibers to slide to the left or right of the needle point, making the stitches ever so minutely off center. Test this by doing a straight row of stitches with the universal point next to a row with the sharp or topstitch point needle. The sharper needle pierces the fabric exactly in front of the needle, forcing the fibers to either side. A universal point needle is made for all kinds of fabrics and chooses the path of least resistance.
—*Janie Viers*

# Pressing equipment

*Good pressing is as important as sewing straight seams, so keep your iron in topnotch condition, say goodbye to gummed up soleplates and scorched fabric and fingers, and be as clever as the PatternReview.com members in supporting your work while you press it.*

## IS YOUR IRON ON OR OFF?

**44** To remind me that the iron is on, I plugged it and a small desk lamp into a power strip and turned the light ON. Now, when I see that the light is on I know the iron is on also.

*—KathySews*

## HOUSEHOLD HINTS FOR A CLEAN SOLEPLATE

**45** If your iron has gunk on the soleplate, let it cool, then scrub it lightly with a soft cloth (I use a microfiber cloth) and damp baking soda. Neither the cloth nor the baking soda will scratch the soleplate. Another suggestion I've never tried is warm vinegar and salt.

*—Debbie Lancaster*

**46** My Rowenta Professional iron had sticky, melted-on gunk on the soleplate from the fusing web I was using. I sprayed Dawn Power Dissolver (available in supermarkets) on the soleplate, let it sit about ten minutes, and wiped it clean with a Handi Wipe. No scrubbing at all. I ran a half-tank of water through the steam tank to be sure none of the foam had gotten inside the iron through the holes.

*—mommietothreeo*

**47** When I get gunk on my iron, I run the hot iron over a fabric softener sheet, and all that glue comes off.

*—SueV*

## NO-SPILL FILLING

**48** A gravy separator, the kind with the long spout that pours broth from the bottom of the cup below the fat, is perfect for filling the steam iron without spilling.

*—Debbie Lancaster*

**49** Use a small houseplant watering can to fill your iron—easy!

*—Deepika*

**50** Use a sports-water bottle for a no-drip method of filling a steam iron's reservoir—you can direct the stream of water accurately into the small opening. Depending on the size of the bottle, it will hold several refills and won't spill if accidentally tipped.

*—Lizz*

## SCORCH REMOVER

**51** I removed the rust stain and a big scorch mark from the white shirt I was making by soaking it about 20 minutes in a gallon of warm water and one scoop of OxiClean.

*—cindy-lou*

## THINGS THAT MAKE FUSING EASIER

**52** Using a Teflon pressing sheet on fusibles keeps the mess off the bottom of the iron. The fusible glue goes against the sheet of plastic instead of the iron and, after it cools, any little blobs can be peeled off the sheet. I have even laundered it; with a quick press it's back to normal.

*—anetjay*

**53** Much of the appliqué work and crafts that I do require spray or iron-on adhesive. My new best friend is Reynolds Wrap non-stick aluminum foil. I place it on my ironing surface with the silicone side, which is embossed with "Release Non-Stick Side," facing up—it offers total protection. Stray adhesive bits get on the Release foil, not on the ironing surface, and I just peel them off. The foil is reusable—just wash it off. Use a lower setting on the iron until you see how the temperature changes with the foil underneath.

*—ohsewnutty*

**54** It's much simpler to apply Steam-A Seam fusible web with a mini iron. The fusible comes off best while still warm, and giving it another pass with a mini is easier than using the big iron.

*—ryansmum*

**55** My mom taught me to use a moistened paper towel as a pressing cloth for fusing interfacing. Squeeze out all excess water from the towel, and re-moisten it as you fuse.

*—Jennifer shaw*

## SOOTHE BURNS, OR BETTER STILL, PREVENT THEM

**56** Recently, I grabbed my hot iron in the wrong way and got a second-degree burn on my finger. I treated it with lavender essential oil (Lavandula angustifolia). The pain was relieved immediately, and I could go back to sewing. If you want to keep some on hand, be sure to get Lavandula angustifolia essential oil as there are other kinds of lavender oils.

—*CSM--Carla*

**57** No more burnt finger tips for me! I use a Cool Finger, made of heat-resistant fabric, on my pointer finger as I press along the narrow edge of a fabric or press open seam allowances.

—*anetjay*

**58** Wear an oven glove designed to resist higher temperatures to protect your fingers when pressing open small seams in difficult places, such as the curved seam between the outer and inner brim in a sewn hat. This is easier than arranging the seam over a pressing ham or seam roll.

—*petro*

## INVENTIVE IRONING BOARDS

**59** My sewing area is not huge, so I devised a more efficient ironing area. I bought two heavy-duty, rolling plastic storage units with pull-out drawers and, after removing the rolling feet, placed the units side-by-side with my folded ironing board on top. This extra storage is a real bonus. The pattern master binder and rolls of tracing paper fit between the units. My patterns in Ziploc bags fit the drawers perfectly, and each drawer front is labeled with the numerical sequence.

—*ConnieBJ*

**60** After my experience with having green dye in a pretty ironing board cover transfer to a white shirt, I feel that a plain, white or muslin-color cover is the best choice.

—*Stilltheone*

**61** Accurate pinning and pressing of a hem is an important finishing step and sometimes I need more work surface than my ironing board provides. So I made a pin-able, portable pressing board: I cut two 2' × 2' (0.63 m × 0.63 m) squares from the sides of a heavy cardboard box, and used a temporary adhesive spray to attach a 2' × 2' (0.63 m × 0.63 m) piece of batting to one of them. I stacked the two pieces with the batting on top. I then cut two pieces of muslin about 27" × 27" (68.6 × 68.6 cm) and layered them on a table. I placed the cardboard, batting side down, on the muslin and wrapped the muslin over the cardboard, securing it with staples. I covered the staples and the muslin edges with sealing tape. I set this pressing board on my cutting table with a vinyl chair mat underneath as a waterproof barrier.

—*patsijean*

**62** My ironing board cover is easy to put on and take off, and is rock solid on my board. I made the cover from a wool fabric and cotton to cover it, both cut to size plus several inches to wrap over the edge of the board. I serged the edge of the cotton and added buttons about five inches apart all around. To affix the cover, I connected the buttons with buttonhole elastic in a zigzag underneath the board.

—*Orsi*

**63** The best money I ever spent was for a 1/3-yard (0.32 m) piece of 60" (152.4 cm)-wide wool batting to back my ironing board cover. It reduces my need for a pressing cloth, and shirt buttons sink into it when I iron them from the back. I don't have the burning or boiling problems from high-heat ironing, and the wool seems to make the fabric recover faster when I'm pressing easily stretched items.

—*SJ Kurtz*

## TEMPLATES: LOVE THEM, MAKE THEM, STORE THEM

**64** Pocket curve templates are not only good for pressing curves in pockets—you can also use them for tracing and for pressing other types of curves. I've used them for pocket flaps and for cuffs with curved edges, but my favorite is for pressing that little curve in the collar stand.

—*Irene Q*

**65** I cut hem-pressing templates from poster board, making them about a foot long and the desired width. Whenever I make one, I punch a hole in the end and add it to a ring with others. Don't use colored poster board—the dye may transfer to your fabric.

—*nanflan*

**66** Make yourself a quick set of pressing guides from manila folders. Cut a folder on the center crease and, starting from the cut edge, make strips with the rotary cutter at common pressing widths: ½", 5/8", ¾", 1" (1.3, 1.6, 1.9, 2.5 cm), etc. Label each strip width. I also make pressing guides that are more specific to a certain project and label them with the width, pattern number, and name. Manila colors don't bleed with the heat of the iron or get hot like metal pressing guides do.

—*jbsew*

**67** I designed a hanging bag to store my pressing templates made from manila folders. First, in each of several large, lunch-size Ziploc plastic bags, I made about five channels to fit the different template sizes, sewing from below the zip section at the top to bottom of the bag. I use one color manila folder for metric templates and a different color for imperial, and use different bags to store each. I clip the tops of the bags together with a plastic binder clip that has a hanging hole, and mount the collection on my display board on a cup hook. They are visible at all times, yet neatly stored.

—*Aless*

**68** For pressing long seams like trousers I made a long clapper/pressing tool from a piece of steamed beech wood 33" × 4" (83.8 × 10.2 cm) and 1" (2.5 cm) thick. Beech is needed for a pressing support because it doesn't warp when you apply steam and heat.

—els

**69** I couldn't figure out how to get into a tight pant leg to press open the second seam. Finally, I rolled up a stiff magazine, wrapped it in a fluffy dish towel, pinned the towel snugly, and slipped it into the leg.

—Ann B

**70** To keep seam allowances from showing when pressing open long seams, use a tightly rolled-up towel. Tie the ends with some fabric scraps, and you've got a seam roll. Another good seam pressing support is a long dowel, cut or sanded down to keep one side flat. For low-plush fabrics like cotton velveteen and crushed velvet, a really thick towel prevents the nap from flattening out—just don't press too hard.

—Dale C

**71** A tightly rolled, thick newspaper can serve as a pressing roll. Cover it with cotton fabric, sewn together on the long side, then cover the roll with a single layer of wool fabric. Sew this together on the long side and across both ends. My pressing roll is about 12" (30.5 cm) long and has a diameter of 5" (12.7 cm).

—els

**72** Use the handle of a wooden spoon to press open small seams. A skewer or wooden chopstick helps press open a small dart.

—els

**73** Instead of a pressing ham, I use a roll of paper towels to shape rounds when ironing and when pinning; it helps ease in my cap sleeves beautifully. It also helps keep the shape with pinning neck and arm facings. Plus, I can flatten it slightly when necessary.

—ladybirdlove

**74** Cardboard tubes from gift wrapping paper are the perfect free tool for pressing long seams. Slit several other tubes and slip them inside the original for more stiffness. A bathroom tissue tube, with three others inside it, does smaller jobs. I've collected various sizes, including some very long tubes that aid in pressing pant and curtain seams. All free.

—patsijean

**Deepika adds:** Another way to stiffen cardboard tubes is to fill them with batting or fabric scraps.

**75** When pressing or ironing trousers, the pocket pieces, especially at the front, are hard to manage and threaten to mark through. I made some thin, lightly padded boards to place between the pocket and the top section, or to slide under the zip guard where the edges tend to mark.

—petro

# Dress forms

*A dress form is an invaluable aid for fitting patterns and garments-in-progress. Here are some hints for getting one in your size.*

**76** For those of us who enjoy sewing but have a difficult time tailoring for ourselves and just cannot afford $200 for a dress double, I have a cheap trick. Put on an old T-shirt that fits you snugly, and have someone wrap you in duct tape, enough to cover the shirt entirely. Cut a seam in the back to remove the T-shirt, and retape. Stuff the shirt with polyfill and, voilà, an instant dress double. I put mine on a dowel rod, and my husband nailed a stand for it. I couldn't ask for a better proportioned dummy.

—FauxZenaChick

**77** I did a Google search on making a Duct Tape Dummy and found a few useful links with instructions. My dear husband spent about an hour wrapping me in two layers of heavy-duty duct tape. Word of warning: take care of all bathroom issues before cocooning yourself in duct tape! When he finished wrapping me, he very carefully cut it open up the back so I could step out. I closed it back up by lacing it using crochet thread and a heavy-duty curved needle.

—SandraB

**78** I have more dress forms than I want to admit. Wolf ones. I constantly gain and lose weight in a 20-pound range, so I dread measuring and fitting. I realized that I can just pin-fit using the dress form closest in size to me. I mark the pattern where it needs adjusting, smooth out the lines, and end up with a near perfect fit. For Halloween I put costumes on my dress forms, and on birthdays they wear clown suits.

—ryansmum

# Cutting tables & tools

*Anyone who's really into sewing will tell you the floor is not the best place for cutting out a project. Here are some smart ideas for making elevated and easy-to-stow cutting tables, recommendations for surfaces to top them, and tips for getting the most from your cutting gear—including your seam ripper.*

## CUTTING TABLE IMPROV

**79** My sister-in-law (who is 6' [1.85 m] tall) needed a high cutting surface when we were cutting out six bridesmaid dresses and two flower girl dresses. Her husband placed a set of bi-fold closet doors on two pairs of tall sawhorses and, presto, a temporary cutting table. We put my folding cardboard cutting boards on top to keep the surface pristine.

—*Janie Viers*

**80** I made a great cutting table at the perfect height—for under $10. I bought a buffet at a yard sale and an unfinished, 36" (91.4 cm)-wide door at our local home improvement store, and painted them. The door is attached to the buffet top with stick-on Velcro, in case I'll want to use the buffet for another purpose. The drawers are perfect for cutting tools, marking materials, tape measures, rulers, and such.

—*Roxie5166*

## RIPPER POINTERS

**81** I had been using the same seam ripper for years when, on a whim, I bought a new one with a slightly larger handle. Wow! The new sharp blade made an amazing difference compared with the old one, which was obviously blunt. I know to change needles and sharpen scissors, but for some reason it never occurred to me to change my seam ripper.

—*Allie in Hong Kong*

**82** Sometimes the point of a seam ripper is too sharp and might cut or slice the fabric. In my craft supplies I have several embossing styluses, which can grab threads in seams without danger of cutting the fabric. They have slender metal ends (double pointed), each end with a ball tip. I slide the ball under the thread, and the thread can be lifted or loosened without sliding off the tool.

—*kkkkaty*

**83** We expect those hard-used seam rippers to last for years or until we lose them. But their blades get dull, and many of us are sewing with tough polyester thread. Although seam ripping is never going to be a fun thing, we can give ourselves a break by replacing our rippers occasionally.

—*beginagain*

## OUR FAVORITE PATTERN WEIGHTS

**84** **Nice rocks.** They add decorative touches to my sewing room and are free. Look along river banks and shorelines for smooth, flat stones in a variety of sizes and shapes.

—*Dale C*

**85** **Utility hooks.** I hate pinning down pattern pieces and then having to unpin them for repositioning or marking. Instead, I hold my pattern pieces in place with large plastic-coated metal utility hooks from the hardware store. Sometimes called bike hooks or ladder hooks, they are about 6" (15.2 cm) long and come with curved or squared ends. The PVC coating keeps them from snagging or marring patterns and fabric. Curved ones fit nicely into curved pattern pieces and square ones form almost a right angle, making cutting corners and curves a little easier. I still have to pin when cutting with scissors, but the hooks work fine with a rotary cutter.

—*patitude*

**86** **Hockey pucks.** They're heavy, smooth, semi-flat, round disks and make the BEST pattern weights. My children would bring home stray ones they found near our community hockey rink, and once the pucks were in my hands they never saw the rink again, just many yards of fabric.

—*Busy Mom*

**87** **Ceramic tiles.** I do my cutting in the kitchen and always used food cans as pattern weights. But the cans had to be put back into the cabinet, and the table looked as if I was both cooking and sewing—organza here, can of olives there. I switched to a set of ceramic subway tiles (3" × 6" [7.6 × 15.2 cm] rectangles), which weigh about four ounces and stack neatly. They fit on narrow sleeve pieces and, when I need more weight, I layer them. A tidy stack of them now waits on top of the microwave.

—*utz*

## The Ironing Board Make-Do

*Several PatternReview.com members suggest using ironing boards as a base for a cutting table. Here's the drill:*

**88** **MaryLynn in Long Beach's system.** I'm old and cranky, with a bad back, so I craved a nice big cutting table. Two problems stood in the way: too little money and too little space. My solution: two ironing boards and a piece of $3/8$" (1 cm)-thick plywood cut to exactly fit under my cardboard cutting pad. The table is the right height, but adjustable, and I can get around it on all four sides. The cost was less than $25, and the ironing boards and plywood fit behind doors.

**89** **SandraB adds:** My sewing room is really tiny, with no space for a cutting table. However, I make a temporary, portable table by placing two ironing boards beside each other, the pointed end of one behind the square end of the other, and setting my large cutting mat on top.

## ROTARY CUTTERS: SHARP & SAFE

**90** I am always leery about changing rotary blades because those things are sharp, and you can really cut yourself. So I use a piece of masking tape to remove the old blade from the cutter and to pick up the new blade.

—*Mary Stiefer*

**91** Today I was cutting out a pattern and needed to mark my forward shoulder adjustment. As I grabbed my pencil to mark the line, I noticed my rotary cutter and decided to cut the line instead. It suddenly occurred to me that I could cut all my pattern tissue with a rotary cutter. Duh! It's faster than using scissors, and it navigates sharp turns easily. You won't want to use your "good" rotary cutting blade for this, because cutting paper tends to dull blades faster than cutting fabric.

—*MelissaB in WA*

**92** I have been using rotary cutters for a couple of years and had purchased sharpening kits to prolong the life of the blades. My hand and wrist still got shooting pains after cutting lots of fleece. Then I put in new blades, and the fleece cut like butter. I realized that the blades I had sharpened were not nearly as sharp as a new one. So, long story short: new blades save on pain and speed up your rotary cutting.

—*Restarto6*

**93** To protect my fine Queen Anne mahogany table when I'm cutting fabrics, I cover it with a cheap vinyl/flannel tablecloth and two full-size pieces of rigid foam core from the art supply store. The foam boards are very light and easy to stow away.

—*jadamooo*

## GOOD CUTTING SURFACES

**94** The most important accessory for rotary cutting is a good cutting mat, but most are small or, if large, expensive. Instead, I use a smooth-bottom, vinyl chair mat available at office supply stores. The smooth surface is great for moving the shears along. I put an old cardboard cutting mat under it and use the inch marks to line up fabrics but not for accurate measurement. Many office mats have a chair lip at one end that can be removed with a circular saw: sand the edges and you have a second, small mat. I've been using my cutting mat for at least fifteen years, and probably will use it for at least fifteen more.

—*patsijean*

## SNIP TIPS

**95** I needed a way to hold my craft scissors closed, so they wouldn't damage things in the tote, and for safety. I sewed the ends of a squib of elastic together, reinforced them with reversed stitching, and voilà!—an elastic loop that holds the scissors closed, but stretches enough for a quick snip.

—*Elphaba*

**96** My tiny sewing scissors were always on the move until a sewing neighbor at a quilting retreat gave me her retractable lanyard (sometimes called a zinger). The scissors are attached to the end of the lanyard, and the other end is pinned to my shirt. The scissors can extend about 18" (45.7 cm) on the reel and will retract back to their original position when released.

—*lisaquilts*

**97** An electric carving knife is the BEST tool there is to cut foam. Many of us have one lurking somewhere, and they can often be found really cheap at tag sales. I learned this tip from an upholsterer many years ago, and I still bless his name.

—*MaryLynn in Long Beach*

**98** When I was making a duct tape dress form, the scissors got quite sticky. I took them apart, put sewing machine oil on them and, to my surprise, the gummy stuff wiped off with a cloth!

—*Orsi*

## RAISE IT TO SAVE YOUR BACK

**99** I was at band camp, cutting out sixteen dresses for the color guard. The table was a great size but regular height, and my back was killing me. I mentioned that I missed my own cutting table because it was higher, so one of the men put patio bricks under each table leg. It was now the perfect height, and I carried those bricks back and forth to camp for three years. Best six dollars I ever spent.

—*svetlana*

**100** Here's a cheap and easy way to raise your worktable: Buy PVC pipe in the diameter that fits your table legs snugly and long enough to make four risers of the desired height, plus four PVC slip-on caps of the same diameter. On bare floors, add self-stick floor protectors. Cut the PVC pipe (I used a hacksaw), or ask the hardware store to do it. Slip a cap on one end of each pipe, add the floor protector, and slip a table leg into the open end. The risers are easy to put on or remove.

—*Tamtay*

# Marking & measuring tools

*Whether you're tracing patterns or marking match points and darts on fabric, you want the lines, dots, and notches to be visible, stay put for as long as you need them, and disappear when you don't. Here are gadgets and everyday items to help you mark with aplomb, plus some suggestions for measuring tools that may be unfamiliar.*

## STICKY MARKS STAY PUT

**101** Freebie self-stick address labels are put to good use in my sewing room. A small piece of one label helps me match pattern dots; another piece folded over the fabric seam-allowance edge becomes a single notch, and a larger piece is the double notch. Check first that the sticker leaves no residue on the fabric.
—*Oopsy-Daisy!*

**102** On fleeces and other "problem" fabrics, the pencil or chalk marks disappear as soon as I move the pattern piece. Instead, I mark them with the sticky dots available at stationery and office supply stores. I can draw notches on them or use numbers and/or letters.
—*PVA*

## TAKING MEASURE

**103** A quick way to measure an approximate yard is to hold one end of the fabric, ribbon, or trim in one hand, with your arm outstretched to the side and at shoulder height. Turn your head in the other direction. The distance from the item you're holding in your hand to the tip of your nose is about one yard. My mom taught me this a long time ago.
—*LoriB*

**104** I measure fabrics and seamlines with a double readout plan measuring wheel, left over from my husband's work as an architect. It's perfect for measuring curves such as the armholes and necklines of patterns: I just set the wheel to zero, and roll it along the edge or line I wish to measure, and it displays the correct length in both inches and centimeters. It's ideal for measuring bindings and trims too. Look for one wherever drafting tools are sold.
—*mikkim*

**105** Make yourself a body mold from aluminum foil to help you draft a better crotch curve on your next pair of pants:

- Tear off a piece of kitchen foil long enough to fit through your legs and up to your waistline at the front and back. Roll this piece lengthwise into a long, tight tube.
- Thread this flexible ruler from the front waistline through your legs to the back waistline, and mold the foil to your body contours.
- Make a notch or deep pinch at your front waist and back waist, and another between your legs where the inseam should intersect.
- Carefully step out of the foil mold and place it on a table. Take your body measurements: body space, length, crotch depths, etc.
—*kethry*

### Trace on the double

*Tired of tracing the seamline and then measuring to rule on the seam allowance? Take this advice:*

**106** **regine's speed-tracing tip.** I trace patterns from sewing magazines and found it a nuisance to add the seam allowance. With a double tracing wheel (available from good notions vendors), it takes seconds and is very accurate. Just run one wheel along the pattern edge (seamline), and the other wheel automatically marks the cutting line.

**107** **So So's D.I.Y double wheel.** My husband made a double tracing wheel for my pattern work by gluing two identical single tracing wheels together with a piece of wood sandwiched between. The wood piece was cut precisely to set the wheels exactly ⅝" apart.

**108** **Deepika's measure.** To trace ¼" (6 mm) seam allowance, just put a rubber band around two pencils (measure to double-check).

## HANDY MARKING AIDS

**109** A pizza cutter marks fabric more clearly than the smooth tracing wheels that leave only a faint line of the carbon. Be careful, though, because its sharp wheel can cut delicate material.

—*Janie Viers*

**110** Flexible plastic cutting mats from the housewares department make inexpensive templates that you can draw around or use to guide your rotary cutter—no more sliced paper patterns. The mats can be cut to shape with regular scissors. For larger templates, I use wide, clear mailing tape to tape sheets together. This is great to do for frequently used pattern pieces.

—*MelissaB in WA*

**111** It's easy to assemble a light table or box from everyday items. Place a power strip with a plug-in fluorescent light into an open storage box, cover the box with a picture frame and then tape translucent paper (vellum, tracing paper, etc.) on the glass in the frame. Plug in the light and start tracing. Use a fluorescent bulb equivalent to a 25-watt (or less) incandescent bulb—NOT an incandescent bulb, which gets hot and is a fire hazard.

—*Patzee*

**112** The only place in my house big enough for my cardboard cutting board is my dining room table. I often want to do pattern alterations on a smaller table, so I made my own mini cutting board by marking a flat piece of cardboard with a 1" (2.5 cm) grid (using a quilter's ruler as a guide). It is barely large enough to do a full bust alteration on but it is so much more convenient than the big board. Actually, my portable alterations board is the lid to a box that I call my "pattern queue" where I keep patterns for upcoming projects.

—*mikkim*

## FINE LINES, VISIBLE DOTS

**113** I mark dark colored fabrics with blackboard chalk, which is a pain to keep sharp. When I saw a two-hole pencil sharpener for 30 cents at an office supply store, I had a light-bulb moment. The chalk fits perfectly in the larger hole and gets a nice, sharp point.

—*Mary Stiefer*

**114** My son's Crayola washable markers are a boon for transferring pattern markings to fabrics. The colors wash out with cold water and dish soap, and did not heat-set when ironed. However, I wouldn't use these pens on fabric that is not washable or is extremely valuable.

—*michellerene*

**115** Remnants of soap bars mark your fabric with a white line that will wash away easily. The soap can be sharpened just by washing your hands with it. Hotel courtesy soaps are also great for this purpose.

—*Tini*

**116** I always wrap a rubber band around the middle of my marking chalk to keep it from rolling off the table. You can put a rubber band around pens or sewing markers to keep them from rolling off as well.

—*Maria Hatfield*

**117** I like good chalk wheels, but sometimes I need to mark points, not lines, on dark fabric. I've used Dixon Washout Cloth Markers for such occasions, but I've noticed that as they age, they harden, and seeing a faint mark on the fabric requires an optometrist and the gift of clairvoyance. This morning I was practically engraving fiddly little (unseen) dots onto sleeve vents, when out of sheer frustration, I moistened the white "lead" in the pencil. Okay, truth be told, I stuck it on my tongue. The white marker sprang to life and left perfect visible dots exactly where I wanted them.

—*Karla Kizer*

## MARK-REMOVAL MAGIC

**118** Don't use blue marking pens on red and pink fabrics! There is a chemical reaction with the ink and the dye, and the mark just won't go away. For other colors of washable fabrics, a little fabric softener in a spray bottle of water gets out the marks without laundering.

—*anncie1*

**119** Use a Tide to Go stain remover pen to remove marks made by fabric-marking pens. It's important to do this before pressing, because the markings can become permanent. If the marks reappear when you add steam, go over them again with the TTG pen. They will wash out when you run the garment through the washer.

—*GirlWhoGames*

**120** I was having a hard time removing tailor's chalk from a sandwashed fabric until I rubbed it with a leftover piece of heavy flannel. The chalk was gone after a few strokes.

—*Robie Kentspeth*

# Pins & hand-sewing needles

*They're little things that can make you crazy when they're lost or seemingly impossible to thread. Plus just tossing worn needles in the trash where they might poke and prick the unsuspecting is not a smart option. Here are simple ideas for controlling these sharp, elusive, and essential sewing aids.*

## IMPROMPTU PIN & NEEDLE HOLDERS

**121** A dry, unused sponge is an excellent pincushion. There's more area to hold pins than on the regular kind, so it's easier to grab pins one at a time. Plus, the sponge doesn't move when I use it on the cabinet of my machine.

—*Coot*

**122** I stick my sewing-machine needles into a pincushion clamped to the machine. The stretch needles for knits get a dot of red nail polish.

—*els*

**123** The magnetic side of those little skinny refrigerator magnets is just strong enough to hold needles so they don't fall into the carpet or chair. I set one on the coffee table, magnet side up and place my needles there, threaded or not.

—*Mary Stiefer*

## PIN SUBSTITUTES

**124** To avoid pin holes when sewing with plastic on my last project, I clipped the layers together with scunci barrettes.

—*Jennifer shaw*

**125** Binder clips worked really well to hold sleeve seams together on my latest knit top project. They're terrific for fabric that gets damaged by pins.

—*Jennifer shaw*

## THIS & THAT FOR NEEDLE USE

**126** Reading glasses one diopter too strong magnify the needle hole on my sewing machine enough for me to thread it easily. For a hand needle, I use tapestry needles—the holes are long enough to thread them without any eyesight assistance at all.

—*Joey in Katy*

**127** In order to identify a needle size once I've removed it from its packet, I mark the packet with a colored felt-tip pen in the color that's on the needle shank. I also keep an index card with my needle supply as a cross-reference to the color code, size, and purpose of the needles.

—*PattiAnnSG*

**128** To keep the needle from getting gummy when I was sewing adhesive-backed Velcro, I ran a bead of Sewer's Aid lubricant along the edge of the Velcro where I would stitch. The lubricant really came to my rescue.

—*PattiAnnSG*

 *Safe needle disposal*

*To avoid nasty pricks from used needles tossed loose into the trash, store them in a small container. Here are some options.*

**129** I keep a used spice bottle on my sewing table to hold discarded old sewing needles and pins. The holes in the shaker tops are big enough to slip the needles through, and the screw-on lid prevents any spills.

—*Jerry P*

**130** I found a new container for used needles that is safer than an empty film canister, which if opened accidentally can spill all the needles. It's an empty toothpick container with a swivel top that dispenses one toothpick at a time through a small hole.

—*Janine S*

**Deepika adds:** This may not be readily available in the States, but similar types with screw-on lids are. Or purchase toothpicks in a similar dispenser and repurpose it when empty.

**131** The tiny closed containers for the gloves in hair-coloring kits are the perfect size for the disposal of old needles, and they close securely.

—*Katharine in BXL*

**132** My used and broken needles go into an empty cylinder of pre-moistened kitchen wipes. The needles can't poke through the hard container, and the top snaps shut. When the container is full, I seal it with shipping tape and toss it in the trash.

—*PKPudlin*

**133** I put my used sewing machine needles in an empty prescription pill bottle. Since the lids on these are childproof there is no chance that they will open up in the trash.

—*Deepika*

# Useful odds & ends

*You know those lists of essential gear found in every sewing book? Scissors, marking chalk, ruler, pins, needles, thread, and machine? Well cruise the following and you'll find some unexpected items intended for other purposes that make sewing easier. Most of them are already in your home, so they're easy to add to your setup.*

## WAXED & ADDING MACHINE PAPER PLUSSES

**134** I was separating the layers of fleece-backed micro suede to use the micro suede as binding, but the adhesive remaining on it gummed up my presser foot. I put waxed paper strips under the foot to help slide the fabric under the foot. The wax paper didn't stick to the adhesive like regular tissue paper would, and tearing it off was easy.

—*beginagain*

**135** A roll of 2¼" (5.7 cm)-wide adding machine paper has a million uses in my sewing room. I use strips to prevent seam show-through when pressing and when I need a scrap of paper for notes. To space buttonholes or other topstitching and trims, I cut a length equal to the distance from top to bottom buttonholes, then fold the paper in half, fourths, eighths, or whatever number is needed. A button placed at each end of the paper, and one placed at each fold, gives me an odd number of evenly spaced buttons. And, I use the paper to create a template for hem scallops by cutting a piece the exact width of a skirt or curtain hem, and then start folding.

—*Karla Kizer*

## Three hands are better than two

*Some hand-sewing tasks are easier if the fabric is held taut, but two hands aren't enough to apply tension and sew at the same time. Other tasks require control in spots your hand won't fit. A "third hand" is a clamp of some sort that solves these problems.*

**136** **Mary Stiefer's gadget of choice.** My third hand is a hemostat, a scissor-like clamp used in surgery and by fly fishermen to make flies or pull out a hook. I have a 10" and a 5 ½" (14 cm) pair. If I need to turn something through an opening too small for my hand, I use my 10" (25.4 cm) hemostat. I use hemostat tips to poke out the corners of an item. And, to fill pillow corners, I put small amount of fiberfill in the teeth, push it into the corner, hold the corner on the outside of the pillow and release the clamp. I purchased mine a fishing supply store.

**137** **ryansmum's pragmatic solution.** My sewing machine presser foot sometimes doubles as a third hand. I can rip out seams by lowering the foot on the fabric next to the seam. Then I pull the other side taut to see the stitches and rip them out, using a razor blade. I don't use this technique on all fabrics; the lighter-weight ones don't appreciate it.

**138** **Sew it seams' handy device.** A spring clamp I picked up at Home Depot comes in handy (pun intended!) whenever I need a third hand. Just recently, it made hand-rolling a hem on a long georgette flounce much easier. It allowed me to hold the section I was working on taut.

## TAPE TRICKS

**139** My homemade dress form is made from brown paper tape, and pinning into my paper twin is darn near impossible. In desperation, I tried taping the pattern to the form with medical-paper tape, which has a low tack, and found it is easy to reposition on the dress form and the pattern. Medical-paper tape is found in the pharmacy section. Blue painter's tape might also work—it has a low tack and is probably cheaper.

—*Kim Winson*

**140** The ½" (1.3 cm)-width of Scotch Magic Tape is the perfect size for testing the position of a welt pocket. Simply cut a 5" strip and position it on your garment until you've found the right spot.

—*nancy2001*

**Deepika adds:** Always test to make sure the adhesive won't damage your fabric.

**141** I tape pattern instructions to the wall in front of my sewing machine. Blue painter's tape doesn't mark the wall, but it can tear the instruction sheet. I solved this by putting a piece of transparent Satin Tape (the kind for wrapping presents) on the top margin of the instruction sheet in two places, and taping the painter's tape to that. The painter's tape peels off the instruction sheet easily, and my pattern instructions still look new.

—*Nancywin*

## HANDWORK COMFORTS

**142** If you can't find a comfortable thimble, use a Band-Aid. It should be tough, durable, and made out of so-called cloth. Put one on the finger that gets the most use while hand sewing.

—*NanJones*

**143** A laptop desk turned cushion-side-up is a great surface for beadwork, and I can poke my threaded needles into the firm stuffing. I like it for any detailed handwork that I do while sitting in a comfortable chair.

—*Sew it seams*

## THOSE POWERFUL RAYS

**144** Keep your magnifier lamp covered when not in use! One bright day the sun burned a hole in a thick pattern book that was beneath my uncovered magnifier. Luckily, I was at home and noticed the smoke in time to prevent serious damage.

—*els*

## GLOVES FOR A GOOD GRIP

**145** My bottle of body wash came with a pair of gloves that were to be used to exfoliate your skin. However, I found that their rough texture is perfect for machine quilting

—*elsie Keaton*

**146** I can't see buying expensive gloves to quilt when inexpensive ones work even better! I use cotton gardening gloves with rubber dots on the palms and fingers. The cotton keeps my hands cool, and the dots allow me to "get a grip" on the quilt fabric. Trim off or serge the cuffs to make these gloves even lighter and cooler.

—*Lizz*

## SKIRT HANGER IMPROV

**147** In South Africa it is difficult to buy a good skirt hanger, so I made one out of an ordinary dry cleaner's steel hanger, three plastic clothespins, and a length of plastic tubing. I cut the tubing into pieces to keep the clothespins evenly spaced along the hanger and slit each lengthwise so it could slip over the wire.

—*regine*

# Organization & cleanup aids

*Whether you've a dedicated sewing space or stash your gear in a closet until you need it, you're no doubt as challenged as the next person to keep things tidy and at the ready. Pattern-Review.com members have some clever ideas for what to use to control clutter and pick up thread clippings.*

## TO HOLD SMALL THINGS YOU NEED AND THOSE YOU DON'T

**148** The little revolving desk organizer I purchased at an office supply store takes up minimal space and keeps my sewing stuff within arm's reach, each in its own section. Marking pens, stilettos, bobbins, thimbles, and my sewing machine needle case are in there. Common pins removed while sewing get tossed into a section. The big center section could hold a pair of scissors, were I organized enough to put them in the same place every time I set them down.

—*costumecarol*

**149** Convert clean, empty, plastic gallon jugs into mini waste-cans to place on your sewing and cutting tables, ironing board, and handwork chair. With a Sharpie marker, draw a line around the jug to meet the bottom edge of the handle; then cut around the handle and along the marker line. Your new waste can is about 6" deep with a handle that's easy to grab for moving around and emptying.

—*elizajo*

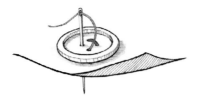
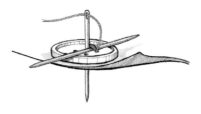

## SELTZER TO THE RESCUE

**150** I keep a small bottle of carbonated water at hand to remove stains on fabrics like wool crepe. Carbonated water doesn't leave a ring as tap water does.

—*els*

**151** A magnet board on an easel keeps my pattern instruction sheet visible while I sew. The boards, made by LoRan, come in various sizes and are sold in the needlework section of craft stores. The one I bought came with a folding stand and magnet strips.

—*LoriB*

## PROP DIRECTIONS WHERE YOU NEED THEM

**152** Although my sewing/craft room has a counter at sewing machine height, base cabinets on each end, and cabinets overhead, I had nowhere to put my current pattern but on the counter. So I put two corkboards that I can pin the pattern to on the wall behind my counter. I added strip magnets around the outside to hold bobbins, safety pins, needles, whatever, and the corkboards also hold miscellaneous gear like scissor pockets and hemostats for turning tubes.

—*Mary Stiefer*

**153** I picked up a sturdy, wood-based wire photo/card holder at a yard sale for a buck and use it to hold pattern directions at eye level on my sewing table.

—*Shinobu*

**154** The mirrored wall in our formal dining room, which does double-duty as my sewing room, is very handy when fitting and hemming. The wall also serves as an inexpensive bulletin board for pattern instructions that can be taken down when guests come over: I put the pattern instructions and the pattern envelope into binder clips and hang them from the hooks of suction cups affixed to the mirror.

—*PattiK*

## MAKE A CLEAN SWIPE

**155** I was giving my sewing room a major cleaning and wanted to pick up the thread crumbs on the carpet before vacuuming. I had a used dryer sheet balled up in my hand to dust dog hairs out of the corners. I swiped the sheet across the Berber carpet—and the threads clung to it. I decided I needed to share this idea!

—*BeckyC*

**156** A pen-sized, telescoping magnet provides a slick way to pick up dropped pins and needles. My husband suggested this mechanic's tool and bought it for me at an auto parts store.

—*Celie*

**157** I tried using my adhesive lint roller to clean the cutting mat when I was working on a little pincushion project. It worked like a snap! No mess, and no pulling out the vac to clean the carpet.

—*Jennifer shaw*

**158** My husband purchased a long-handled toilet brush recently. Since we already had one, I hid it in my sewing room. After finishing a sewing project and wanting to clean up all those threads, I spotted the new brush in the corner, and a light bulb clicked on—I reached for the brush and whisked up all those threads.

—*gorgeous*

**159** I wrap packing tape, sticky side out, around old, dry sponges. One I keep by my sewing machine to pick up threads. Another, near the sofa where I hand sew, is especially nice for dab-dabbing the small threads that collect on fabric during a serger "rip" session. When the tape on both sides of the sponge is filled, I replace it. I think these little sticky tape wraps are worth the bother to make because I have fewer threads flying about.

—*j222b*

**160** A handful of those small, unusable scraps of fusible interfacing removes thread and fabric "fuzz" from your cutting table, sewing machine, scissor blades, and elsewhere. The tacky surfaces gather up debris better than vacuuming or painter's tape, and there's no need to buy sticky peel-off rolls. I collect the scraps in a small container.

—*lilyofthevalley*

**161** I sweep fallen threads off my studio floor with the special broom that hairdressers use to sweep up hair on the salon floor. I attached a magnetic piece to the broom's opposite side; any dropped pins stick to it and are easily removed.

—*els*

CHAPTER **TWO**

# Set Up Your Sewing Room

> " *I savor everything about sewing: reading, planning, browsing, shopping . . . and sometimes I actually cut and stitch! Have a moderate stash (immoderate?) of fabric and patterns. Notions junkie.* "
>
> —*SewFar*

# Get your gear in order

*There are lots of tools and materials required for almost any sewing project and it's easy to become mired in disorder when the fabric starts flying. Here are strategies for keeping your projects organized and supplies tidy and always at hand.*

## ORDER + EFFICIENCY = MORE SEWING!

**162** The clear plastic bags for sheet sets and other household linens have a zipper or a button closure. They are perfect to store a pattern and fabric as well as any buttons, thread or trim I bought for the project. When I am ready to start sewing, everything is together in one neat package.

—*terrilee*

**163** Here's how to speed up the time spent sewing seams. Don't stop, take out a pin, and put it in a pin cushion. Instead, insert pins horizontally in the seam before sewing, pin head facing right and to the outside edge of fabric. Keep a large, flat container directly behind your sewing machine; and, as you sew, take out each pin just before getting to it and toss it to the back of your sewing machine. No need to look where you are throwing it: 99% of the time it lands in the container. I also keep an empty container on my sewing table and switch them when the one behind the machine gets full.

—*Kirstenw*

**164** I sew standing up at a laundry counter that is about 37" (194 cm) high. I seem to get in more sewing time because it's easier to handle large pieces, to get to the ironing board, or to stop and do laundry, make beds etc. Give it a try!

—*j222b*

**165** So that useful tools are within arm's reach, I have multiple seam rippers and small scissors (for snipping threads) in the various places where I sew. I keep a set next to my machine, on the ironing board, on my worktable, and in the bathroom where I check fittings.

—*meanjean*

**166** If you have a folding TV tray or other little table, set it next to your machine chair as a place to keep a container for those little things that seem to walk off just when you need them. This should place the container where it can't be knocked over when a big piece of fabric (or your hand) comes sweeping its way.

—*Nancy Anne*

**167** I get so engrossed in the project I'm working on that I can work right through important mini deadlines. Now I have a timer in the sewing room and set it as a reminder to take care of life's annoying sewing interruptions, such as food, work, laundry, etc.

—*Karla Kizer*

**168** Nothing screams "homemade!" like loose threads dangling from every garment seam. Clipping is much easier with a pair of thread snips or small scissors always at hand, so I leash them to the sewing table with a length of ⅛" (3 mm) wide elastic. One end of the elastic is tied to the thumb hole on a pair of embroidery scissors; the other end is tied into a loop that slips over the cord where the foot pedal plugs into the machine. My elastic stretches far enough that I can use these scissors at the ironing board, but is short enough when relaxed to be manageable at the machine.

—*Michelle in Oaktown*

**169** I was constantly misplacing my tape measure or dropping it on the floor. To keep it handy, I hung it from a small nail inserted in the wall next to my cutting table.

—*BJ1400*

## HOORAY FOR LARGE DIVIDED CONTAINERS

**170** I don't have a space dedicated solely to sewing, so I need a large container to corral my sewing tools and supplies in one place. I bought a large household tool box (21" × 10" × 12" [53.3 × 25.4 × 53.3 cm]) that was half the price of a sewing box and twice the size. It also has compartments in the removable tray for small items.

—*Jane M*

**171** Although I have great places to store my tools, they gather on my table when I sew and are a chore to clear away to make space for cutting or to spread out a project. I found a basket with three compartments for rulers, pencils, tape measure and such, and one large section in the back for my sewing notebook, pattern envelope, instruction sheet, even the latest sewing magazine. It's easy to whisk away this caddy or carry it to the TV room to do my hand sewing.

—*KarmenG*

## MAXIMIZE YOUR LIGHTING

**172** I needed more light in my sewing room but had maxed-out the available wattage. My husband advised changing to the lower-energy daylight bulbs that put out 100 watts of light, but use only 23 watts of power each. WOW!! I even see differences in blacks, now!! Only drawbacks: the light is very bright, compared to other rooms, and the bulbs are expensive. Look for compact fluorescent bulbs with two tubes coming out from the thick, white base with three full spirals that cross over at the top. They fit a standard light socket.

—*SewTwin*

## NEEDLES AT THE READY

**173** I had been using a piece of masking tape on my machine to hold the machine needle when I was temporarily switching to a different one, but the tape left sticky residue on the needle. I discovered that the soft loops on the Velcro scraps in my sewing box make the perfect no-stick little needle holder.

—*KatieN*

**174** I buy needles whenever they are on sale and store them in plastic business-card sleeves in a three-ring binder. The little pockets are just the right size for several packs of needles, and there are 10 or 12 pockets on a page. Makes it much easier to find them and to see what I'm running out of.

—*ValerieJ*

## SEWING ROOM CLEANUP STRATEGIES

**175** For trash control, keep a small, lined trash can beside you and drop in threads, fabric notches, and other stuff that would normally land on the floor. With a lining (I use plastic shopping bags), you can quickly toss the whole deal out. Put several bags in the bottom of the can, slip another over them as the liner, and you'll eliminate trips to the cupboard for a new one.

—*Nancy Anne*

**176** Before vacuuming your sewing room, be sure that all bobbins and spools of thread are off the floor. They can jam the machine, and invisible thread can melt inside it. I realized I had missed some when I smelled something burning in my vacuum. Needless to say, I had to buy a new sweeper.

—*NanJones*

## PRESSER FEET AT THE READY

**177** I collect presser feet the way some sewers collect notions. Problems arise, however, when I have a special need and think I have the correct presser foot for the job, but can't be sure. Inspired by sewers who organize their fabric stashes, I purchased a divided box at a container store. I put a card in the box lid and added labels corresponding to the feet in the little cells below. I also penciled in the page number of the usage instructions in my sewing machine book. What a timesaver—it was worth the effort to get organized.

—*meanjean*

**178** Sew a divided bag customized to hold all your presser feet. Make one that folds up and ties shut; it will be just the right size to store near your machine.

—*Summerlea*

---

### ✂ *Task-driven organizing*

*Your sewing will be most efficient if you sort and store your gear according to the way you use it. Here are some suggestions:*

**179** **Debbie Lancaster's cat-proofing fix.** For years I've kept my things in one of those cheap, multi-drawer carts to keep the cats from using small items as ping-pong balls when I wasn't there. Just recently, I realized I was using the cart in the wrong way. I had carefully separated all the notions by type, was going to the cart at least a dozen times every time I sewed, and when I finished, each item had to be put back into its own little drawer. So I dumped out everything and redistributed items according to tasks. I put small boxes into one drawer to hold things I frequently use; when I'm sewing I remove the entire drawer from the cart. When I'm done, I put the drawer away where the cats (unless they get a lot smarter) can't get the contents.

**180** **elizajo's out-of-sight system.** Something I learned teaching second grade: organize materials by task, not by category of supplies, and place them for easy access. I am reorganizing my sewing supplies/materials into tasks. "Cutting" is one example: My folding cutting board, table leg extenders, cutting mat, and large measuring tools slide under the guest room bed. I also have a lidded box under there with my good scissors and other cutting gear. And a sweater box with fabrics ready to be cut out.

**181** **Elaray's portable thread-marking box.** I'm doing a lot more basting, thread tracing, and tailor tacking than ever. I find these marking methods are the most accurate and they really don't take a lot of time. I use an inexpensive pencil box to keep all the necessary hand sewing items (needles, thread clips, and topstitching thread) in one place. I don't have to search for each item separately.

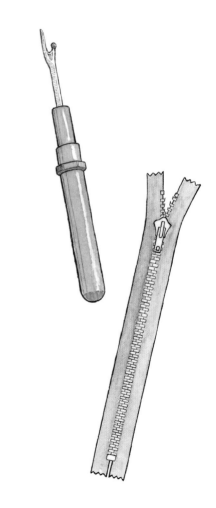

# Keep track of information

*Can't remember which sewing book had the best explanation of binding? Forgot which notions you already own or must buy in order to make your next dress? Tired of hunting through a pile of magazine clippings to find that collar you wanted to copy? PatternReview.com members take the prize for good ways to organize the information they need in order to sew.*

## RECORD IDEAS & INFO IN A

**182 Tip index notebook.** I made a Where to Find It notebook to index sewing information. The pages have three columns, made on the computer, labeled as: Tip, Source, and Page Number. In the Tip column, I write the tip; in the Source column, the magazine, book, or wherever I found the tip; and I enter the page in the Page Number column. The notebook is divided into four sections: Sewing Garments, Home Decorating, Quilting, and Miscellaneous.

—*Beth Pierce*

**183 PDA.** My PDA (aka Palm Pilot, personal data assistant) helps me to keep track of sewing tasks and/or lists—such as a thread inventory, a pattern wish list, and things to buy when they come on sale—and I delete the items as I pick them up at the store. Other uses include inches-to-fractions and fabric-width conversion charts, my current measurements, and books I'd like to buy/borrow from library. I also keep a to-do list and a spending tracker. Unlike bits of paper, I won't lose my data as long as I do regular back-ups.

—*candyo*

**184 The pattern envelope.** I file printouts of reviews (from PatternReview.com) of the patterns I plan to make in their pattern envelopes. This way, I have the benefit of other people's comments, solutions, or challenges right at my fingertips.

— *OP Gal*

## KEEP MANUALS ORDERLY

**188** All my sewing machine manuals are stored in a three-ring binder. I brought a binder to an office supply store and had the clerk drill holes in the bound side of each manual that matched the binder holes.

—*PattiAnnSG*

**185 Portable binder.** Organizing my projects into a 7" × 9" (17.8 × 22.9 cm) three-ring binder has made sewing more satisfying for me because I'm using my time more efficiently. My portable notebook has five sections:

- Section 1: Patterns I'm interested in buying. I print a picture from an online catalog and trim it to fit. This is a good place to include fabric ideas.
- Section 2: Projects in the Works. Each page here is marked in a grid, six to the page. Each square has a pattern number and a description of the item I'm planning to make. When I buy the fabric or choose it from my stash, a swatch gets taped here. This is a perfect resource for choosing thread, trims, and linings and for planning any coordinated future projects. Behind each project page is a photocopy of the back of each pattern envelope, showing yardages and back views.
- Section 3: Completed Projects. Part of the fun I'm having comes from writing up the finished projects, which I post to PatternReview.com and to my own Website. I print my Web site pages and include them in the notebook, with swatches of the fabric I used for the item. This is a great reminder and helps match coordinating or contrasting garments or items in the future.
- Section 4: Tips. I record the settings (with samples) for serged finishes for particular fabrics, special stitches I used with their settings, as well as tips and tricks I want to remember for upcoming projects.
- Section 5: The Sewing Room. Here's where I track possible changes to my sewing area; functional notions and tools I'm considering purchasing, etc.

—*Noile*

**186 Magnetic photo album.** I have an ever-growing collection of pictures cut from catalogs and magazines, showing outfits I like or details such as a collar or a ribbon belt. To organize these scraps of paper, I put them in a large but inexpensive magnetic photo album and sort them roughly by categories: necklines, color combinations, pants, accessories, etc. The papers can easily be rearranged or removed.

—*Karla Kizer*

**187 Digitize it.** One way to save something from your Internet browser to a word-processing document, or to preserve the entire Web page, is to click File on your browser task bar and then choose Save As. A box pops up and prompts you to select a folder in which to store the file. I have a folder called Sewing, which includes subfolders by topic. Then you type a File Name for the page and, below that, you have to Save as type and choose Web Archive, single file (*.mht), which in my version of Windows is the second choice on the drop-down list, and press Save.

—*Pat K*

**Deepika adds:** The process on a Mac is similar but may vary depending on the browser you use. Consult the Help function if you need assistance.

# Organize your fabric

*If you're like most sewing enthusiasts, you've got a collection of wonderful fabric stashed somewhere in your home. Can you put your finger on the whereabouts of specific pieces, or recall how many yards you bought? Fabricholics one and all, read on for the best ways to store and keep track of the goods you will someday turn into a wardrobe—or two!*

## CATALOG YOUR STASH WITH SWATCHES

**189 Four-to-a-page in a binder.** I created a fabric organization form that holds four fabric swatches per sheet. I tape the swatches onto the sheet, labeling each with the fabric name, source, yardage, width, fiber content, and price. The forms are three-hole punched and put in a ring binder. To keep the binder balanced, I made a mirror image of the form so that the swatches are on different sides on alternate pages. This swatch notebook is also handy to keep in the car trunk for fabric shopping. If you'd like to use my form, download it from http://images.PatternReview.com/siteimages/forms/FabricOrganizer.pdf.

—*Deepika*

**190 In photo-sleeve pages.** Catalog your fabric stash in a three-ring binder in clear plastic photo sleeves. Cut small fabric swatches and insert one into each pocket. When you shop, everything will be in the binder for matching and coordinating.

—*Barbara H*

**191 In a business card wallet.** I use business-card wallets to hold fabric info on cards that fit into the pockets. I staple the fabric on one side of the card and write a description of the garment on the reverse. The wallet fits in my bag and makes it easy to match fabrics, thread, buttons, and accessories when shopping.

—*LiZ*

**192 In an embroidery-floss organizer.** The best swatch-carrying idea I've found is Floss-A-Way, an embroidery-floss polybag organizer system. It contains 36 5" × 3½" (12.7 × 8.9 cm) Ziploc bags and a binder ring. The bags have a space on the front for info and are big enough to hold a good-sized swatch. The binder ring is easy to open, in case you want to take along just one or two swatches.

—*Lou*

**193 In a zippered CD case.** I catalog my fabric swatches in an 8" (20.3 cm) CD case. It's compact, has deep binder posts to handle the extra thickness of fabrics, zips closed, and has a carrying handle. Additional sleeves are available, too. I put a swatch of fabric in each sleeve along with a 3" × 5" (7.6 × 12.7 cm) card for notes. When I have fabric cut, I ask them to cut me a small square, which I put in a sleeve, and I write down the fabric info on a blank card. I include a sample of trim or anything else I plan to use with the fabric. I keep the case in the car so I'm always prepared.

—*EveS*

**194 Coded to your storage boxes.** I use page protectors that hold baseball cards. The 4" × 6" (10.2 × 15.2 cm) index cards cut in half slide perfectly into the pockets and leave ½" (1.3 cm) sticking up to staple the fabric onto. The card has yardage, content, price and other information; and the pages are organized by fabric type. I store fabric in boxes labeled A, B, C, D, etc., so I write the box letter on each card.

—*Nancywin*

## STASH CATALOG AS PROJECT PLANNER

**195** These tips will help you keep track of your stash and plan what to sew with each fabric:

- First, lay out all your fabrics in some logical manner—I do mine by type (suiting, knit, sheer, silky, etc.).
- From each fabric cut a swatch exactly 4" × 4" (10.2 × 10.2 cm). Launder and dry the swatches; then re-measure.
- Glue or staple each swatch to one side of an index card. On the card list the length and width of the fabric, content if known, noted % of shrinkage, and any other observations.
- Once you decide what to make from a specific fabric, note on the swatch card what else will be needed to create the garment.

- Stack these cards in the order in which you plan to start the project: store them in a card file box, or punch holes in the corner of each card and put them on a binder ring.

Now you know exactly what's in your stash and how to best use it. You have examples of fabric at hand when shopping for patterns. When snoop shopping, you can check to see if you have a fabric that fits the garment that intrigues you. For me, having all that ready information encourages me to finish one project and start the next!

—*Nancywin*

**196** When I buy fabric, I cut a small 2" × 2" (5.1 × 5.1 cm) square with pinking shears and staple it in a spiral notebook. Under the swatch I write the fabric content, width, yardage, cleaning info. I put coordinating fabrics on the same page, and sometimes note the pattern I was thinking of when I bought the fabric. After the garment is finished, I jot down what I made. This helps me remember how much yardage I bought, and I can check my notebook if I have a new pattern to try.

—*JudyP*

## FILE CARE-TEST RESULTS

**197** When ordering online, I print the fabric care and content information, and the Web site's address on a piece of three-hole notebook paper. I cut a 2" × 3" (5.1 × 7.6 cm) swatch and glue its top edge to the paper with the info, so that it hangs loose on-grain. To reference how an individual fabric reacts when it is washed or steam ironed, I cut several swatches and treat them differently. For instance, one is just pressed with a press cloth, another is pressed without the cloth, another is steam pressed with a press cloth to pre-shrink—and one is washed in Woolite, air dried, and steam pressed with a cloth. I label each and add it to the notebook page. This really lets me know if something I make could be washed or has to be dry-cleaned.

—*alicia*

## SOLVING STASH MYSTERIES

**198** I often receive bundles of mystery fabrics from online companies. By going back to the site where I got the bundle and browsing the offerings, I've solved several of those mysteries and was able to note exact fiber content and laundering instructions. Besides, it's exciting to see how much $$ that "free" fabric is worth!

—*Nancywin*

**199** I cut the swatches for my stash catalog from the selvage, across the fabric, because sometimes the selvedge marks are the final clue to identifying similar fabrics.

—*Aless*

## Organize your patterns

*You're not alone if your love of sewing patterns has produced an embarrassment of envelopes, tissue, magazines, and tracings. Here are clever ways to keep track of which patterns you own— and add comments if you like—and to store them efficiently.*

## CONVENIENT FABRIC STORAGE

**200** My rather large fabric collection is kept in cardboard records storage boxes (from an office supply store) to avoid dust and fading; each box is labeled to indicate the contents. I set the empty box on end, with the open side vertical and facing me, and stack the folded pieces one on top of another. When the box is filled to the top, I set it back on its base and cover it. When I remove the lid, all the fabrics are on display.

—*Brine*

**201** Storing a large length of polyester knit is easy when you roll it around a cardboard wrapping paper tube. You just unroll what you need for a pattern, and snip it off.

—*Mary Stiefer*

**202** I have a dedicated sewing room, but storage space is still a problem. I recently started rolling up my fusible interfacings and storing them in 24" cardboard mailing tubes. I use a dowel to start the rolling process; it makes rolling the lightweight interfacing much easier. I put labels on the outside of the tubes so I can identify the contents (lightweight, midweight, etc.). I store the tubes in a large cylindrical basket along with my rolls of tracing paper.

—*elaray*

## MAKE A PRINTED PATTERN CATALOG

**206** Here's a pattern cataloging suggestion: Scan and print the pattern envelopes, then have them laminated and bound in books. If you lose or damage one, you have the CD of the master scans. Also, the original envelope stays fresh.

—*Lou*

**207** I carry photos of my pattern info on a looped cord like an oversize key ring so I can bring patterns and yardage info to meetings and for shopping.

- I laid out the patterns in three rows, four to a column, and snapped a digital pic in the highest resolution. I printed them on

**203** A wall-mounted, wine-bottle rack holds my rolls of stabilizers and interfacings. It keeps them organized, easily accessible, and out of the way.

—*SueV*

**204** The sofa in my sewing room now has some decorative cushions filled with my hoard of fabric scraps that are semi-organized by color, weight, etc. These pillows look better than a heap of plastic bags and take less room than baskets; I zip or baste them closed so I can retrieve the scraps if I like.

—*petro*

**205** Safety pins keep track of my interfacings. I use a sticky label to mark each interfacing with the manufacturer's name, fiber content, etc., then I fold it in half (sticky-sides-in) and attach it to a safety pin that is unpinned and moved as I use up the interfacing. I mark another large safety pin with the same label to hold scraps of that interfacing—it's a handy way to store small pieces of interfacing to test on a fabric before I commit to cutting into the big piece.

—*Karla Kizer*

8" × 10" photo paper and cut out each individual pattern picture.
- Using a glue stick, I mounted each pattern pic on poster board cut slightly larger than the photo to make a border for the hole punch. I reinforced the holes and wrote the pattern's fabric recommendations and yardage on the back of each card.
- I strung the photos on a thick serged chain and tied both ends together. This loops easily through my handbag strap.

—*ryan's mom*

## MANAGING PATTERNS FROM MAGAZINES

**208** A portable filing folder organizes my children's and toddlers' pattern originals and trace-offs, and saves me lots of search time. I placed the original pattern (and the book or magazine it came from) in the first pocket; in each subsequent pocket I placed all the traced-off pattern pieces for each size (one pocket per size). I repeated this to file other patterns in the remaining empty pockets.

—*Hilary*

**209** I photocopy my BWOF sewing instructions. Then, I physically cut out the needed instructions from the other instructions on the page. I arrange and tape the instructions to another sheet of paper and photocopy again. One piece of letter paper is easier to manage than the magazine and this leaves plenty of room to write notes to myself to augment Burda's minimal instructions. I usually include references to books that explain the instructions more clearly. I store this augmented instruction sheet in a Ziploc bag with the pattern pieces.

—*elaray*

## FOLD, PRESS, RETURN TO ENVELOPE

**210** To fit a pattern neatly back into its envelope after use, I iron as I go—fold in half, press, fold in half again, press. The pattern goes back into the envelope, just like new!

—*SexiSadi*

## EASY REFERENCE, EASY RETRIEVAL PATTERN STORAGE

**211** After I hit 100 patterns, storing them on hangers was no longer practical—now I keep them in manila envelopes. Each is labeled with the pattern number, company (sometimes different companies have the same numbers), and a brief description. I store them in copier-paper boxes in numerical order. The pattern envelopes go into a clear plastic Sterilite ShowOffs box, sorted by type (fall/winter, spring/summer, purses, home dec, kids, etc.)

—*candyo*

**212** I copy my pattern pieces onto plastic and make lots of notes when I alter a pattern. Instead of stuffing all this back into the pattern envelope, I put them into comic book protectors. These clear plastic sleeves fit the pattern envelopes beautifully with lots of flexibility to hold any extras. I store them in three-ring, comic-book binders.

—*jadamooo*

**213** When storing patterns, I scan the photo from the pattern envelope front and stick it on a 12" × 16" envelope, which is big enough for the original pattern and the one I have traced off.

—*regine*

**214** I instituted this easy-to-use system for organizing my pattern stash. By the way, this system took a while to set up so pace yourself—do a few every night and you'll be done soon:

- Separate the pattern tissues and instruction sheet from the pattern envelope. Slip the pattern envelope into a plastic sleeve made for three-hole notebooks. Place the pattern tissues and instruction sheet into a one-quart Ziploc clear plastic bag, putting the instruction sheet on top of the pattern tissue to display the pattern number. Some pattern numbers weren't prominent so I hand wrote them in the upper-right corner.
- Store all the Ziploc bags numerically in boxes. I file patterns with no number alphabetically by name at the beginning.
- Store the plastic sleeves containing the pattern envelopes in notebooks, by garment type. In my Blouses and Dresses notebooks, I sort the pattern envelopes by sleeve length. If the pattern has multiple options, I file it by the garment style that attracted me.
- It's so cool to pull out the notebook and reference my collection in an easy manner.

—*KarmenG*

### ID clues for pattern pieces

*Ever unfold a traced pattern, stare at the pieces, and realize you've forgotten what sort of garment it makes? Here are two tips for tickling your memory:*

**215** **MaryLynn in Long Beach's system.** If I'm drafting a pattern, or significantly changing/morphing a commercial pattern, I assign the new pattern a number based on that day's date. For instance, the pattern number for June 1, 2009, is 060109. If I happen (rarely) to make more than one pattern in a single day, I add a hyphen and the ordinal for that pattern. Example: 060109-1, 060109-2. I put that number on every piece. Each pattern is stored in a gallon-size Ziploc bag and may include a sketch or written description.

**216** **Sherril Miller's visual clues.** When I traced a pattern from a pattern magazine, I later had trouble identifying the pattern. So I started tracing the line drawing of the garment onto each pattern piece. This helps me immediately identify which pattern the pieces belong to.

## MAKE A DIGITAL PATTERN CATALOG

**217** I use Picasa Web albums (Google pictures) to organize my patterns online. I find a picture of my pattern or scan my copy and save the photo to my Google photo album. Each photo is identified by the pattern name; then I add info about the pattern, indicating whether it has been cut, cut apart, if I have made it, and any changes I made. This lets me browse my patterns easily.

*—1handfull*

**218** I carry around an electronic catalog of my patterns in my Palm Pilot. It might take an hour at first to add 50 patterns to your catalog, but only a few minutes later, when you're just adding recent purchases:

- My catalog uses images downloaded from the pattern manufacturer's Web site. I pull the cover image plus the diagrams, which are organized by garment type in folders within the Palm's photo album software.
- The images are also on my desktop, so this process functions as my at-home pattern catalog, too.
- I also copy the yardage requirements for each into a separate text editing file.
- My physical patterns are organized by pattern number, regardless of manufacturer, so it takes only two seconds to find one after I spot it in my electronic catalog.

*—J-Girl*

**219** I made an electronic version of my pattern wish list/catalog, so I could refer to it more easily in the store from my PDA. Here's what to do: Install CutePDF, a shareware program, on your computer; this allows you to convert documents to PDF files. There's a free version on the site. Open your wish list or catalog, and select the print version. Select Print, or Send to Printer. When the menu opens to select a printer, select CutePDF. Pick the directory where you want to save the PDF version and select Print.

The program will create a PDF version of your catalog and save it in the directory you chose. Move it onto your portable electronic gadget, and you'll have it handy when you are in the store. If you already have the Adobe Professional you can use that to the same effect.

*—kkkkaty*

**Deepika adds:** There is various free software available for creating pdf documents; search online if you do not have any.

## FIND THE PIECES YOU REALLY NEED

**220** When you fold up your pattern pieces for storage, make each fold so that the words identifying the piece (e.g., "sleeve") face up. This silly tip has actually saved me more minutes than I'd like to admit.

*—bkool*

**221** If you have a favorite sewn item to make from a particular pattern, fold the parts that you use with the instructions around them, separately from the ones you don't use, and slip them into the envelope. You don't have to take out EVERY pattern piece to find the few you actually use!

*—Janie Viers*

**222** Some accessory patterns have up to six items in each envelope, often with several small pieces per item. I separate out the pattern pieces for each accessory item and put them in a quart-size freezer bag, writing the item name on the bag's white strip. These quart bags, the instructions, and the envelope all go into a gallon Ziploc bag. This keeps the small tissue pieces safe, and I can pull out exactly what I want to make.

*—redsquid*

## CREASE-FREE PATTERN STORAGE

**223** When I don't want to put a pattern away in its envelope, I pile all the pattern pieces, with the smallest ones on the top of the pile and the largest on the bottom. Then I lay a long gift-wrap cardboard tube on one end of the pile and carefully roll all the pieces onto the tube. I secure the wrapped pieces with an elastic band, label the outside piece, then slide the cardboard tube out for reuse. I store the rolls of pattern pieces on a shelf.

*—Elaine Dougan*

**224** The local copy shop gave me some of the rigid, black cardboard tubes that blueprint paper comes in. These 36" (91.4 cm) tubes are about the same width as pattern pieces. After ironing the patterns flat, I roll them up and slide them into the tubes for storage. Bonus: no re-ironing the pattern.

*—Mary Reed*

**225** After ironing my pattern pieces, I hang them to keep them wrinkle-free while I'm working on the project. I run an 8" (20.3 cm) piece of string through the two handles of a large binder clip, tying the ends to form a loop. I clip on the pattern pieces and hang the loop over a hook or tack it to a cork board.

*—meanjean*

# Keep thread tidy

*People who don't sew may think thread storage an odd thing to obsess over, but hunting through disorganized, unwinding spools and bobbins of unknown content can spoil the pleasure of a good sewing session (or anyway, delay it). PatternReview.com members prefer their threads to be neat, with bobbins attached. Join them.*

## RECORD THE THREAD ID

**226** To keep bobbin thread from unwinding, I tape the thread end to the outside of the bobbin and write the number of the thread color on the tape; masking tape works very well for this. I only use one brand of thread, so I always know which thread spool matches which bobbin. If you use more than one brand, figure out a coding system so you'll know which spool is which.

—*Robie Kentspeth*

**227** The gadgets for linking a spool of thread to its matching bobbin don't work well for me because putting things back where they belong is not my strong point. Instead, I label bobbins with reinforcement rings for notebook paper. I write the thread brand/type and the color code on the ring before sticking it on the bobbin and position the ring so its hole lines up with the one on the bobbin. Check first to make sure that the reinforcement won't be peeled off by moving parts on your machine.

—*Karla Kizer*

**228** When I pierce the spool on my thread-holder, the little label gets destroyed. I replace it with a reinforcement ring and write the color number on the "O" with permanent ink.

—*Rhonda in Montreal*

## Write on the bobbin

*Two PatternReview.com members use Sharpie pens to label their bobbins:*

**229** **Oopsy-Daisy! says:** For colors that you use often, write the thread color number with a Sharpie marker on clear plastic bobbins. I have five colors of navy that are slightly different and, when sewing late at night, it's hard to match up an already-wound bobbin.

**230** **Leslie in Austin adds:** On metal bobbins, the Sharpie marks are removable with rubbing alcohol.

## KEEP SPOOLS & BOBBINS FROM UNWINDING

**231** Commercial bobbin keepers, which prevent bobbins from losing their thread, are expensive and I never seem to have enough. I bought a length of plastic aquarium tubing (15mm or about ⅝" outer diameter). I cut off little rings, cut the side of each ring open, and then slip the ring around the thread on the bobbin. I actually like these better—they are softer as well as cheaper and don't crush the thread on fuller bobbins.

—*Astrostitcher*

**232** There are no more tangled threads in my thread box. When finished with a project, I wrap the thread back onto the spool, wrapping it over my thumb a few times. This creates a little gap. I poke the end of the thread through this loop and tighten it.

—*Beth Pierce*

**233** To keep bobbin thread from unwinding, wrap a small piece of Glad Press'n Seal around the bobbin, making sure to overlap and press securely. The food wrap is easily removed when you want to use the bobbin and can be reused many times.

—*Lizz*

## THREE THREAD RACKS, ONE TRAY

**234** My thread storage unit cost only $10. I bought an unfinished wooden shelf on sale, stained it yellow, and hot-glued white plastic spool holders on it. If you want to make a holder for serger thread, buy a larger shelf.

—Clev

**235** I built a sturdy rack to hold coned thread from pegboard and dowels. I used a Dremel to cut the dowels and glued them on a slight angle.

—Diane Slade Inc

**236** Small spools of embroidery thread fit perfectly into a kitchen drawer cutlery holder.

—Mary Stiefer

**237** I mounted thread racks on over-the-door hooks. To keep the spools from slipping off the rack, I cut plastic straws approximately in thirds and used them as dowel extenders. Eureka!

—Patti B

## STORE THE SPOOL WITH ITS BOBBIN

**238** There are handy little plastic gadgets that snap a bobbin to the top of a thread spool to keep them together, but this trick is fast, really cheap, and works just fine for me. Loop a rubber band through the bobbin, then wrap it around the thread spool enough times to keep it secure. The rubber band keeps the bobbin thread from unwinding, but I still have to secure the spool thread in its little keeper.

—Diana M

**239** The old wood trays printers once used to hold lead type are divided into compartments, each the perfect size for storing a slender thread spool and its matching bobbin. They're generally easy to find at flea markets. If you hang them so the long dimension of the compartments is vertical, you can rest the spools on the horizontal dividers and top each with its bobbin. This makes a pretty display and it's so convenient.

—donna mel

## CONTAIN YOUR BOBBINS

**240** Cocktail ice cube trays are the perfect size for bobbins. The trays stack and can be labeled for easy identification.

—Lizz

**241** I store my bobbins in metal AOL software boxes. The boxes are very shallow, so the bobbins fit in a single layer in the box; the lids are marked to indicate thread colors. I also keep a box just for empty bobbins.

—Robie Kentspeth

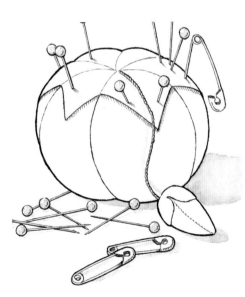

# Keep notions tidy

*By nature, long and skinny ribbons, elastics, and even zippers are challenging to store. But tangled trims aren't nice—even if you can find the one you want, it might be crushed, twisted, and hard to use. And while the idea of a button box is romantic, you'll be happiest if you can tell at a glance how many of each type you've got. Try these tips to keep your trims accessible and in good form.*

## GROUP BY SIZE, TYPE, OR COLOR

**242** My grandmother was a very efficient seamstress. At the end of a project, she strung the unused buttons through a safety pin. Sometimes she bent the pin to accommodate the diameter of the buttons. On pins, the same buttons all stay together. Keeping them on the papers they come with takes up too much space, and dumping the loose ones in a can makes it really difficult to find all the matches.

—*meanjean*

**243** When I see a good sale on buttons, or some that are unique, I buy them in sets: usually six to eight for shirts, four for jackets, plus smaller ones for the sleeves. I keep track of them in an old hanging jewelry organizer. Jacket buttons go on one side and shirt buttons on the other; buttons are separated by matching groups and/or colors and put in the individual pockets. I only use this method for carded or specialty buttons: bulk buttons go in food storage bags in a drawer.

—*Nancywin*

**244** Storing all the zippers I bought on eBay had me stumped, until I got the idea to put them over hangers so I can see what I have. All my zippers are the same length and are sorted by color, but zippers of different lengths could be stored by length instead. I secure each bunch with a twist tie.

—*MelissaB in WA*

## RIBBONS AT THE READY

**245** The "ribbon stick" holding all my ribbons reminds me of those I saw in a cheerleading movie. I wrap individual ribbons (single width) around empty wrapping paper rolls and tack each end in place with pins from store-bought clothing.

—*celeste*

**246** I use metal plant hangers to store all those rolls of gorgeous wired ribbon that I can't resist buying: I loop the rolls through the long, hooked rod of a plant hanger, which I then hook on an upper shelf. When I need a length of ribbon, I unroll it from the stack or take down the holder, lay it horizontally, and measure off what I need.

—*granny geek*

## TANGLE-FREE ELASTIC AND LACE

**247** I love using clear elastic but have often thrown the whole jumbled mess away because I couldn't find the end and it seemed stuck together. My new supply was in danger of heading down the same path, until I gave it some thought. I threaded the end through a plastic drinking straw; then put the wrapped elastic, threaded through the straw, into a Ziploc bag with the straw sticking out a little. Now I pull out what I need and store the bag in my elastics treasure box.

—*sewingripper*

**Deepika adds:** See Chapter 4 for tips on using clear elastic.

**248** Several yards of loose stretch lace or smaller elastic can make a bit of a mess. After I find a free end, I put the rest into a plastic bag—zipper top or twist-tie types both work. Leave the free end sticking out of the bag so you can find it. Don't pack too much lace in a bag as this will keep it from feeding out easily.

—*Kathy in NM*

# Secrets for Sewing Knits

Whether it's a T-shirt or a ball gown, if Sarah Veblen makes it, the sewing will be flawless. A custom fashion designer with a home-based business in the Baltimore metropolitan area, Sarah is always busy teaching, creating clothing for her clientele, and writing in several venues. One of her many areas of expertise is sewing knit fabrics. Here she shares some techniques for working with knits, demonstrating the key steps for designing and making her hoodie dress with flounces. Visit sarahveblen.com to learn more about Sarah, her classes, Web store, and newsletter.

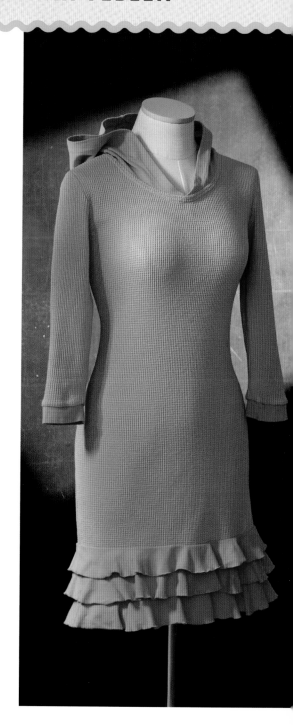

*"When sewing with knit fabrics I like to utilize a pattern I have already developed. This way I know that the garment will fit, or at least be close since each knit fabric is a little different. I wanted this dress to look like an elongated hoodie, but with some interesting details to give it pizzazz and to make it just a bit girly. I envisioned the silhouette as shapely rather than loose and baggy. To solidify these ideas, I drew a quick sketch and quickly saw that I could start with my basic T-shirt pattern. I tested and modified a hood pattern to get the shape I wanted in my chosen fabric."*

# Choosing a suitable knit

*There are so many wonderful knit fabrics—and if you've ever sewn them, you know the structure of the knit, the weight of the yarns, and the way the fabric stretches all affect the shape and fit of the garment you make. Take time to analyze a knit before using it, and test your pattern: this isn't difficult, here's how.*

## SELECTING PATTERNS AND FABRICS

Patterns for knits are sized differently from patterns for woven fabrics, since the amount of wearing ease is dependent on the degree of give or stretch of the knit fabric. I use these two words to mean different things: All knit fabrics have inherent "give" resulting from the way the knit stitch is formed. I use "stretch" to convey that the fabric contains spandex—this is what is meant when a pattern calls for "stretch knit" fabric. This is why it's important to develop and fit a pattern with a certain category of knit fabric in mind, making the mockups and finished garments

from the same type. (To test the give or stretch of a particular knit, refer to Assessing Knit Fabrics below.)

Since I was using a familiar T-shirt pattern for my hoodie dress, I knew how much give the knit fabric for the body needed to have. And because the hood and flounces are really just decorative elements and do not affect the fit of the garment, I knew I could use a different knit for them.

While the amount of give of the fabric for the body of the dress was dictated by the pattern I had chosen, I also considered the

weight and thickness of the fabric. The knit needed to be thick enough so that I would feel sufficiently covered when wearing the dress, and it needed to have enough body (structure) so that it would hold its shape and not cling to my body.

In order for the dress to make sense visually, I wanted to use the same fabric for the hood and the flounces. The hood could be just about any knit fabric, so I made sure I selected a fabric that would make really nice flounces: it needed to be a bit soft and drapey.

## Assessing knit fabrics

Learning to assess knit fabrics will increase your confidence—and your success rate—when making knit garments. The process shown is a good way to assess the amount of give or stretch in a knit fabric. If you perform the test on a number of different knit fabrics, you'll see they differ quite a lot.

This assessment demonstrates how much knits can vary, which in turn illustrates how the amount of give or stretch can affect sizing. For example, if you made the same T-shirt pattern in each of the fabrics shown in the test photos, the shirt made in the interlock knit, which is the more stable of the two, would be tighter than the one made in the rib knit.

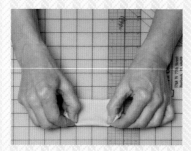

1. Fold the knit fabric along the cross grain, grasping the fabric between the thumb and forefinger of each hand, and leaving a 2" ( 5.1 cm) space in the middle.

2. Now, keeping one hand in place, gently pull the fabric with the other hand, noting how much the fabric easily stretches. Don't pull or stretch the fabric to its max—just to where it comfortably expands. These photos show a rib knit (top) and a stable interlock knit (bottom)

# Mastering the construction

*Whether you plan to make a garment similar to my hoodie dress, or something different, the techniques I explain here cover the basics needed for assembling almost anything in knit fabric. I think you'll find them versatile and easy to adapt.*

## DRESS BODY TECHNIQUES

1. I like to use my serger in a 4-thread configuration for many of the seams of knit garments. However, a serger is not necessary when working with knits. In fact, I like to sew shoulder seams with my conventional machine so that I can press the seam allowances open, thereby balancing their weight.

2. Pin the sleeves to the garment and serge construct with a 4-thread configuration. On many knit garments, this method of "flat construction" (versus setting in a traditional sleeve) usually works well. I use ⅝" (1 cm) seam allowance, but it's fine to use any seam allowance you prefer. Press all seam allowances toward the sleeve.

3. Serge construct the underarm/side seam of the garment and press toward the back.

4. Hemming the lower edge of the garment could be done in a number of ways (and may be done before or after you attach the flounces):

- Using a cover stitch machine; this stitch has built-in ability to stretch.
- By hand using a catch stitch; if the catch stitch is loosely worked, it will have the ability to stretch just a bit.
- Using a serger and a rolled or narrow hem setting; both of these stitches will stretch.
- Using a conventional machine and a zigzag stitch setting; even a narrow zigzag stitch enables a stitch to stretch a little. This is the method I chose, first serge finishing the raw edge with a 3-thread configuration, since the bottom flounce covers the stitching.

## HOOD TECHNIQUES

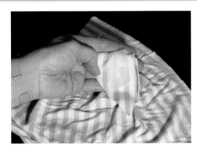

1. First make the buttonholes for the drawstring. A small piece of silk organza is the perfect stabilizer for perfect buttonholes in knits. Because my hood fabric was so stretchy, I first applied a thin, stable fusible interfacing and then pinned two layers of silk organza in the buttonhole area.

2. To sew the center back seam of hood, I used my serger with a 4-thread configuration, but a cover stitch could also be used.

3. To hem the hood and form the drawstring channel, I used a straight stitch on my conventional machine. To prevent the fabric from being stretched out of shape while stitching, reduce the pressure on the machine's presser foot. If your machine does not have this capability, try a walking foot or roller foot.

4. To attach the hood to garment, I used my serger with a 4-thread configuration.

5. After inserting the drawstring in its channel, I set my conventional machine to a short straight stitch and stitched-in-the-ditch of the center back seam, just across the channel, to prevent the drawstring from being pulled out.

## CUFF TECHNIQUES

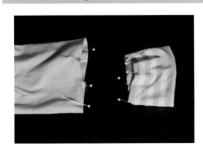

1. To make the cuff, use a straight stitch (no stretch needed) on your conventional machine and then press the allowances open. Then fold the cuff in half, right side out.

2. For maximum control, baste the open edges of the cuff together using a zigzag stitch so the cuff will stretch. Divide and mark both the cuff and sleeve opening into quarters.

(continued)

3. Turn the sleeve inside out. Insert the cuff into the sleeve, aligning the cut edges and matching the pins. Pin together.

4. For maximum control, machine or hand baste the cuff to the sleeve opening, stretching the cuff as necessary. Then, with the cuff oriented in the serger as shown, sew the seam using a 4-thread configuration.

5. Stitch over the beginning stitches for about ⅝" (1.6 cm), then serge off the work, leaving a long thread tail. Using a blunt needle, pull the thread tail into serged stitches and clip.

## FLOUNCE TECHNIQUES

1. Refer to Deepika's tip #272 for making a flounce pattern on page 46. Making one or two mockups will quickly tell you how much fullness looks the best to your eye. Decide how many flounce tiers you want and choose the length of each.

2. To join the flounce sections (the side seams), use a conventional machine so the seam allowances can be pressed open in order to control bulk. Sew the sections of each tier together before attaching to the garment or hemming.

3. To pin the flounces to the dress, mark the center front and center back of each flounce and of the garment. Pin the flounces in place, right side down on the garment with the flounce hemline toward the garment neck.

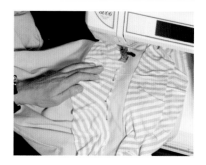

4. To sew on the flounces, I chose a 2-step zigzag stitch, which secured the seam allowance well, and has built-in stretch, preventing popped or broken stitches during wear. But a cover stitch could also be used.

5. To prep the flounce for hemming, stay stitch across the side-seam allowances at the lower edge. This will prevent the allowances from flipping over when you stitch a rolled hem.

6. To hem the flounce and enhance the wavy effect, use a rolled/narrow hem setting on your serger (I used a 3-thread configuration). Stretching the fabric while stitching will produce extra waviness or lettuce leafing: the more you pull, the more pronounced the lettuce leafing effect.

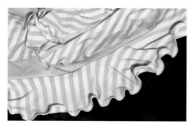

Here is the finished flounce.

*The hoodie dress is just as fun in fresh blue and white as it is in pink.*

CHAPTER **THREE**

# Design & Pattern Prep

> " *Love to design, hate to sew, love results. Have an enormous stash that my kids think should go. We haven't downsized yet, so I think my stash has wonderful possibilities.* "
>
> —*filichirp*

# Start with inspiration

*Absolutely, a truly custom wardrobe is one of the best things about sewing—the best for some of us. Figuring out what we want to sew is sometimes easy and enjoyable, but other times it can be difficult to think through the details or visualize the results. Here are tips to help you indulge your creativity.*

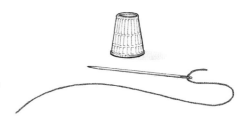

## FIND YOUR FASHION INSPIRATION AT

**249** **Your screen saver.** I was fooling around on my computer the other day and, having no idea how much it would inspire me to action, saved a picture of a pattern illustration as my monitor background. This is very easy to do and to change (consult your operating system help menu for how to customize the monitor background). I plan to change the picture as I work on different projects—it makes me find time to work on whatever I'm sewing. A new definition of "nag screen."

—*LaurieEm*

**250** **Get Lucky!** The magazine, people! ☺ Seriously, *Lucky* is one of the best sources for the latest fashions and trends that translate into great sewing ideas. Close-up photos, similar styles (skirts, tops, dresses) grouped together, with fabric types, etc. It features up-and-coming designers too. It's my favorite inspiration source for making my sewing projects more like ready-to-wear.

—*Oopsy-Daisy!*

**251** **Online Ready-to-Wear Sites** When I can't quite visualize how a design element or type of fabric will look, I use the search feature on the online sites that sell RTW to get examples. Of course this only works if they've used the term in describing the item, but give it a try. For example, I wanted to compare how plaid looks on garments when on the diagonal vs. horizontal/vertical. I simply typed in "plaid" and browsed the inventory. Many "brick and mortar" stores have online sites, so even if you could never afford to shop in them, you can browse their inventory for ideas.

—*LoriB*

**252** **A custom storyboard.** I put together a storyboard of the patterns and garments I plan to sew. I can see at a glance what will go with what. The board is taped to the wall in my sewing room where I can see it. I can't draw so I copied the line drawing for each garment from the pattern company Web site and then put them into a Word document (you can use many different programs to work with the images). I resized each drawing to the size I wanted and then traced it by hand, making design changes when I wished. Then I just glued my fabric choices to the paper.

—*Sherril Miller*

**253** **TV fashion programs.** My husband and I recently invested in a high definition, large, flat screen TV and the HD satellite programming to go with it. I think I have died and gone to heaven. Instead of being the front row seat to the NFL, it has become, for me at least, a window into the world of couture. It's a window far clearer than anything I have enjoyed on the Internet. To see the moving clothes on a live body with the detail of high definition photography is just amazing. So if hubby is claiming he needs one of these to watch football, agree all the way. Better yet, just go out and buy one for yourself. You will be glad you did.

—*solosmocker*

## DISCOVER DISCONTINUED PATTERNS

**254** The sewing pattern companies reuse their pattern numbers. So, when you are searching for an older pattern by its number, you need to know when it was printed or a description of the item so that you can find it. Simplicity 1234 could be a dress one year and a few years later it could be a shirt pattern. If I can't locate a discontinued pattern through a Google search, I try an advanced eBay search:

- There is a trick to search for sewing patterns on eBay: Enter the pattern brand and number and then check the box labeled "search title and description." If the item is on eBay, you should be able to find it that way.
- eBay has a feature for buyers called I Want It Now. You can put your wish list there. Tell the sellers what pattern brand and number you want, of course, but also identify the kind of garment it is and the size you are looking for.

—*oldpatterns*

**255** Remember those paper dolls you used to play with when you were little? Well, this way of capturing fashion inspiration is kinda like that . . .

- Make a design template: Trace a lady's figure, front and back views. I traced one out of the Vogue catalog. Photocopy it. Zoom it to get several different sizes. Or make a croquis of yourself (see the tips on page 47).
- Every time you see a design or design detail that you absolutely love, race home and sketch it onto one of your photocopied templates.
- Jot down a few notes to remind you where you saw it, why it caught your eye, the fabric, the color, etc. Design ideas can strike at any time—walking down the street, at the movies, cruising RTW—so BE PREPARED!
- Affix the drawing to your sewing room wall. I loosely separate the sketches into tops, skirts, etc., and put them up alongside magazine clippings/postcards/labels, etc. I know it's messy, and if you sew in your dining room this may not be possible, but I love having all that inspiration around me as I sew. Sometimes I just look around the room and marvel at the amazing details those talented designer types come up with.

*—Helen near Sydney*

**256** When I start getting creative with a new pattern I try out ideas on the line drawing provided on the instruction sheet: I make a photocopy of the drawing, increasing the size as much as possible, and then make a number of copies to play with. I sketch patterns from possible fabrics like stripes, flowers, etc., or possible embellishments. Or I draw changes or modifications I'm considering. This is a good preview that helps me make design choices. The line drawing is much more accurate than the fashion drawing on the front, which is usually elongated and stylized.

*—marycds*

**257** If you have Photoshop or Photoshop Elements, you can combine a photo of your fabric with the line drawing of your pattern:

- To do this, open your fabric photo in Photoshop. Make it an appropriate size, which will usually mean downsizing it (you don't want the fabric texture/design to be huge on your line drawing).
- Then select a square of the photo or the swatch, go to the edit menu and choose 'define pattern.' This will make your fabric appear as a pattern in the paint bucket pattern collection.
- Now open your line drawing in Photoshop, click on paint bucket, select "pattern" in the fill field, select your fabric and "paint bucket" your line drawing. Kind of like dressing the paper dolls we used to play with as children.

*—franticfashion*

## Clone RTW favorites

*Here are two approaches to taking a pattern from a garment you love to wear.*

**258** **Liana's method.** If you want to quickly copy a simple garment, it's easy to do using a needlepoint tracing wheel. (The type with longer, very sharp points that will pierce fabric.) This is a quick method that will give you a "close enough" pattern for things like nightgowns, T-shirts, PJ pants, etc., and can be very handy as a starting point for making a garment without a commercial pattern, or for copying details to add to another pattern:

- Lay a piece of paper on top of a surface such as a cardboard cutting mat.
- Place your garment to be copied on top, and run the tracing wheel around the edges of one piece, through the seams, etc. The points will go through into the paper, marking the seam lines.
- Write the size and a description on the tracing so you'll know what it is in the future.

**259** **Janie Viers' method.** I had a blouse that fit like a dream. I wore it to death. I loved it to death. I washed and ironed it and took it apart and compared the pieces with many patterns that had come up lacking! Then I adapted the closest one to reflect the lines of my perfect shirt. If you have panties, pants, tops, or dresses that have bitten the dust, use them as the basis for altering commercial patterns so you can have them live on forever. An item has to be really unwearable for me to feel free to pick it to pieces, though!

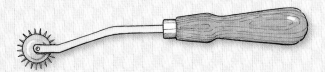

**260** **Faux two-piece sleeve.** Here's a way to shift the seam of a one-piece sleeve toward the back, so that when viewed from behind, it resembles a two-piece sleeve. Why would you want to do this? 1) Less bulk at the underarm. 2) I think doing a placket is much easier if the sleeve is seamed this way; you can even sew the cuff on while the sleeve is flat. Please, please make a muslin to make sure you want to use this technique before cutting into any good fabric! Follow the drawings below to make the change:

- First draw a line parallel to the lengthwise grain from the notch on the back of the sleeve cap to the bottom edge; cut the pattern on this line.
- Transfer the cut-off section to the opposite edge of the pattern, aligning the two underarm seamlines.
- Add seam allowance to the new vertical edges (and to the rest of the pattern if necessary).

—*blue mooney*

**Deepika adds:** This puts the vertical edges on different grain lines—watch for interesting effects with vertical stripes and think twice about using with plaids or horizontal stripes.

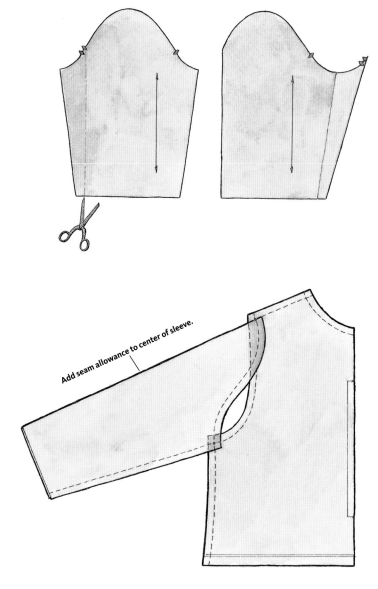

Add seam allowance to center of sleeve.

**261** **Reversibles.** I have found during my short year of sewing that many items may be made reversible! Try sewing two skirts together, a jumper, or a sleeveless top! All can be made reversible by simply sewing the right sides together and leaving an opening for turning. I like to topstitch to keep pieces neatly in place.
—*shesflipped*

**Deepika adds:** Make that nearly all. But she's right, omit facings and hems and make two garments alike, then sew together along the perimeter. Think through how you'll handle armholes or wrists, or pants hems: you can't turn a "donut" through an opening in the perimeter if the center is closed.

**262** **D.I.Y. Dolman.** I saw a cut-on sleeve on various RTW tops and I liked it, plus it makes a knit top even easier to sew, as there is no sleeve to set into the armhole. How did I draft it?

- I began with a knit top pattern that fits me. I folded the sleeve in half lengthwise.
- I laid the bodice front pattern piece on my table. I lapped the folded sleeve pattern on it, aligning the seamlines (not the cut edges) as follows: I matched the top center of the sleeve cap to the intersection of the armscye and shoulder seams, and matched the top of the underarm seam on the sleeve to the top of the side seam on the bodice—as shown in the drawing at bottom left.
- Then I traced the perimeter of the overlapped pieces to make a new front/sleeve piece, adding seam allowance to the folded edge in the middle of the original sleeve pattern.
- I did the same process to create a new back/sleeve piece.
- I compared the results with one of my RTW tops and it's exactly the same shape, so I must have been doing it right!
—*LauraLo*

**263** **Adjustable T-neck.** For years I have tried to make a decent tall collar (like a turtleneck) on a T-shirt. At last I have found a method that works for me: I attach the bottom edge of the collar to the neckline in the normal way, then instead of folding down and attaching the top edge, I just leave it free. When I wear the shirt, I fold the collar to the inside and can make it taller or shorter as I please.
—*regine*

**264** **Facings to the outside.** Neckline and armhole facings don't always have to go on the inside of a garment. They can be used on the outside as a decorative feature of your project—this won't change the facing's function as an edge finisher and stabilizing element. But all the world will see it! Use interfacing in a compatible weight for the fabric as usual. Sew the facing right side to the garment wrong side, trim and clip the seam, and then fold the facing onto the right side of the garment.

Following are a few things to consider when reversing your facings.

**265** Do you like the shape of the facing? If not, try reshaping the outside edge.

**266** Consider cutting your facing from a contrasting fabric to add emphasis.

**267** For added zip, finish the facing edge with a flatlock stitch in pearl cotton thread or with piping.

*—ShereeSews*

**268** **Cinch the back.** I saw this recently inside a jacket at Anthropologie and thought it was a great idea. It was a casual boxy type jacket, but on the inside, in the back lining, at the waist, there was a narrow casing with a drawstring to cinch in the waist lining as much as you want. The casing was not on the jacket itself, but just in the lining. And it went from side seam to side seam, just in the back and the tie part was in the middle back and came through a buttonhole. Similar to what you see on drawstring pants. I thought this was a neat idea for cinching in a boxy jacket without losing any of the style.

*—SueV*

**Deepika adds:** If you want to try this, add the casing and drawstrings before you sew the lining fronts and back together so you can secure the drawstring ends in the side seams.

### Eliminating the side seam on pants

*No-side-seam pants are fast to make; if you don't have a pattern, follow these tips to convert your favorite casual pants pattern—you'll have to omit any in-seam side pockets.*

**269** **Deepika's straight leg version.** I am a lazy sewer so I decided to convert my favorite yoga pants pattern to a no-side-seam pattern to make it even quicker! I was able to make these pants in less than an hour including the cutting time! You gotta love that. This is how I did it:

- First I straightened the front and back pieces by drawing a line parallel to the grain line from the point where the leg began to flare to the hemline. Grain line is very important for this.
- Then I placed the front and back side-by-side, overlapping the side seams slightly (the crotch curves faced out). There was a gap at the top, where the hip curves.
- I taped a piece of tissue paper under that gap—it became a curved dart. So later, when I stitched the pants, I had a nice hip curve without a seam on the sides!
- To finish, I straightened the hemline, which became distorted when I aligned the side seams.

**270** **Kim Winson's tapered take.** The credit for this tip goes to the fabulous ladies at PatternReview.com. I wanted to convert a pattern for regular jammies to one seam—meaning combine the front and back pattern pieces to eliminate the side seam. I just couldn't figure out how to add a taper to the legs. Here's what I learned:

- Lay the front and back pieces side-by-side on a pinnable surface; overlap the seam allowances at the fullest part of the hips and insert a pin through the seamline at this point.
- Next overlap the pieces at the hemline to create the taper you want—the pin at the hips allows the tissue to pivot at that point. A crazy huge gap will open at the waistline.
- Trace this new shape to make a new pattern piece. Draw a straight line across the bottom of the leg, between the inseam edges. Draw along the side seamlines of that gap at the waistline to mark a big dart. From the bottom of this dart, draw a line perpendicular to the new bottom edge. This is the new straight grain line.

- I trimmed the excess fabric after I sewed the dart. I really enjoyed doing this pattern modification. And my jammies came out very nicely.

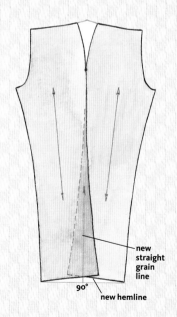

new straight grain line

90°

new hemline

**271** I love making knit tees like the beautiful ones that run $50-plus in ready-to-wear. I have found that I can redesign the neckline shape easily with waxed paper. It's fun to get creative and try different shapes:

- Cut a piece of waxed paper large enough to span from shoulder to shoulder.
- Draw a line perpendicular to the "shoulders" down the center with a Sharpie—this is your center front line.
- Fold the paper in half on the line and cut a 4" (10.2 cm)-deep wedge out at the top to create room for your neck. Unfold.
- Press the waxed paper against your collarbone area—it will stick to your skin if you wear only your bra.
- Stand in front of mirror and with the Sharpie, draw a neckline shape you like. If the paper isn't smooth, clip it more at the neckline area. Mark the top of the "shoulder seam" at the base of your neck on each side.
- Transfer the shape to your pattern. Remember to add seam allowances.

*—ryansmum*

**Deepika adds:** To be more accurate, you might want to trace your original pattern neckline, shoulders, and armscye onto the waxed paper first.

**272** A flounce—a ruffly looking piece used at the bottom of a skirt or sleeves—is one of the easiest things to draft from scratch. Being able to do so enables you to create quick patterns and pattern modifications. Here are easy steps for creating a flounce. Once you've read them, make a muslin sample to see how this works.

- Measure the edge (all the way around the skirt hem or sleeve) to which you wish to add the flounce; divide this measurement in half. This is half the top edge of the flounce.
- Decide how deep you want the flounce to be (from top to bottom).
- Draw a rectangle of these dimensions on scrap paper. On it, draw lines at half-inch intervals parallel to the ends.
- Cut the rectangle on the drawn lines but stop just before you reach the top edge—you're creating a sort of fringe.
- Place the paper fringe on a larger piece of paper. Tape one end down. Now move the top edge in an arc, spreading the fringe apart. Spread to create a quarter

circle or even a half circle. Because the top edge of a flounce is not gathered like a ruffle, all the fullness is created when you spread the rectangle. The more you spread, the more the flounce will drape and flute. Tape the fringes down.

- Now trace the pattern onto tissue paper. Smooth out the curves if they aren't neat, mark one short edge "cut on fold,"

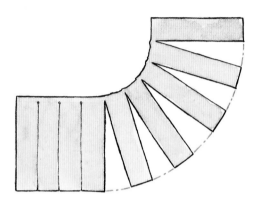

and add seam allowances to the other edges. Then cut out the pattern.
- That's it! You have your flounce pattern. Cut from fabric, sew to your garment, and you're done.

*—Deepika*

## WORK YOUR STASH

**273** I often use older patterns, but end up altering them for a more up-to-date fit. Even the slightest change in neckline can make the difference in how *en vogue* something can look. Look at new fashions and patterns with a close eye and note design changes; then incorporate them on older, similar ones if you don't want to buy new.

*—Nancywin*

**274** For those of us who are fabric- and pattern-addicted and have mountains of both everywhere: DO NOT FEEL GUILTY, BAD, OR OUT-OF-CONTROL. You do not have too much in your stash—you have lots of choices! You do not have to sew every pattern or piece of fabric purchased. You get to cherry-pick the best and eventually you will pass along anything not selected to some lucky person—which counts as a good deed.

*—ryansmum*

## LOOK AT 3D EXAMPLES

**275** When thinking of sewing a new style, particularly a time-consuming item, try on a ready-to-wear item with a similar cut and detail to see if you like it on you. You could save yourself doing hours of work done only for disappointment.

*—KathleenS*

**276** If you have pattern drafting software, (I use My Pattern Designer), and like to experiment, you can print your pattern at one-quarter size and then cut it in fabric and put the pieces together to get an idea of how your creation will look.

*—PattyPrice*

**277** I learned this tip way back when: When selecting patterns, look for ones with the finished garment shown in photographs, not drawings. Often, the drawings are how the designer HOPES they turn out and not how they REALLY are.

*—Phoebe*

## ZIP DETAIL FOR SKIRTS

**278** I made a very tapered, calf-length skirt to give a slimming look to an outfit with a wide jacket. Although I made a muslin skirt first, I never thought of testing it in the ladies' room. When I wore the skirt I discovered I couldn't lift it over my hips . . . So, the next day I ripped out the back seam from the hem to 3" (7.6 cm) below the back zipper. Then I put in an extra long invisible zipper—upside down. The problem of sanitary stops is solved. I can close the zipper completely or leave a bit open for a walking slit. And I will never again forget to experiment in the ladies' room.

*—els*

**279** I was given a wool skirt a few years ago that has a really nifty detail. The skirt is lined and faced (no waistband), and one side seam has a separating zipper inserted the entire length from hem to waist. The zipper is set in upside down, so you can unzip from the hem as far as you like for an adjustable side-slit. It's a fairly basic, conservative skirt otherwise—straight and knee-length, with an invisible zip at center back. The side-seam zipper, on the other hand, is the kind you'd find in outerwear, heavier-weight with big plastic teeth. It's a fun look overall, and easy to copy.

*—gabrielle*

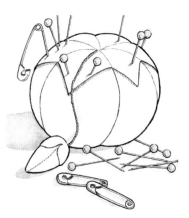

## CHIC CHEATS FOR KIDS

**280** I love sailor-style button-bib front pants for children. However, they're cumbersome for small fry to manage, especially in the bathroom, and also require a lot of work for something so quickly outgrown. I get the same look with NONE of the work by simply doing this:

- Choose an elastic waist pants pattern that has slant front pockets (not in-seam or patch). Bell the pant bottoms slightly.
- Make the pants as directed by the pattern instructions.
- Attach buttons along the slant edge of each pocket to mimic a button front. If you want it to look even more authentic, sew (but do not cut) buttonholes along the pocket edge before assembling the pants.

*—CharityAK*

**281** If you're sewing for a little girl and are in a hurry or haven't yet mastered collars, set-in sleeves, and facings but can make a skirt, then take this shortcut to an "advanced" design. Buy a RTW denim shirt (I got one in a thrift store for next to nothing). Cut it off slightly above your child's natural waist. Then cut a fabric rectangle for the skirt, making it about 2½ times longer than the bottom circumference of the cropped shirt and deep enough to create the desired length plus a hem. Gather the top (long) edge. Pin and sew to the bottom edge of the shirt. Presto! A fancy dress in next to no time at all. Add a belt if you like.

*—CharityAK*

 *Digital croquis for "Truth in Fashion"*

*A croquis is a silhouette drawing of your figure—head to toe—over which sketches of various garments can be superimposed so you can gauge how they suit your shape. Digital cameras and photo editing make it easy to create one that won't lie to you.*

**282** **Franticfashion's technique.** I use the line/technical drawings of patterns superimposed on my croquis. If you are artistic, you can print out your croquis and draw your designs on top. There are various instructions on how to make a croquis online (Google to find them), but I made mine using Photoshop:

- I took a photo of myself in my underwear (that's the scary part, I hope no one ever gets a hold of this, lots of blackmail potential!) and deleted the background. I then ran the photo through a variety of Photoshop filters to get an effect that appealed to me and looks good with clothing.

**283** **Tonya's technique.** A word of warning: you won't get a very flattering image of yourself. I remember the high school art teacher explaining that artists draw the human form eight heads high rather than seven like we really are because the change from 3-D to 2-D makes the form look shorter and squatter than reality. That's what I'm comforting myself with at this point. But if the design looks good on your croquis, it will look even better in reality, right?

- I had my husband take a digital picture of me in my foundation garments (you should have seen the strange look on his face with that request).
- I opened the photo in Paint Shop Pro. I created a new vector layer, and on that layer I traced around my body shape and added some style guides such as a waistline and princess seamlines.
- I then deleted the picture layer and was left with just the outline. I resized it to fit on letter paper and printed out a few copies to sketch with.

# Painless pattern prep

*Multisize options to decipher. Trace it how and onto what? Seam allowance on or not? These are just a few of the challenges you meet before you even spread out your fabric and lift your scissors, let alone sew. PatternReview.com members love, hate, or simply tolerate this part of sewing—whichever is the case, they've come up with smart ways to make it easy and efficient.*

## FAVORITE PAPERS FOR PATTERN TRACING

**284** For tracing patterns I have discovered a cheap tracing paper. I go to the medical supply store in town and buy the paper that medical offices use to cover exam tables. It's about 21" (53.3 cm) wide so it's wide enough for most pattern pieces. It's also pretty transparent so I lay my original pattern underneath it and then trace the lines. It's fast, it's easy, it's cheap: Maybe $5 for a HUGE roll that lasts forever.

*—cynthia w*

**285** I've started using pastel tissue paper—the kind you have on hand for gifts—for tracing patterns for interfacings. The colored paper is my clue that I shouldn't cut the piece out of the fashion fabric. (Yeah, I've done it . . .) This system would also work for pattern pieces that should be cut out of contrasting fabric, or for lining pieces.

*—Karla Kizer*

**286** When I decide to make an item, I trace the pattern onto freezer paper. Because it's coated, you can use a Sharpie to trace the pattern without worrying about the ink bleeding through. But the best thing about this stuff is when you are ready to cut the pattern out, just iron the freezer paper pattern to the fabric! It stays in place and NO need to pin. If you have a piece that has to be pinned with the reverse side down, just trace it that way and you don't have to worry about remembering to invert it on the fabric. To store these patterns without folding, I just hang them on a clip-style skirt hanger.

*—Heidi H*

**287** I find greaseproof paper and waxed paper to be a great tracing paper for small garments/ kids' clothes and crafts. I'm not sure if these come in different widths but if they do, they'd be good for all patterns.

*—Lou*

**Deepika adds:** Greaseproof paper is a food-wrapping paper not commonly available at retail—ask your local market if they can source it for you.

**288** Here's an inexpensive paper that works well for tracing: Butcher paper, which can be found at local restaurant suppliers or out-of-business liquidation sales. One large roll of this stuff will last you forever. White butcher paper is thicker than tissue, pretty much the same weight as printer paper. Butcher paper isn't transparent, but is usually thin enough to trace with providing you have adequate contrast. (You can place a white sheet under the tissue, and then the butcher paper on top. That usually provides enough information for tracing purposes.)

*—twistedangel*

## ADJUST LENGTH PROPORTIONALLY

**289** I've struggled getting skirts to the proper length for my petite figure. Trial and error in front of a mirror works for some designs but if the skirt has a separate yoke the yoke must be shortened before assembly. One day I did the math: At 5'2" (157.5 cm) I am 94% of the 5'6" (167.5 cm) height of Burda's design model. If a skirt is 30" (76.2 cm) long for someone 5'6" (167.5 cm), the appropriate length for me would be about 94% of this, or 28.25" (56.5 cm). If the yoke and lower portion are 10" (25.4 cm) and 20" (50.8 cm), the correct proportions for my height are about 9½" (24.1 cm) and 18¾" (47.6 cm),

respectively. This approach can also be used by tall gals to estimate how much to add: a 5'10" (177.8 cm) figure is 1.06 times as tall as a 5'6" (167.5 cm) model and would be suited by a skirt 1.75" (4.5 cm) longer than the 30" (76.2 cm) skirt.

This method of proportional adjustment works well for skirts. For other garments, it provides a starting place for estimating the amount to adjust when tissue fitting. I'm not a 94% scale everywhere: I tend to need more shortening between the waist and hip than between the shoulder and waist, for example.

*—Seamingly Simple*

**290** I have three predetermined lengths for skirts I wear, based on my ready-to-wear garments. Knee-length, mid-calf, and ankle. I keep the dimensions noted in a file so I don't have to measure my clothes every time. The result is always flattering, regardless of the length suggested in the pattern.

*—Deepika*

**291** **Carpenter's pencil.** While tracing a pattern today, I made numerous trips to the sharpener in the office. I know I need to get more exercise, but this was not the time. I found a carpenter's pencil and tired it. WOW! No more frequent trips to the sharpener. No more sharp points to poke through the tracing material. No more broken leads. Simply use a utility knife to remove the wood to expose the lead, and then a piece of sandpaper to refine the tip. I was able to trace fine and bold lines easily. It worked great. You will find these little gems at the local home improvement store.

—*Talleymom*

**292** **Sharpie marker.** Sharpie markers are great for tracing onto plastic. In fact, if you want to get really creative, buy them in different colors and color-coordinate your tracing. I have even found sets with "tropical" colors of purple, turquoise, orange, etc. in the office supply stores, particularly during back-to-school promotions. For the first trial pattern tracing/fitting, I'll use blue. Red is good for making the alterations. When I finalize the fit or want to make a final copy, I'll use green (for go!).

—*Oopsy-Daisy!*

**293** **China marker.** I was getting frustrated with pencils and (even worse) pens for tracing patterns onto tracing paper, and felt-tip markers of course bleed through. So the other day I tried out a china marker. I was slightly nervous about trying this, since the name in French is *mine grasse*—greasy lead—so I tried it first on a scrap of tracing paper. Not only was it not greasy, it didn't smear even when I tested it by rubbing one piece of marked tracing paper with another piece. It's also very smooth to write with, and—not that you would need this with paper!—waterproof. And it doesn't seem to bleed through at all to the other side of the tracing paper.

P.S. These markers have a paper wrapping next to the lead, and when they get stubby you "sharpen" them by pulling the string back a bit and peeling away some of the paper.

—*Joan1954*

**294** **Serrated tracing wheel.** Sometimes patterns have such light ink that I can't see the lines through my tracing paper. Here's what I do: I lay my freezer paper on top of my cardboard cutting mat, lay my pattern piece on TOP of the freezer paper, and trace around with my serrated tracing wheel. The little teeth make a dotted line that is easy to see on the freezer paper. Using tracing paper in between works too, but this way you don't have to lift your piece to reposition your tracing paper and risk moving your pattern.

—*Sew it seams*

**295** **Inked tracing wheel.** I finally figured out a way to trace Burda WOF patterns that works for me. I pin vellum tracing paper to the pattern I want to trace. I make all of my internal markings (grain lines, ease markings, pocket placement, etc.) with a pencil and then I ink my Clover double tracing wheel (set at ¾" [1.9 cm]) with water-based crafts ink (I used a Stampin' Up ink pad). I outline my chosen pattern with the inked wheel, marking the cutting line as well as the seamline.

—*Krystal aka Pirouette*

**Deepika adds:** You could use an inked single wheel to trace the grain line and darts, and of course, the pattern outline if you don't need to add seam allowance.

## *Colored pencil has a tracing advantage*

*LoriB picked up a colored pencil to trace a pattern one day and was amazed how such a simple change could be so helpful.*

With colored pencils you can:

**296** Colored pencils are often softer than a #2 pencil and therefore glide easier on the paper. The color is easier on the eyes and also gives you added benefits.

**297** Trace the pattern entirely in one color and use a different color to mark your alterations.

**298** Color-code sizes when you've cut multiple sizes from one pattern.

**299** For Burda WOF patterns or others without seam allowances, trace the seam line in one color and then go back and use a different color for the cutting line. If you make a habit of always using the same color for the cutting line, perhaps it'll jog your memory when you forget to add the cutting line and go to cut your fabric.

**300** Mark the stitching line on patterns that include seam allowances to help with altering. When you tissue-fit or make adjustments, it's important to know where the seam line is.

**301** I used soil separator fabric this weekend to trace off some patterns. It is thin, very see-through, and not as stable as the Swedish tracing paper (read: sometimes it "gives"). And it marks well with a dark ink pen or gel pen; pencil drags too much. The only real problem I see with soil separator fabric is that you won't be able to see it on some fabrics, so I retrace the lines with a Sharpie. Plus, it folds flat so storage won't be a problem! At less than 11 cents a yard for the 48" (122 cm) wide variety, soil separator fabric gets my vote: You can copy an entire sheet of any pattern without having to piece the tracing.

—*audsews*

**Deepika adds:** This material sews well too. It can be found in the plumbing supply aisle of most hardware and home improvement stores.

**302** I was about to toss a torn, clear-plastic shower curtain liner, when it occurred to me to use it to trace some complicated Burda WOF and Ottobre Design patterns. (I first washed it to get rid of the soap scum.) It worked very well. I used a fine point Sharpie pen to trace. If you press too hard with the pen, the plastic will stretch and the tracing will become distorted, but apart from that I had no problems. For the first time, my blood pressure didn't increase dramatically while trying to trace an Ottobre Design pattern.

—*SandraB*

**303** Most sewers will know this, but beginners won't. I copy patterns on 100% nylon tracing material that I buy at the fabric store. This material will not tear. But the good part is that you can mark your garment fabric right through this tracing material using a fabric-marking pen (after you test it on the fabric). No need for dressmaker's tracing paper. Makes cutting patterns go much quicker.

—*Mary Stiefer*

**304** I trace patterns onto the cheapest non-fusible interfacing, which I buy by the 25-yard (23-m) bolt. A bolt (really a roll) runs about $30, lasts me for a year or longer, and takes up little room. When I lay out these interfacing patterns, they stick to the fabric just a bit; if I secure them with weights I can cut quickly. I keep each pattern in a Ziploc bag, along with an annotated file card to which I've stapled a swatch of the fabric I made it in. It works really well.

—*TEC*

**305** When my daughter got married, we bought an aisle runner on eBay, 75 (69 m) yards of 36" (91.4 cm) non-woven cloth-like material for about $25. After the wedding I used it to trace patterns! It has a vine pattern on it, but it is easy to see through, and it's easy to write on, doesn't tear easily, you can sew it, and it's much less expensive. It worked so well that I recently bought another roll.

—*Rosie who use to be Rose*

### Trace onto painter's plastic drop cloth

*Clear plastic (polyethylene) sheeting, sold in home and hardware stores, is a favorite tracing material of several PatternReview.com members. Here's the how and why:*

**Oopsy-Daisy! has it down pat:** The "Medium Duty/4 mil" weight is best: it's durable, won't tear, and stays in place. Here's what I like especially:

**306** You can get a roll (3' × 50' [.92 × 15.3 m]) for less than $2. It lasts just about forever and is wide enough so you don't have to tape bits together for those large odd-shaped pattern pieces.

**307** I use Sharpie markers to trace—they don't smear and move easily when tracing, no sputtering nor skipping.

**308** The plastic holds up to repeated pinning, and stays in place very well with pattern weights too.

**309** The see-through plastic makes it so much easier during pattern layout and cutting to match stripes, prints, etc.

**310** The easiest way to store your plastic patterns? Roll them with the smaller pieces inside the larger ones, secure with a rubber band and stick a Post-it note identification underneath one of the layer rolls or the rubber band.

**311** **Tessa spins it this way:** The plastic is about 100" (2.84 m) wide, folded in half on the roll. I'm not sure how long. A roll costs less than $10. To copy a pattern I use weights to keep the plastic in place and an overhead-projector marker to trace and add comments such as the date, elastic length, who it was made for, how much I lengthened, etc. I have found it best to use a black marker, as blue and red seem to fade.

**312** The plastic pattern pieces are easy to fold, and the roll is easy to store. I use weights to secure the patterns when cutting my fabric too.

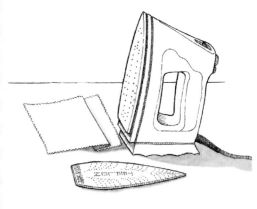

## CUSTOM SEAM ALLOWANCE SIZE

**313** When I cut a pair of fitted pants, I increase the seam allowances in the following areas and then fit and adjust the pants as I sew them.

- Side seams: add 1" (2.5 cm)
- Front crotch: extend ½" to 1½" (1.3 to 3.8 cm). This'll depend on how full your thighs are.
- Back crotch: extend by 1" (2.5 cm). This is dependent on how big your derriere is.
- Hem allowance: add 1" to 2" (2.5 to 5.1 cm)—just in case you decide to wear a heel.

Hope this is useful.

*—Dale C*

**314** Some people think that you shouldn't trim seam allowances before stitching. However, there are some cases where you have to. I am making patterns for leotards. The pattern has ⅝" (1.6 cm) seam allowances, but I want to serge a ⅜" (1 cm) elastic to the edge and turn under to topstitch. I have to trim the allowance off the pattern or off the garment prior to stitching. I personally find it a lot easier to trim the pattern.

*—Fluteplayer*

These are my insanity reasons for not adding seam allowance to a pattern:

**315** I like having stitch lines traced onto my garment pieces. It makes it easier to alter a pattern and to sew more accurately where it really shows (matching collar points for example).

**316** It makes it easier to fit a garment and helps to show the final adjustment I need to make to the pattern for future use.

**317** I change the allowance width according to seam, fabric, and finish. I vary the width within the same seam allowance sometimes (crotch seam, for example).

*—Nata*

## REINFORCE FOR DURABILITY

**318** I have patterns that I use over and over, and they tend to get pretty tattered where the pins go. I cut small squares of soft iron-on interfacing and ironed them to the pattern corners and edges. Sure helps make the patterns last longer.

*—JO913*

**319** When I find a pattern that I really like and want to use over and over again, I trace it onto a piece of poster board, use a paper punch to punch a hole in it, and set a grommet into the hole. Then I can hang it on a cup hook on the wall for easy access. The stiff cardboard makes it easy to weight and cut out with a rotary cutter, the grommet keeps the hole from tearing, and I can just lift down my favorite patterns instead of having to unfold (and maybe even iron) them.

*—xenophea*

**320** If you don't want to take the time to make a traced copy of a multi-size pattern, it's possible to just fold away the bigger sizes to reveal the one you want to use. However, on some lines, especially places like waist and yoke curves, you have to at least snip in to the curve, across the various size lines, in order to fold away the excess, and this makes the pattern a bit fragile if you later spread it out for a larger size. A quick fix occurred to me when I was doing this recently: In those curves where you have to make crossing cuts, if you first run some ordinary clear tape over the area near the edge, it will survive being chopped around better. It's not an elegant solution, but it's quick and it works.

*—petro*

**321** As a costume designer/maker I tend to use the same pattern several times. To prevent it from getting ragged and possibly becoming inaccurate, I first press the pattern piece with a dry iron and them press it to freezer paper—wrong side of pattern to shiny side of freezer paper. I then have a pattern that will last for years: Freezer paper ROCKS and costs approximately $6.00 a roll (150 square feet [13.94 square meters]).

*—raggedyandrew*

**322** I hate to trace patterns. Hate it. Hate it. Hate it. I'm a new sewist, so most patterns I make only once; then they go back into the envelope to collect dust. However, I'm finding once in a while I come across a pattern that I really like. When I do come across a pattern that I'm going to make a million times, after I cut it, I iron it onto some fusible interfacing. It certainly makes the cheap tissue stronger, and keeps me from tracing. Grr, tracing!

*—SexiSadi*

**323** I recently subscribed to Burda WOF and therefore began tracing my patterns. Since these magazine patterns don't include seam allowance, I would dash in a cutting line ⅝" (1.6 cm) from the seamline. Finally a eureka moment: 2 pencils held together with a rubber band. I cut cardboard spacers and inserted them between the pencils until the points were ⅝" (1.6 cm) apart. It's not pretty, but it sure gets the job done . . .
—*monahan*

**324** I don't add S.A. to patterns because I like having stitching lines. I trace patterns onto fabric and then cut outside the traced lines with a rotary cutter. I don't try to cut uniform S.A. I then put the fabric pieces through an unthreaded serger, guiding the edge of the serger foot along the traced stitching lines. This trims the S.A. evenly. You could add S.A. to patterns traced onto the Pattern Ease or other similar fabric-like tracing medium this way if you prefer not having stitching lines on your fabric.
—*Nata*

**325** I traced off and cut out my first Burda WOF pattern. After carefully cutting out the pattern pieces from the pattern paper and laying them on the fabric, I discovered that it would have been a whole lot easier to mark the seam allowances on the paper rather than the fabric. (The magazine suggests adding the seam allowance and marking the cutting line directly on the fabric.)
—*Gloria Allender*

**326** Last night, while I was preparing a muslin, I wanted to give myself 1" (2.5 cm) seam allowances instead of the ⅝" (1.6 cm) that came on the pattern. I realized I could use a good compass to customize the allowance. I set mine to ⅜" (1 cm) and traced the metal point along the original cutting line so that the pencil point marked the pattern 1" (2.5 cm) from the seamline. A center wheel compass (from an art supply store) is important for keeping the separation right. Mine also allows me to replace the metal point with a second piece of lead, which is nice. All in all, I've found it easy to use and I didn't have to go buy something new.
—*mit*

**327** I have always found adding seam allowances to Burda WOF patterns rather tedious. The Olfa rotary cutter can be used with a little adjustable extension arm, but even though I really tightened the screw that holds it to the cutter I couldn't seem to keep it from moving and messing up my measurements. I discovered that if I visually lined up the black screw on the right hand side of the cutter with the pattern's seamline (I am right handed), the blade would cut a ³⁄₈" (1 cm) seam allowance. I then tried my Ergo rotary cutter and found that by sighting the clear projection on the right side along the seamline, I could cut a ⅝" (1.6 cm) seam allowance. Try experimenting with your cutters on some scraps and see if this works for you.
—*Brine*

**328** I recommend reinforcing patterns with inexpensive, nonwoven, fusible interfacing because it is polyester, so you don't have a problem with it shrinking as you fuse it to the pattern. One hint, though, use a dry iron instead of steam for fusing interfacing to pattern tissue.
—*Deepika*

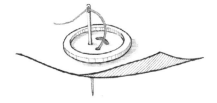

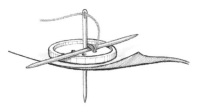

### To mark the seam allowance, just sew!

**Fluteplayer** suggests this easy way to "rule" the seam allowance onto a pattern: Use your machine to straight stitch the cutting line at the desired distance from the seamline.

**329** First trace your pattern onto tracing paper and rough cut it, eyeballing about 1" (2.5 cm) seam allowance. Then set your machine to sew along the desired cutting line either by aligning the left edge of a wide foot with the seamline and moving the needle to the right, or by using a stitch guide. I use an old needle that I have discarded. I use a small stitch length. You don't need thread. When you are done, the needle will have perforated the paper enough so that the excess paper simply tears away from the pattern. I get perfectly trimmed seams every time.

If a full pattern piece is to be cut on folded fabric, I fold it on the fold line and stitch though both halves at the same time, using a few pins or tape to keep the layers from slipping.

## COOL TRACING METHODS THAT WORK

**330** I know everyone has her own way of tracing patterns, but I am so happy with my current technique that I thought I would pass it along. This method gives you a heavy-duty copy of a flimsy tissue original; the result can be rolled or folded.

- Lay out a large piece of Foamcore board on a table. Top it with a piece of kraft paper large enough for your pattern.
- Arrange sheets of 8½" × 13½" (21.6 × 34.3 cm) carbon paper (the kind used by offices before photocopies were common) over the kraft paper in a single layer, with the carbon side down.
- Place your pattern on top of the carbon paper. Pin these layers to the Foamcore.
- "Trace" your pattern with something that will not mark or perforate your tissue pattern—I use the wrong end of my sewing machine's lint brush. Use a French curve, ruler, etc., as needed.
- The carbon reproduces your original pattern beautifully but it will smudge. Protect your new copy by spraying it with Krylon Workable Fixatif (the stuff that artists use to preserve pastel drawings).
  *—Tailypo*

**Deepika adds:** Instead of traditional carbon paper, use large sheets of dressmaker's carbon, which doesn't smudge (available from online notions vendors). And trace with a smooth tracing wheel—this is what it is designed for. ☺

**331** Trace patterns easily and quickly by using a window as a lightbox. Use Blu-Tack (you know that sticky stuff you used to put posters on your wall as a kid?) to stick your pattern pieces to a big window. Also using Blu-Tack, stick a piece of tracing paper over the pattern pieces. Trace your pattern, working from the top left, smoothing down your tracing paper as you go. I find it helps to slide a large ruler over the pattern, holding it all flat to the window with one hand while you trace with the other. The great thing is you don't need a sunny day for this to work well: just a little light makes the lines on your printed pattern show through enough for you to trace them easily.
  *—.x.Helen.x.*

**332** After each round of alterations, I mark the changes on my pattern and date it. Then I use that pattern to trace out a new one. I use four very small pieces of blue painter's tape to secure the edges of the old pattern to my table. Then I lay a new clean sheet of pattern paper on top of that and anchor it with four more pieces of tape. I find this technique easier than using weights since the weights can get in the way of markings and if I shift them, they sometimes also shift the paper. The painter's tape does not hurt my table (no sticky gum left behind), nor does it hurt my pattern paper. Sometimes I pull it off the pattern and sometimes I leave it.
  *—meanjean*

**333** When I trace, I secure the tracing material and pattern to a board with thumbtacks, which I place around the outside shape of the pattern piece. This makes it easier to see which shape to follow and keeps everything in place.
  *—sew2006*

## CLUE IN TO THOSE BURDA WOF PATTERNS!

**334** I learned with my first Burda garment that the line styles that indicate various sizes are not consistent from one pattern to another, even within the same WOF issue! After I determined my size (40) and looked up the pattern key (which, in addition to which line style to trace for your size, tells you what color line to look for on which lettered sheet, as well as the pattern piece numbers for your garment), I reminded myself as I traced each pattern piece, "My BWOF tracing line is the alternating long dash-short dash." I decided to use the lower sleeves from a different pattern from the same issue and breezily traced the pattern piece in a size 40—or so I thought. It wasn't till the construction stage that I noticed something wasn't quite right. When I pulled out the master pattern sheet to check, I was surprised to find that I had, in fact, cut a size 42 in the second pattern.
  *—SewFar*

**335** As you know, patterns in Burda WOF magazine are printed on top of each other. The lines are color-coded to each pattern but did you know they print the color-coordinated numbers of the pattern pieces on the edge of the sheet to help you find them? I didn't! Guess I've just been in such a hurry to trace that I never noticed them before.
  *—LoriB*

**336** With lines for about 25 pattern pieces, each in five sizes, all on one sheet, it is easy to become confused while tracing Burda WOF patterns. The mistake I make most often is to miss tracing some construction symbols like pleats or notches. To avoid these omissions, I refer to the schematic diagrams of pattern pieces that are printed with the sewing instructions, where all symbols are clearly indicated without the distraction of 99 other lines. I compare my tracing of each piece with the diagram before moving the tracing paper. If a symbol is missing, it is easy to find it and add it to the tracing before it is too late.
  *—Elaray*

## FOUR KNOCK-OFF TECHNIQUES

**337** Sometimes I have a special garment, but I don't have the pattern for replicating it. If that garment is too worn to wear, I take it apart and use the pieces as a pattern. First I make marks for each seam—it's very important to make them so you don't lose the way; make them with permanent markers or little cuts. Second, carefully, un-seam the garment and press each piece. Then transfer the shape to paper or Pellon, including all the marks, grain line of the fabric, etc. Also, I make notes and pin them to the corresponding piece so I'm sure to remember any details and how the garment was constructed. Once I have the complete pattern in paper with annotations, I use it to reconstruct that special item I loved in a new fabric.

*—Iris*

**338** Maybe others already came up with a good way of doing this, but I always have a hard time copying pants with elastic waists. Now I use a skirt hanger that has clips: I clip the waist and slide the clips to stretch the elastic just enough to make the fabric smooth. After that it is easy to copy the pattern with any method you like to use. And you still have two free hands to do that!

*—Orsi*

**339** When I worked in the garment industry, we used clear cellophane wrap (the type used to wrap gift baskets) to trace off a pattern from a garment we wanted to copy. Using a Sharpie, you trace around the garment one section at a time; then label each section. I still use this great technique as a starting point for "knocking off" a garment. I transfer the tracings to grid patternmaking paper and add any alterations needed, and then I true up the pattern and add seam allowances.

*—ryansmum*

**340** Use your digital camera to take photos of a garment such as a tailored jacket that you are taking apart for the purposes of sewing up a copy. It is so easy to go through the stages of taking apart a complicated garment, and then find you've forgotten exactly how it went together. Photograph the construction, labeling each piece as you take it apart, and get a printout photo on ordinary paper immediately, so you can label that too, noting any special techniques. You will then have a set of labeled pattern pieces that tell you which way up they go—and by your photos, how they fit together.

*—Pocket Venus*

## TRICKS FOR TRACKING THE CHOSEN SIZE LINE

**341** I always trace my patterns and many times have found myself veering onto the wrong size on multi-sized patterns. I found that if I first place dots on the correct line at strategic points such as corners, crotch points, hemlines, etc. I am able to trace the proper lines using a styling curve to connect the dots.

*—Brine*

**342** I find Jalie patterns very difficult to trace. I especially have difficulty finding my line after a notch. This was driving me insane. (That's my professional opinion.) I decided to use a thick-tipped highlighter pen to mark my cutting lines on the original pattern. When I lose track of my line while tracing, I can find the nearest highlighted line, move there, and then trace back to where I had lost it (kind of like going backwards in children's mazes). If you use different sizes of these patterns you could highlight different sizes in different colors as long as the size outlines are not too close together.

*—drsue*

**343** I am so pleased with myself. I wanted to reuse a pattern that I had previously cut out at a different size than I presently am. Some of the seamlines had been cut off, but I had saved and labeled the trimmed parts. Now that I want to cut out a different size, I don't have to guess at the missing parts; I can just fit the trimmed pieces back where they belong.

*—Elaine Dougan*

**344** I was looking at my Burda WOF pattern sheet in dismay, as I wanted to make my standard alterations while tracing, but moving back and forth between three sizes was confusing me. So I used brightly colored Post-it flags, the type shaped like arrows with black outlines, to "point" to the correct cutting line and guide me while tracing. While these flags are highly visible through the tracing paper, I think any Post-it-type product with a mark to help orient you would do the trick. Best of all: they leave no residue, and they are reusable many times.

*—redsquid*

### Adapting a pattern from woven to knit fabric

*Patterns intended for woven fabrics will be too large if cut in a knit with a lot of stretch. Here are tips for scaling them down. Warning: math aptitude helps.*

**345** LauraLo uses a photocopier. To find the stretch factor, first cut a 4" (10 cm) square of your fabric. Stretch the horizontal grain line as much as you can without forcing it, and measure it. Let's say it is 15 cm. Your horizontal stretch/scale factor is your initial 10 cm divided by the 15, or 0.66. Do the same vertically. Now, if you're lucky, you got the same stretch factor and you can take your pattern to a copy machine and reproduce it at 0.66%. (If you weren't lucky, you need pattern drafting software or the patience to rework the pattern mathematically.)

## CONQUER CURVES

**346** This is probably incredibly obvious to everyone but me, but I was drawing wobbly lines while tracing a pattern last night and it suddenly occurred to me: use the curved end of my Fashion Ruler! And lo and behold, although I have no idea how to actually use the curve properly, or what the various notations on it mean, if I slide the thing up and down, and maybe flip it over, any gosh-darn curve on my pattern will line up with some part of the thing! My traced pattern came out looking exactly like the original.

Newbies, I think the thing cost $15, so even if you never plan to alter your garments, which is what this tool is designed for, think about buying one just for accuracy when tracing.

—*Tailypo*

**Deepika adds:** You used the curve correctly! French curves, which are sold at most art supply stores, also make perfect guides for tracing or for refining curves in areas you alter—and they're usually inexpensive.

**347** It's easiest and most accurate to measure a curve on a flat surface if you hold your tape measure on its edge.

—*Diana M*

## PHOTOCOPIER TO THE RESCUE

**348** This summer, I bought my first ever Burda WOF magazine. I didn't care for how the patterns were arranged—pattern line over pattern line was almost enough to make me throw this magazine in the garbage—so after trying to copy the pattern using various techniques I finally found a way that worked for me. I simply copied and printed the pattern with my all-in-one printer, which has scan, copy, and print capability. While it did take some time to organize the pieces, this technique worked beautifully!

—*newlywedws*

**349** Copying the small pattern pieces on the desktop copier is a great idea. Foundation paper used for paper-piecing quilt blocks is thinner than regular printer paper and feeds very nicely through my printer. If you want the advantage of non-stiff copied pieces, this may be the way to go. It is available in many sewing catalogs and at fabric stores that cater to quilters. It comes in packs, usually of 30 or 100 sheets.

—*vasallese*

## GET A GRIP ON PATTERN ADJUSTMENTS

**350** If a pattern piece has to be shortened or lengthened, patch it with fusible interfacing instead of adhesive tape. Use the type that is applied without steam, this way you can iron the pattern to remove the creases without it shrinking. You can also use this technique to repair a torn pattern.

—*els*

**351** I make lots of changes to patterns to get them to fit. I had a roll of the blue freezer Press 'n Seal (heavier than the clear) that I stuck to my pattern in various places and drew in my changes with a Sharpie marker. I was then able to trace the corrected pattern and remove the Press 'n Seal, leaving my original pattern unspoiled. I did this on my muslin also to sketch in facings, which were easy to trace once I had them drawn as I desired. I had to share this—it would also be great in areas where you want to add length or width to a pattern so there won't be oops moments if you forget in the future.

—*mssewcrazy*

## TEMPLATE MATERIALS

**352** Decorating firms and wallpaper stores often have discontinued wallpaper books for free. I've been using the pages for small pattern pieces and templates. I like using the vinyl samples because they don't tear and I can pin and re-pin them over and over. Samples in checkered prints help with lining everything up nice and neat. If you find the really big sample books, even better.

—*Maria Hatfield*

**353** I have used my daughters' old school folders made of poly-vinyl to make templates. They are sturdy, easy to mark on with a Sharpie or ballpoint pen, easy to trace around with either a chalk marker or rotary cutter, and recycled. They are great for pocket patterns, quilt templates, and small pattern pieces you use frequently. And they're free!!

—*audsews*

**354** A lot of us trace our patterns, and I've been plagued at times with facing pieces that don't accurately match the body piece. So this is what I'm doing now: I trace and cut each piece, then put them together to see if they match, and trim or retrace and recut to make sure they match. This was a "duh" moment for me!

—*Debbie Lancaster*

**355** When I trace a pattern, I label the tracing with the size I've traced and also the piece name or number and the pattern brand and number. That way, even if I wait a while to cut it out (and the measurements change), I won't have to rely on my memory to know what I traced. I'm working on a swimsuit that I cut out months ago, and I can't find the original pattern. Since I wrote down the size I used on the tracing, I was able to get elastic length from a helpful PR member. But from now on, when I trace a pattern that needs something like elastic, I'm going to record the length of the elastic on the tracing too.

—*Muria*

**356** A light bulb moment came this week when I was cutting out a dress for my granddaughter. If you have a pattern piece that says "cut 4" and you know that you will have to use the same pattern piece twice to do so, simply trace two copies. This will keep you from having to make sure that all marking are transferred to the cloth before you reposition a single copy.

—*NanJones*

**357** I like to work efficiently. I sew a lot of knit pullover dresses and shirts and I've noticed that the front and back are often the same except for the neckline and the sleeves are often symmetrical front and back. When this is the case, I transfer the pattern with my length alterations onto sturdy butcher paper, making just one full front/back pattern that has a high back neckline only and one pattern for each sleeve length option. Over the years I have also copied an assortment of neckline treatments: a cowl, a V-neck, turtleneck, a scoop neck, etc., each with a front and back pattern.

I use the shirt front/back and sleeve patterns to cut generic shirts or dresses, sometimes 8 or 10 at a time; it only takes about an hour. They can sit in a pile until I'm ready to sew them. When I'm ready to finish them I choose a neckline pattern for each and cut it. The result is a collection of knit shirts and/or dresses in which each is different.

—*filichirp*

**358** It's sometimes so difficult to fold knit or slippery fabrics double for cutting, I decided to make a full pattern so I could cut with the fabric spread in one layer. I was amazed at how much faster I could cut since I did not have to fiddle with folding the fabric evenly. Give it a try. You won't be fighting with wide big pieces of fabric.

—*mssewcrazy*

**359** When I have a pattern that has multiple views, I press out the pattern sheets, find the view I will be using and apply round sticky dots to the pieces to identify them. If I make another view at a future date, I use a different color sticky dot. This makes this job so much easier!

—*Enid E*

**360** I tend to forget what adjustments I made where on a pattern, so I developed a system that lets me look at a pattern later and tell what I did. It involves using markers (or colored pencils) of various colors. When I'm done, I've got a rainbow colored pattern, but I can easily see what I did where to adjust it. Here's an example of how my system works when I adjust a top pattern to be size 8 at the shoulders, size 12 at the bust, and size 14 at the hips—a common alteration for me:

- Use a green marker to trace the size 8 lines at the shoulder and all the common-to-all-sizes lines, such as the CF fold line and the hem.
- Use a blue marker to trace the size 12 lines at the bottom of the armhole and down the side seam for an inch or so.
- Use a purple marker to trace the size 14 lines at the hip.
- Then use a French curve to guide the transition between the different sizes, tracing with an orange marker.
- Make a key on the pattern to indicate which color represents which size.

—*Lisa Laree*

**361** When tracing off patterns for children, I use a different color for each size to make it easier to find. This eliminates using the wrong pieces/wrong size the next go-round!

—*Oopsy-Daisy!*

**362** Jalie pattern instructions are usually found in the middle of the large paper that includes all the pattern pieces to be traced and there is so much information on the original page that it is easy to get lost. I take time up front to photocopy the instructions. It takes a little effort to fold the large sheet and get it on the copy machine correctly, but later, the copy is so much handier at the sewing machine than the bulky pattern. I make a copy of the written instructions and a copy of the picture section too. I store them with the pattern. With all that said, I love the Jalie patterns and the great range of sizes given. I think they are easy to sew and have great style.

—*jbsew*

**Deepika adds:** Even easier—go to jalie.com, locate your pattern, and simply print out the directions.

**363** I prefer the neckline facing for a top or tee to be made without shoulder seams. There is no need to double up the seam allowances at the shoulders. Start by tracing the front and back facing patterns, abutting at the shoulder seamline. I add a seam allowance at the center back and cut the center front on the fold. I mark the shoulder seamline on my new pattern so it is easy to see how the facing aligns with the garment.

—*els*

**Deepika adds:** This puts the back facing off-grain from the garment, which probably won't affect the results, but if your fabric is unstable you might want to sew a tape into the neckline seam or interface the facing with a nonwoven material.

**364** If you like contour waistbands for trousers this may be of interest: In order to reduce the bulk at the end of the waistband, elongate the band pattern at the center front by a couple of inches, and reduce the band facing pattern by the same amount. Then sew the pieces together at their ends. Fold them, right side together and center backs aligned, before you sew the seam on the top edge. You'll see the top piece is folded back and the seam lies a couple of inches from the end. This reduces the bulk where the waistband overlaps for the fastening and makes it easier to get a neat end. The band now finishes in a fold, instead of a seam. Just make sure the seam doesn't fall where you want to make a buttonhole!

—*petro*

**Deepika adds:** This is nice for skirts too and can be done at a back or side closure as well as at the front; if there is an underlap, you can make the same adjustment on it too.

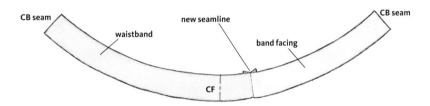

CHAPTER **FOUR**

# Fabric, Thread & Notions

> " *I started sewing while working at a JoAnn Fabrics for extra money. Anyone who's worked at this type of store can tell you I probably spent more than I made while I was working there.* ☺ "
>
> —Muria

# Shopping savvy

*Before you can sew, you must acquire pattern, fabric, thread, and various notions. Seems so matter-of-course, but there are approaches to shopping that make the experience so much easier—especially now that the Internet is a major resource or when the things you need are somewhat special.*

## RESOURCEFUL IDEAS

**365** This tip requires a sense of adventure! There is a freight recovery/salvage business in our area called NPS; they purchase and then resell lost or rejected freight shipments. No frills here but sewers can find great bargains. There are many bolts of very attractive fabric, patterns (99 cents), notions (Mettler thread!), even sewing machines. Now I know most of you will never be anywhere near this particular store, but without a doubt there is such a business somewhere near you, so if you can find one in your local phone book, or by word of mouth, check it out.

—*kkkkaty*

**366** I'm making spa accessories (head wrap, bath pillow) for a dear friend. So I looked at the terry cloth at my local fabric store. Found costly, thin, sickly fabric. Light bulb!! Why not check out towels? There's a great selection of beautifully colored, fluffy ones available—everywhere from big box stores to nice department stores. And, the price is so much less than yardage. Maybe I'll make a set of accessories for another friend.

—*Rhonda in Montreal*

**367** If you want to know whether a fabric will end up being scratchy, just cut off a small piece and tuck it in your bra. Walk around the fabric store for at least 10 or 15 minutes and if you forget it's there, great! It should be fine to wear all day next to your skin. You could also tuck the swatch in your waistband or sock if you don't want to fuss with your underwear in public.

—*Summerlea*

**Deepika adds:** For me the best way to test is to rub the fabric on my face. Find your most sensitive area.

## HOW MANY CENTIMETERS IN ONE YARD?

**368** A yards-to-meters conversion chart helps me and probably other non-U.S. sewers when using American patterns because we use the metric system rather than inches. Search online for "convert yards to meters" to find sites that provide charts or do the specific conversion for you.

—*els*

**369** Long car trips have me staring at the horizon, mentally tracing and altering patterns and planning adjustments. Since I've become increasingly intrigued with European patterns, I often find myself trying to convert centimeters to inches in my head. I don't "speak" metric system, much less "think" in metric. All I know is the rough translation: 2.5 cm is approximately 1 inch. Because dividing by 2.5 is more than I can do while attempting to stay in my traffic lane, I switched to a simpler method: double the number of centimeters and divide by 5. Yes, I know . . . it's basic math, and since my name is not Pythagoras, it's definitely a "recycled" idea. Anyone who laughs gets to balance my checkbook.

—*Karla Kizer*

**370** I found a chart that shows the equivalent yardage for different width fabrics online and think it invaluable. Search for "yardage conversion" and you'll find a number of sites that post this information.

—*Lou*

**371** If you need to know the approximate yardage of a piece of fabric but don't have a tape measure handy, you can hold your fabric up to an exterior door. The standard width of an exterior door is 36" (91.4 cm) (1 yard, obviously). I'd say that's a pretty good estimate for those of us who can't eyeball a yard. Another method I use quite often: I'm completely dense and can't tell the difference between 45" and 60" (114.3 and 152.4 cm) widths. I'm 64" (162.5 cm) tall (5'4"), which means my arm span is 64" (162.5 cm). If the fabric is nearly the width of my arm span, then it's 60" wide. If not, it's 45" (114.3 cm).

—*jacalhoun*

**372** I recently discovered that Google has a super-simple way of finding measurement equivalents. Let's say you're reading a European pattern that says it's for someone with a hip measurement of 92 cm. "What the heck does that mean—it sounds HUGE," you say to yourself. Well, in the Google search bar just type "92 cm to inches" and you'll learn that 92 centimeters = 36.2204724 inches: Just under 36 ¼". Definitely not huge. ☺ This works the other way too, of course—imperial to metric. Cool, eh? ☺

—*Joan1954*

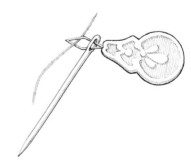

**373** If I need notions for a particular project, I cut a swatch of its fabric, staple it onto a page in one of those little spiral notepads (the kind that can be found in a drug or grocery store), and write notes next to it saying what is needed (e.g., 9" [22.9 cm]) zipper, buttons, etc.). Once I have purchased everything on that page and don't need it anymore, I tear it out of the notebook. This keeps me from buying things that don't match, or coming home from a store and realizing I forgot to look for something.

—*Margaret*

**374** I keep a small case with my swatches in my car. In it are photocopies of the front and back of pattern envelopes I plan to use with each fabric, so if I need trim, elastic, etc., I have the info I need right there. In the back of the case is a sleeve with copies of envelopes of patterns I really want to make but need the right fabric for.

—*EveS*

**375** If you're like me and you always have a couple of projects in flight, plus fabric bought for the next couple, plus you're sewing to coordinate with a garment you made a couple months ago, then you need a swatch baggie. I keep a sandwich-size Ziploc bag with a collection of my swatches permanently in my purse. That way, when I'm out and have a couple extra minutes to run into a fabric store, I can easily pick out matching threads, zippers, buttons, linings, trims, etc.—whatever it is I need. Try it. You'll find yourself doing fewer of those double trips to the fabric store just because you forgot your swatch.

—*meanjean*

**376** I can never remember the fabric content, care instructions, price, etc. when getting caught in a "too good to pass up" fabric purchase. My solution is to utilize my stash of old adhesive labels. While the fabric bolts are in the shopping cart, I note the fabric content, care, price, length, store, etc. on a label, then I stick the label on the fabric edge as it's being cut. I transfer the info to my swatch book at my leisure.

—*Patzee*

**377** Having one-too-many times spotted some fabulous home dec fabric while shopping and not known if it was right for a project, I came up with a solution: I took digital photos of all of the rooms in my house and printed them out. I slipped them into plastic sleeves, added paint chips (when I had them), fabric swatches, and rug samples and placed them in a binder. That way, I have the complete picture in portable form. Plus there's the added bonus of sales staff commenting, "Ooh, you're so organized," which makes me feel competent.

—*OP Gal*

## THE SCOOP ON DISCONTINUED PATTERNS

**378** To discover which patterns are going to be discontinued, look in the pattern drawer at your fabric shop. When the contrast side of the little divider that has the pattern number is turned forward, it means the pattern won't be included in the next book. When patterns are 99 cents, I often pull up a chair to the drawer (when it's not super busy at the store OF COURSE!) and look to see if there are any I should buy now.

—*Janie Viers*

## PLAN FOR EXTRA TO MATCH A PLAID

**379** To estimate the amount of exta fabric needed to match plaids, calculate the following PER GARMENT (i.e. jacket, coat, vest, skirt, pants):

- Working along the selvage of your fabric, determine the length of the plaid repeat. Specifically, find the dominant horizontal line and measure the distance from it to the next identical line. For example: 6" (15.2 cm).
- Count the number of major pattern pieces in your garment. In a jacket, you'll have four major pattern pieces: front, front facing, back, sleeve.
- For security's sake, add one additional piece to your total of major pattern pieces. In my example, 4 + 1 = 5 major pattern pieces.

- Multiply the number of major pattern pieces (5) by the length of the plaid repeat (6" [15.2 cm]) to find the extra length needed to match the plaid. In this case, 30" (76.2 cm) of additional fabric needed for your jacket.
- If you wear and/or sew a small size jacket pattern, and know that you can fit both the front and back pattern pieces on the same width of fabric, you need only one extra plaid repeat for these two major pattern pieces. Likewise, if you know you can fit the sleeve and front facing on the same width of fabric, you need only one extra plaid repeat for these two major pattern pieces. DO add the extra (security) major pattern piece. In this example, you would need only three extra plaid repeats for your small size jacket.

—*lilyofthevalley*

## THE ONLINE EXPERIENCE

**380** Sometimes I purchase fabric online, and so am not standing at the counter as material is measured. Mostly I've had good experiences, but unfortunately twice I've run into yardage shortage. In both cases the vendors took care of me for costs. But I had spent lots of time figuring, planning, etc., based on the yardage on the receipt—wasted time. Now I will always measure the yardage upon receipt, and won't plan or layout the pattern until I do that.

*—utz*

**381** I have found that if I want to find a specific kind of fabric for sale online, I get good results if I type, for example, "silk organza fabric" into Google, and then use Search Images, rather than just Search or Search Web. Since most fabric sellers have a photo of the fabric, I tend to find what I want without all the unusable search results.

*—Liana*

## INDULGE THE RECYCLE JONES

**382** Finding rib knit yardage can be difficult, especially if you are looking for an odd color, or a certain weight, fabric content, or a chunky rib. Most rib knit yardage for sale comes only in basic colors with narrow ribs, and can be fairly expensive. Instead, look for rib knit garments at the thrift store: cuffs and collars don't need a lot of fabric, so a single top will probably supply enough fabric. You can work around stains or flaws, there are tons of colors available, and the cost is usually less than buying yardage. There are lots of interesting weaves in ready-to-wear, and you may be able to make special use of the integral knit hem (not available in yardage).

*—Nikki*

**383** I have a stash of used silk ties from my husband that I use for the binding when making a Hong Kong finish on a waistband. I take the tie apart and hand wash the silk, which is already on the bias. When it is dry, I press it and cut it into an even strip with my rotary cutter and ruler. It is ready to use for a Hong Kong finish. You can also recycle the tie interfacing: It makes great sleeve headers. If you let people know you collect old silk ties, you might be amazed at how many you receive!

*—Peggy L*

**384** Ties also make excellent handbag handles. They are usually tapered, so you might wish to take the time to find the true bias and cut parallel to it.

*—Deepika*

**385** I am an avid thrift store shopper. I have discovered and then felted numerous vintage wool sweaters in order to use the felted wool as embellishments on a variety of projects. (My first was a charming sweater with an ice skater motif that I used for a winter pillow). Here is the technique I use for felting wool garments:

- Remove buttons, zippers, and any other hardware.
- Cut apart the garment along seam lines so that you have two flat sleeves, a back and front. Leave on the ribbings where possible because they are sometimes interesting to incorporate in projects still attached (such as using a ribbed hem at the top of a Christmas stocking).
- Wash the pieces in your washing machine on the hottest water cycle. Tumble dry on hottest setting.
- Repeat as desired until you have reached your desired degree of felting.
- Incorporate into projects as your imagination dictates. Pieces can be cut and used without any edge finish. I use them to create pillows, sachets, brooches, flowers for package toppers, purses, garment appliques, roll into buttons, etc.!

*—CharityAK*

**386** If you have an old quilt that is beyond salvation, don't just throw it away. Use it to create country-style appliqués to embellish your garments or home decor items. I have also seen these quilt shapes fused onto blank note cards. Here's how:

- Pick open the quilting threads and then separate the quilt top from the batting and backing.
- Create an appliqué template. You can trace around cookie cutters, use shapes from coloring books, draw your own designs, trace over fabric motifs, whatever you like.
- Place your template over the quilt top; pay attention to the piecing and balance seams and patches where they look best.
- Trace around your template using a fabric marker. Rough cut around your shape—don't yet cut on the outline.
- Fuse the rough-cut shape to paper-backed fusible web. Then cut on the marked outline.
- The applique is now ready for fusing on your project. Raw edges can be satin stitched, blanket stitched by machine, or blanket stitched by hand.

*—CharityAK*

# Fabric chat

*Need help identifying fabric content or remembering care requirements? Afraid or lazy about preshrinking? Having trouble with faux fur or fleece, or in need of some tips for sewing knits or velvet? PatternReview.com members have oodles of good advice.*

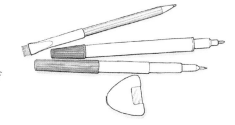

## NOTE THE CARE REQUIREMENTS

**387** If you have a fabric that must be dry cleaned, put a label in your finished garment so you won't forget. I saw that my local fabric store had some "dry clean only" care labels so I bought some. I did a Google search and also found "dry clean only" labels available online from a variety of vendors.

—*LoriB*

**388** I like to mark my notes and a ribbon tag in each garment with the Fabric Care Code for the fabric used (among other info.) These are the numbers inside the triangle on the bolt end of fabrics. Recently I had a terrible time finding a listing of these, and thought maybe others had too, so here is the list:

1—Machine wash, warm
2—Machine wash, warm; line dry
3—Machine wash, warm; tumble dry
4—Machine wash, warm, delicate; tumble dry, low; cool iron
5—Machine wash, warm; do not dry clean
6—Hand wash separately; cool iron
7—Dry clean only
8—Dry clean, pile fabric method only
9—Wipe clean with damp cloth only
10—Care treatment not available; undetermined fiber content

—*Liana*

## TIPS FOR FIBER ID

**389** If you burn swatches in order to determine fiber content, and have trouble figuring out the results, buy small amounts of fabric that you know to be 100% cotton, polyester, linen, nylon, rayon, etc. You can burn these samples and compare them to the burn test of your mystery fabric. Save your burned 100% samples with a notation on what the fiber content is (possibly on cardstock) so that you don't have to test these baseline samples every time.

—*Muria*

**390** There are various ways to test fabric for wool content. If you burn it, you can smell burning hair and it looks like burning hair, for example, but I like to know how much wool there is. To confirm the amount of wool content, cut off a swatch (exclude the selvages) and cover it in bleach in a small container. Thinner fabrics take a couple of hours, allow more time for thicker ones. Wool "dissolves" in reaction with bleach, so any fiber remaining is not wool. This has saved me from disappointment a few times when I wanted a tailored garment and wanted to work with wool, and I found while my fabric looked wooly and felt wooly to the touch, it had minimal wool content and wasn't suitable for my pattern.

—*redsquid*

## D.I.Y. U.P. (ULTRAVIOLET PROTECTION)

**391** Rit Sun Guard Laundry Treatment is a relatively new product that adds a UV protective shield to fabrics. The package states: "... a typical white T-shirt is rated UPF 5. A single treatment with Rit Sun Guard boosts its rating to UPF 30." There are clothing manufacturers that specialize in UPF 50 clothing, but their items are very costly and the selection limited. This product is easy to use and lasts through many washings. I found it at Joann's and at Rite Aid—located in the fabric dye section at both.

—*Patzee*

## SEWING WITH FLEECE 101

These are all the things I learned while sewing yards and yards and yards of fleece one Christmas:

**392** Spend money on good fleece. Splurge on anti-pill. (The pilling doesn't damage the fabric, but it certainly isn't attractive.)

**393** Fleece has a nap! Follow the layout on that pattern guideline.

**394** Use a zigzag stitch or a serger.

**395** Most fleece can be used on either side. If you really want to know the intended right size, sprinkle water on both sides of the fabric (in different spots). The side that wicks the water the fastest is the right side.

**396** I used a size 14 ballpoint needle and it worked like a charm.

**397** If pressing is necessary, use a cool iron and a pressing cloth. Test the setting!

—*salruss*

**398** An easy way to tell the right orwrong side of fleece is to hold your fabric by the horizontal cut edge (the cross-grain) and pull slightly. The cut edge will curl to the wrong side of the fabric. It is sometimes hard to tell just by looking, but this little test works really well.

—*Sew it seams*

## SEW BALLISTIC (NYLON)

**mit says:** After making a messenger bag with ballistic nylon (BN from here on out), I thought I would share what I've learned. First of all, BN is a heavy duty fabric, often used for good quality soft-sided luggage.

**399** Weight: BN comes in multiple weights: I used the medium, 1050 denier (a standard measurement for fabric weight).

**400** Cutting: I used a rotary cutter (of course the blade was dull by the end) and some not favorite scissors.

**401** Stitch length: Use a long (4 mm) stitch length.

**402** Pinning: Textile Outfitters recommends using staples instead of pins. Overall, I found I didn't need to pin or staple much, but when I did, the stapler came in handy. The staples were easy to remove after sewing the seam.

**403** Needle: I used a size 16 jeans needle with good results.

**404** Thread: Upholstery thread worked well for me.

**405** Machine: A sturdy machine is a must. Even with a sturdy machine, I ended up turning the fly wheel by hand to go over some bulky areas.

**406** Edges: BN is often coated to make it water repellent. The coating means you don't have to finish the edges, but I like to. I used a nylon grosgrain ribbon, pressed lengthwise in half, to bind my edges.

**407** Final tip: The fabric is very bulky, so there is quite a lot of width taken up when folding under a seam allowance, etc. I recommend planning for $5/8$" (1.6 cm) allowances, but sewing with $1/2$" (1.3 cm). I learned this when making the top of my messenger bag—what I thought would by 5" (12.7 cm) turned out to be 4½ (11.4 cm)" .

### *Always preshrink fusible interfacing*

*The PatternReview.com members agree a steam iron will do it but disagree on the best way! Here are two suggestions: check them out and see which works most effectively. Maybe it depends on the strength of your iron.*

**408** **comocosews' method.** One way to shrink fusible interfacing is to lay out your pieces on a ironing board. Put your iron on hot steam and go over the pieces without touching the interfacing. About ½" (1.3 cm) away or so. You can just see it shrinking. Then let it cool.

**409** **Diana M's method.** You CAN preshrink iron-on interfacing so it won't ruin the garment by shrinking after it's all sewn. Cut according to pattern, trim as described in the pattern directions, then lay it carefully in place. Hold a good steam iron about 6" to 10" (15.2 to 25.4 cm) above it and give it a heavy dose of steam. Very carefully, pick the interfacing up, then gently lay it back down. You will be able to see that it has shrunk some (how much depends on the kind and the size of the piece).

### PRESSING YARDAGE THE EASY WAY

**410** When ironing yardage or other large, flat pieces (like quilt tops or tablecloths), you'll have more space if you turn the ironing board around, so that the square end is on your left (for right-handers) and the pointy end is on your right.

—*Irene Q*

## BE SMART: PRESHRINK

**411** I always wash my fabrics before cutting and sometimes have several different ones that I would like to wash together, assuming they are colorfast. I have found one quick way to determine if the color is NOT fast is to wet a corner of the fabric, rub some soap on it, squeeze it, and see if the resulting suds turn colored. If the result is tinted suds, I know that this is one piece that I am definitely going to need to wash separately.
—*Brine*

**412** This may be a simple tip but it's something to keep in mind. If you are looking to sew a lined dress, wash and dry the lining before cutting. This will make sure that when the garment is done, the lining will not shrink on you. Cotton linings especially tend to shrink.
—*hemaM*

**413** After preshrinking two pieces of fabric today, I decided to put one tiny safety pin on the selvage of each after the fabric was dry. Voilà. The fabric is discreetly labeled "washed" and can be put into storage. I usually forget whether something is preshrunk and end up washing it or taking it to the dry cleaner again!
—*Jennifer shaw*

## NO-TWIST PRESHRINKING

**414** If you try to machine wash or dry large cuts of fabric (3 yards [2.75 m] or more), they can really twist and bunch up, making a big wrinkled mess! To avoid this, accordion-fold the fabric in about 1 yard (.92 m) lengths. Then tack the layers together (I use several zigzag stitches) at three to four places along one of the selvages. Now, throw it in the washer and dryer, and snip them apart when you're done.
—*Irene Q*

**415** I keep a spare shower curtain rod above my bathtub to hang fabric to let it air dry after preshrinking.
—*Jennifer shaw*

**416** I use mainly natural fibers and most of them fray rather badly, especially linens. I overlock the cut edges of the fabric before I prewash it; this prevents the edges from fraying. I usually just pop the fabric into the washing machine—very practical.
—*regine*

**417** I try to prewash all my fabric purchases shortly after I acquire them. That way, no matter when inspiration or desperation strikes, the fabric is ready for cutting. I have also found that when I wash up several pieces at a time, they tend to get all twisted up in the dryer and get very wrinkled. I had started serging the ends to prevent raveling in the wash, and I got the inspiration of serging the ends of the fabric piece together so it isn't so long. This has really helped: the pieces are easier to press, some hardly wrinkled. When it is time to use the fabric, I just snip off the serging, losing maybe ½" (1.3 cm) of fabric.
—*svetlana*

## YES, YOU CAN PRESHRINK RAYON AND SILK

**418** I am a firm believer in dry cleaner avoidance, so if it doesn't go in the washing machine I don't buy it. I have found over the years that most rayon will wash just fine IF you make allowances for shrinkage of yardage AND you test a strip first. I tear off about a 6" (16.2 cm) strip on the cross grain, pop it into a lingerie wash bag with a dye trapper sheet (Shout makes one) and put into the next washer load of similar color. It goes into the dryer as well (keep it in the bag for that trip as well). If it compares well to the original yardage for color and texture (or if I like the results), the whole thing goes into the wash by itself. The dye trapper sheet gives me a good idea of how much dye has been thrown off. There is so much shrinkage in rayon I don't feel comfortable not preshrinking in any case. One odd thing I have found to be true is that you need to use detergent in the load. Without it, you won't get as much shrinkage NOW but you will later.
—*SJ Kurtz*

**Deepika adds:** Dry cleaner avoidance is good for the environment! The solvent used most frequently is toxic and its residue can seep into drinking water. Not to mention all those plastic bags . . .

**419** To preshrink silk, I hand wash it using baby shampoo, rinse it about a million times, then rinse it again adding ¼ cup (59 mL) white vinegar to the water. According to online fabric vendors Silk Road, "Vinegar neutralizes any remaining soap, and allows it to rinse out completely restoring the fabric's natural sheen; it can make a dramatic difference." Then I rinse it in cool water one last time. Once I was washing several yards of fabric and didn't have the space (or patience) to hang dry it, so I put the fabric in the dryer on fluff (no heat) with a clean, dry, white towel; then ironed it while still damp.
—*monahan*

**420** I find some knit fabrics can be fiddly at times, meaning they don't serge, no matter the differential feed used on the serger or how taut you hold the knit fabric. I place a strip of Solvy (the original, not the ultra) underneath the knit fabric edge while serging. The feed dogs grab the knit better and the result is a nice even serged seam. You can then spritz the seam to remove the Solvy or wash the finished garment to remove it; both ways leave a nice seam finish.

—*Linda L*

**421** I have found that some knits just don't want to be sewn, making stitches skip even with the proper needle, thread, and silicone. To overcome this, I stabilize one layer of each seam by fusing a strip of interfacing to the wrong side: Be sure to use an interfacing that doesn't curl when cut into strips. Use a rotary cutter to make the task speedy. Be certain to lap the interfacing just over the seamline so you are certain to catch it in the stitching. This is a pain indeed. Fortunately most knits don't need this treatment but now you know if you happen to own a misbehaving knit.

—*ryansmum*

**422** My knit fabric rolled up terribly, especially on the cross grain. Before placing the pattern pieces, I first pinned several places along the cut edge. Otherwise I would have wasted several inches of fabric. When sewing, I found it helped to zigzag the seam close to the edge first, then it was much easier to sew or serge the seam with the correct seam allowance.

—*SandyinMO*

**423** I made a knit top where the front and back are laid on folds, for which the fabric had to be arranged with the two selvages folded to the center. The knit was so fine that it was next to impossible to see the ribs to make sure it was folded straight. So I lined up one selvage with the edge of my cutting table and let the other fall off the opposite edge. (Yes, I know this distorts the fabric, but if it is all distorted the same way, it doesn't matter). My table is 30" (76.2 cm) wide and the fabric was 60" (152.4 cm), so I knew the center was approximately at the table's edge. Next I inserted a pin through the fabric every few inches along the table's edge. Then I shifted the pin line to the center of my table—I had a line I could easily fold the selvedges to. Others may already know this, but I feel as though a light bulb lit up in my brain!

—*Ruth C*

**424** The first T-shirt I made from rayon/Lycra knit did not work and ended up in the circular file, but the second is just what I wanted. Here's what I learned: I forgot that rayon is heavy so a knit expands downward. I know to hang the finished garment for several days before hemming to allow for this, but I didn't realize it also affects darts. I made a side dart in this top. I wore the top to work (luckily under a blazer) and by the end of the day, the dart had moved down, way below my bust! On the second top I made, I moved the dart to the armhole as shown below and shortened it some—so it would have room to lengthen. Worked great!

—*Ruth C*

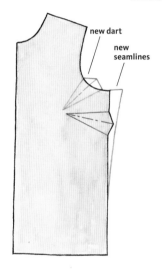

new dart

new seamlines

## Secrets for lightweight drapey knits

*Debra H shares some good tips for sewing lightweight rayon or matte jerseys that have a lot of drape:*

**425** Prewash all jerseys—many will shrink, especially rayon, silk and cotton.

**426** Use ½" (1.3 cm) bias strips of lightweight fusible knit interfacing (Dream Weave, Touch of Gold II, Sewers Dream, etc.) to reinforce any horizontal or bias seams, such as necklines, shoulders, and armscye. Match the length of the strips to the pattern piece, not the cut fabric, and then fit the fabric to the piece before fusing. I do not usually reinforce vertical seams unless the fabric has a lot of lengthwise stretch.

**427** Use either a very narrow zigzag (.5 mm wide and 2.0 or 2.5 mm long) or stretch stitch for your seams (or use a 4-thread serger overlock).

**428** Use a walking foot attachment or make sure you push your fabric toward the foot/needle as you sew to avoid stretching seams too much. I love my Pfaff because it came with the walking foot built in.

**429** Fully interface all your hems with strips of fusible knit interfacing the width of the hem before turning the hem up and stitching in place. I even do this if I use my serger coverstitch to finish the hem, because it helps the garment hang so much better. I use same type of interfacing as noted above but not cut on bias.

**430** Let rayon and silk jerseys hang for a day or two before hemming—they stretch some in length.

**431** If you finish your raw seam edges with an overlock stitch, make sure that you use a fairly long stitch to avoid having too much bulk, especially if you serge the seam edges together. This bulky serged edge can create bumps/waves that show on the outside, especially when you press the fabric.

**432** Use steam more than pressure from the iron to press open seams and to finish your garment. Rayons and silks are very prone to getting iron marks and shiny areas from the iron, even on low temps. I try to steam while holding the seam up off the ironing board or while the garment is hanging. Pressing over a Velvaboard or piece of thick velvet or terry cloth helps too.

**433** I tried unsuccessfully to hem a Slinky knit using the cover hem on my serger. I couldn't avoid skipped stitches. I stopped sewing to go to the grocery store and on the way it dawned on me: "Why didn't you try your blind stitch machine?" As soon as I got home I ripped out the cover hem. I put matching thread on the blind stitch machine and set it for skip stitch. In no time at all I had a PERFECT hem! No stretching, no skipped stitches—it was just right.

—*SandyinMO*

**434** When working with a stretchy knit that doesn't seem to move through the presser foot, I use a rolling foot. And when I use a double needle, I adjust the tension on the bobbin down to a low setting and fill with Woolly Nylon thread. This helps eliminate or reduce the tunneling that can occur with a double needle.

—*okie2thdoc*

**435** I can't believe what a difference using a strip of tissue paper has made when trying to sew a stubborn knit that does not want to be sewn. WOW. Without the tissue I had a very ugly gathered stitch. You just have to place the tissue on top of the seam and sew through it. Removing the tissue was easy: I pulled both edges simultaneously away from stitching.

—*ryansmum*

## Leather and pleather

*Two PatternReview.com members have good tips for sewing real and synthetic leather. Deepika's tips apply to both, CharityAK adds more for sewing the fake.*

**Deepika's tips.** These are not rules for sewing leather, they are just things I discovered while I sewed it and they helped me:

**436** Use a leather needle. For my bag, sewing through four layers of leather, size 14 worked fine.

**437** Use a Teflon presser foot. It won't stick to the leather—especially if your leather is coarse like mine was.

**438** Increase your stitch length. Smaller stitches may cause perforation in leather.

**439** Use a thicker thread for topstitching.

**440** For appliqués or layered construction, a thin coat of rubber cement on one piece will really help keep things in place before you sew.

**441** Use binder clips to hold the seams while you sew. Use the smallest kind.

**442** Sew slowly and carefully, especially if you are using contrasting thread. You cannot redo the stitches since they leave holes in the material.

**CharityAK's tips.** Leathers can be expensive and difficult to sew. While real leather is hard to beat aesthetically, there are some decent synthetics. Here are some tips for working with the new "pleathers" (plastic leather):

**443** Choose a simple pattern without lots of small pieces.

**444** Avoid patterns calling for lots of topstitching.

**445** Use paper clips, clothespins, binder clips, double-sided tape, or even glue sticks instead of basting and pinning.

**446** If you must pin, pin in the seam allowance where the pinholes won't show.

**447** If the pleather sticks to the throat plate or your presser foot, try covering the material with waxed paper or tissue paper.

**448** Sew with the wrong side up when possible as the back bonding is easier to pierce.

**449** Avoid ironing. Use a clapper to set seams where possible. If you must iron use a synthetic setting, no steam, and a pressing cloth. Always test a scrap first.

## NO-SLIP VELVET-TO-LINING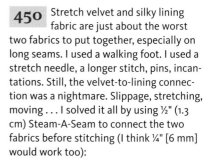

**450** Stretch velvet and silky lining fabric are just about the worst two fabrics to put together, especially on long seams. I used a walking foot. I used a stretch needle, a longer stitch, pins, incantations. Still, the velvet-to-lining connection was a nightmare. Slippage, stretching, moving . . . I solved it all by using ½" (1.3 cm) Steam-A-Seam to connect the two fabrics before stitching (I think ¼" [6 mm] would work too):

- Attach the Steam-A-Seam first to the right side of the silky lining by finger pressing it in place. Then lay the velvet over it, edges lining up.
- Steam press lightly to hold the two fabrics together.
- Then pin the seam and sew. Trim the seam so that most of the Steam-a-Seam is cut off.

—*maryfrana*

## Twelve tips for sewing silk/rayon velvet

*Debra H* says, "Silk/rayon velvet is one of the most exquisite apparel fabrics, almost watery in its drape and softer than other velvets." Here are handling tips she developed sewing seven different garments from the fabric:

**451** **Prewash.** Do this to save your sanity. Test a small area first to make sure it doesn't fade badly. Washing the fabric ensures your garment will be safe in the machine, gives it a soft vintage look and it will obscure iron marks and other imperfections. Wash in cold water on gentle cycle and dry on low heat/fluff cycle.

**452** **Cutting.** Serrated scissors work the best. Cut a single thickness only.

**453** **Marking.** Washable or air erasable fabric markers are great, especially for marking dart lines. Test first if using a light color. Do not press down when using the markers; a light touch is all that's needed.

**454** **Pressing.** Use a steamer or iron that produces a lot of steam heat, which is the best way to press open seams, etc. Lay velvet with the pile facing down over a Velvaboard or towel with the pile facing up. (Make sure that there are no wrinkles or creases in the towel or Velvaboard as this will show up on the fabric, as will the finished edges of these items.) Wrap some scrap velvet or a piece of terry cloth around your index finger to protect it from the heat and to prevent fingerprints on the fabric. Release as much steam as you can about ½" (1.3 cm) above the fabric and quickly use your wrapped finger to press open the seam, crease the hem, finish a collar or cuff, etc. You can also wrap pressing hams, sleeve rolls, etc. in a towel for pressing special areas.

**455** **Restoring a marred velvet surface.** Velvet pile that is almost totally flattened by an iron is not repairable. Moderate to minor marks can be minimized with the help of a second person: Lay the damaged area face up over your Velvaboard or towel. Release steam about 1" (2.5 cm) above the damaged area; immediately have a friend brush the still damp/warm pile with a soft toothbrush or hairbrush, brushing back and forth to raise the pile. This may have to be repeated several times. Hopefully you can get it to the point that it will look like part of the vintage look.

**456** **Interfacing.** Always use nonfusible interfacing. Even interfacing that fuses at low temperatures has trouble adhering without contact with the iron. It also can create a crinkled look on the pile, which you may not want. Washed silk organza works best for me and you can use multiple layers for more support. Washed cotton lawn and organdy also work well, with the latter providing the most body.

**457** **Sewing seams.** A microtex needle size 70/10 works best for me. If possible, use a walking foot or special velvet foot. I use a 2.5 mm long, .5 mm wide zigzag for all major seams. Pin thoroughly, piercing only the seam allowance as pin holes will be permanent. If you see the fabric bunching up in front of the presser foot, stop sewing and lift the presser foot to readjust the fabric or you will end up with tiny tucks in the seam.

**458** **Sleeve caps.** Place the gathered/eased cap over a pressing ham covered by a hand towel (towel pile facing up). Use the steam about ½" (1.3 cm) above to shrink the eased area, using your fingers to spread the eased folds out over the ham. You can use the tip of the iron inside the seam allowance only.

**459** **Hems.** I typically make sleeve hems at least 1" (2.5 cm) and main hems at least 1¼" (3.2 cm) deep. I interface the hem with a bias strip of washed silk organza cut ½" (1.3 cm) wider than the hem depth, serging together at the velvet edge. I then press up the hem using the techniques above. I hand stitch the hem, catching a few threads of the organza and just one or two threads of the velvet backing. The organza provides soft shaping for the hem and also adds strength.

**460** **Closures.** Avoid buttonholes if you can, especially if you have trouble making nice buttonholes with easier fabrics. Button loops, frogs, zippers, and similar options work best. If you must use buttonholes, put a piece of transparent stablizer that does NOT dissolve in water on top of and under the buttonhole area; secure with tape at the edges. Mark the buttonhole on the stablizer and stitch. Then pull away the stablizer from the buttonhole and cut the opening. The stablizer helps hold down the fuzzy pile so that the buttonhole looks more professional and also adds strength.

**461** **Topstitching.** Most topstitching is completely lost in velvet, which may not matter if you need to do this for construction purposes only. If you want the topstitching to stand out more, use a triple straight stitch but remember that this will leave very large needle holes if you need to remove stitches.

**462** **Wrinkle removal.** Throw the wrinkled garment in the dryer with a damp T-shirt of similar color. Do not use towels because they tend to shed fibers onto velvet. Dry on low heat/fluff cycle.

## Steps to success with faux fur

*Working with faux fur presents some challenges. It is bulky, slippery, and usually comes in a 30-inch (76.2 cm) width. Two PatternReview.com members offer help.*

**Hooptastics' keys to success.** I was frightened by long fake fur at first, but it was so easy! Way easier than short fur that wiggles around on you when you are trying to sew it!

**463** Use a sharp box cutter to cut the backing only, not the fur. (Change the blades often—those snap-off blades are a blessing.)

**464** Be sure to leave enough room when cutting near the bottom edge of the fabric—the vendor probably cut the piece with scissors, which means they also cut through the fur.

**465** Use a hairbrush to gently (but you don't have to be too gentle) brush the fur away from the seam allowance towards the center of each piece.

**466** I sewed with a large open zigzag stitch. This made it easy to pull out fur trapped in the seam—I used the blunt end of a needle. With long fur, it didn't matter that the stitch was so wide.

**467** Sew in the direction of the nap.

**468** Be prepared to vacuum—the fur gets everywhere! DON'T be afraid! Go get some ugly stuff from a discount bin and practice on a silly hat.

**Katlewo3's tricks.** I found it best to use a pattern with simple lines that does not require pressing because an iron can cause the fur to melt. Here are some tricks that worked for me:

**469** Trace off two copies of each pattern piece, reversing one. Using two copies kept me from cutting out the same side of the garment twice.

**470** Lay the pattern pieces on the back of the material. Cut through the backing only using the tips of the scissors or a single-edged razor blade.

**471** Use long pins with large heads that won't get lost in the pile.

**472** Baste together seams to keep them from slipping.

**473** I used a 14/90 needle and set my machine for heavy knit fabric, and had no trouble with needle breakage.

**474** Using a blunt needle, knitting needle, or wooden skewer, lift fur that has been caught in the seam. Then, holding your scissors flat against fur, cut away fur close to backing within the seam allowance.

**475** Hem faux fur by hand, using a catchstitch. If the fur is thick, face the hem with a strip of lining fabric folded in half with the raw edges enclosed when the strip is turned up.

**476** Sew loops or fur hooks and eyes in long fur fabric rather than standard buttons and buttonholes.

## SMOOTH THE WAY FOR PLASTICS

**477** I was sewing some plastic totes and having difficulty with feeding the material through the machine. It occurred that I wasn't having foot drag trouble, but table drag! So, I took a big piece of freezer paper and put it shiny-side down/plain paper–side up over the machine bed, cutting a little hole for the bobbin thread. I taped it over the front and under the foot and over the back of the table. I had seen a Teflon version of this, but didn't want to pay the price for something that 1) was expensive 2) I didn't use much and 3) I would probably misplace between the time I bought it and the time I needed it. So, there you are, a non-drag surface for the machine that costs pennies!

*—Janie Viers*

## GOOD TO THE LAST SCRAP

**478** If you are a disciplined sewer fond of perfect fitting, then you probably make muslins before cutting the real fabric and you likely have a great deal of scrap muslin you do not know what to do with. I donate mine to a children's hospital that is always in search of crafts supplies. The kids make gorgeous collages, puppets, and little stuffed animals. I also give them crayons that write on fabric, funny colored zippers, and buttons—here is a costume for a kid who did not ask to be sick. If you do not have a children's hospital nearby, a local public school will also be happy to have those "leftovers". No waste! ☺

*—Mahler*

**479** Whenever I make something out of a nice soft knit, I save the scraps to make underwear. Most underwear patterns take very little fabric and sometimes I have enough to squeeze on a set. Learn how to make these and you can save lots of money! I first practiced on old T-shirts till I got my pattern to fit just right. Now I refuse to buy any undies, and I don't get wedgies anymore. ☺

*—Dale C*

**480** Recently I've been making patchwork blankets from leftover fabric that is too small for a garment. I cut it into 5" (12.7 cm)-wide strips. Then I select similar fabric and coordinating colors for each blanket. I give the blankets to people in need. If I don't have nicely matched scraps, I give them to animal shelters. I feel I've used all the fabric I've bought well. ☺

*—Iris*

**481** Wondering what to do with your fabric scraps? Save them and bring them to your machine dealer. Sewing machine dealers always need fabric strips to test the machines.

*—Deepika*

**482** If you use scraps for doll clothes, try this approach to creating a wardrobe you can give to your favorite doll-playing child: Make a doll garment right after you've finished your primary project. Your machine is already threaded with the right color and you have the fabric right there, not stuffed away in a bag. No last minute rushes to finish doll clothes in December!

*—LoriB*

# Thread chat

*Stymied when you can't find matching thread? Annoyed by tangles? Challenged by needles that seemingly can't be threaded? Chagrined by the cost of threading your serger? Here are answers to these and other common thread issues.*

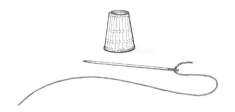

## HASSLE-FREE HAND SEWING

**483** I love using silk thread for my hand sewing. Long pieces aren't likely to tangle. If it does knot up, the knots come out a lot easier. I always hand bind quilts with silk thread. For cotton threads, if you find they tangle a lot, give the spool a spritz of Sullivan's Silicone Spray for Sewing, which will also help it glide through the fabric better. You can easily find this online.

—*papalacios*

**484** When hand sewing, placing a knot at the end of a strand of thread (and making it big enough) can be fiddly. My quilting teacher taught me this fast and simple technique to make a great knot. Reverse hands if you are left-handed (see illustration below).

- Thread a needle and hold it horizontally between your left thumb and index finger with the point toward your right hand. The thread should just dangle down.

- Pick up the end of the thread with your right hand and grip it with your left thumb together with the needle (so a loop of thread hangs from your left hand).
- With your right hand, grasp the thread near the needle tip and wrap it around the needle about three times; then add the wrapped thread to your left thumb/index finger grip.
- Here's the magic: Hold onto the needle with your right hand while your left hand slides the wrapped thread to the left, down and off the needle and along the thread until it forms a knot at the end. It sounds complicated, but it's REALLY easy once you try it. You can adjust the size of the knot by wrapping the thread more or less.

—*Asa Hagstrom*

**485** Topstitching thread is great for basting because it is thick and therefore easy to see and it slides out easily when it's time to remove it.

—*Elaray*

**486** My daughter is now in college, and works part time in the costume shop for the theatre, where she was introduced to Silamide hand sewing thread. It is a hank of waxed thread cut into individual lengths; it comes in a package, you pull out a precut length, and baste away, or hem, or sew on buttons, or whatever. It is fine, yet sturdy, and NEVER knots up on you—which saves gobs of time. Look for it online; it's about $7.00 for a package, which looks like it will last me for years.

—*Lee Ann Hawkins*

**Deepika adds:** This nylon thread is also used for beading, for which it is put up on spools. Look for the precut hanks at a sewing notions supply.

**487** To keep your thread from knotting before hand-stitching, run it lightly through a cake of beeswax. You may have already known that. What you many NOT have known is that if you run a warm iron over it quickly after waxing, it makes the thread even more durable. If you've never used wax in your hand stitching, you will wonder how you got along without it once you start.

—*Nancy Anne*

**488** I know most of you know this, BUT if you are hand sewing with a needle and you want to sew with a double thread: Don't knot both thread ends together at the bottom, instead knot each thread at the end of the thread and it won't get so twisted up. Seems too simple to work, but it does.

—*Janie Viers*

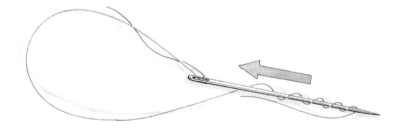

**489** I never seem to have enough empty bobbins on hand, so I usually unwind partially filled bobbins at the end of each project and throw away the extra thread. It's such a stupid little thing, but often I'd get impatient doing this and go too fast and the bobbin would slip out of my hands and fly across the room. So I took a small plastic food storage container and punched a hole in the lid. Now, when I want to unwind a bobbin, I just drop it into the container, thread the loose end through the hole and put the lid on. I can unwind the bobbin quickly without losing it. And the container doubles as storage for my empty bobbins!

—*GwenC*

### Wind it right

**Sarah J Doyle** *has it from a pro: According to my sewing machine repairman husband, the most probable cause of the lower thread breaking is an improperly wound bobbin. Regardless of where you wind the bobbin, the basic "bobbin rules" apply:*

**497** Always start with an empty bobbin.

**498** Don't wind the bobbin so full that it is hard to insert into the bobbin case. Most machines have an automatic "shut off" when the bobbin gets full, but if yours does not, be careful not to fill it too full.

**499** Using bent bobbins can cause uneven stitching and thread breakage. Try rolling the bobbin on the table—if it wobbles, throw it away!

**500** Always use the right shape and type of bobbin for your machine. Check your owner's manual.

**490** I was desperate for a way to make the thread reel off the cone or spool more easily without worrying that the spool would fly off the top of the spindle when I filled bobbins. I put an old empty and dented bobbin on the thread spindle and then stuck a straw through it. The bobbin spins really well to keep the spool from "dragging" and the straw keeps the spool from spinning off, or as in the case of the 1,000 yard threads, keeps them spinning smoothly!

—*Janie Viers*

**491** I hate having to fill bobbins while I'm in the midst of sewing a garment. The problem isn't so much filling the bobbin; it's having to remove the top thread in order to do so and then put it back. I have enough trouble threading the needle as it is! I didn't want to fill two or more bobbins at once—because maybe one would be sufficient. So I now buy two spools of matching thread when I'm preparing for a project. One is dedicated for the top thread and the other is used only for bobbin winding. If I need to refill the bobbin partway through the sewing process, I just pull out the second spool and there's no need to touch the top thread (or rethread the needle!). I find this saves me beaucoup time and frustration.

—*Joey in Katy*

**492** The option to wind the bobbin directly from needle is characteristic for modern and expensive machines, but you may succeed in doing it on a simpler or older machine as I did: Pass the thread from needle under the presser foot and then wind it around the bobbin. Place the bobbin on the bobbin-winder and lock it. Hold the thread with your fingers as you wind so the bobbin fills evenly. Be careful, because some thread can burn your fingers, if you do it too fast. Always place the thread under the foot, because if you don't, you can spoil the needle.

—*Annemari*

**493** If you wind a bobbin with the presser foot raised, keep one finger on it so it doesn't vibrate into the needle. Wind at a slow speed!

—*Joey in Katy*

**494** I found out (the hard way) that winding nylon thread onto your plastic bobbin may make it impossible to remove the bobbin from the winder! To prevent: wind at slow speed and/or don't entirely fill the bobbin. To remedy: unwind the bobbin entirely and you should be able to remove it from the winder. Maybe everyone knows this already, but I panicked after winding the very first bobbin on my new sewing machine and finding an answer online took a surprising amount of searching.

—*Kristi_Dugan*

**495** Sometimes my bobbin does not wind tight enough or it overfills. I had this happen this morning because I was winding a bobbin and reading something else and wasn't paying attention. My usual remedy for this was to grab another bobbin, throw the badly wound one in a case to deal with later (never sure how I was going to deal with it) and just wind another one. This time I was aggravated because I had wasted thread. Then the light bulb flashed on. I popped the badly wound bobbin onto the thread spool spindle. I loaded an empty bobbin in the winder and proceeded to wind a new bobbin from the badly wound one (this time paying attention to what I was doing). Badly wound bobbin totally unwound and thread now on new perfect bobbin. No more wasted thread!!!

—*Mirza*

**496** If you have a Bob 'n' Serge for your serger and would like to use your sewing machine to wind serger thread onto bobbins for it, you can spend up to $30 for a Deelybob thread cone adaptor—or you can fake one for free if your sewing machine and serger are near each other: Simply place the coned thread on the holder on your serger and thread it up through the telescopic thread guide. Then pass the thread across to your sewing machine and through the regular bobbin winder tension guides. Now wind as usual. Now that I've figured this out, I can simply buy one cone of serger thread in each color I need. That saves both money and storage space.

—*nancy2001*

## SAVE $: USE BOBBINS INSTEAD OF SPOOLS

**501** Everyone's probably already figured this out, but it just came to me the other day. I needed two spools of thread for use in a twin needle topstitch application. But I had only one spool of the color I needed. Since I was using Woolly Nylon in the bobbin I placed the regular thread bobbin on my secondary spool holder. The bobbin fit fine and the twin needle stitching came out great. I can't believe I've been buying two spools of thread all this time.

*—drsue*

**502** I used to buy serger thread four cones at a time (for my 4-thread sergers). However, ever notice that you use much, much more upper and lower looper thread than you do needle thread? So, try using only two cones instead of four! Just fill two bobbins from a serger cone and then use the bobbins for the two needles. Instead of buying sets of four same-color cones, you can get by with only two same-color cones—and thus buy many more colors!

*—Joey in Katy*

**503** A serger needs thread: two or more spools depending on the technique. Since I like to have my serger thread colors somewhat match the fabric I'm serging, I came up with this technique so I don't have to buy three to four spools for every color fabric, especially for colors I know I will only use occasionally. The technique requires: empty regular thread spools; one spool of serger thread; blue poster putty (Blu Tak), a sewing machine bobbin and sewing machine with its bobbin winding mechanism and, well, my hands. (My machine has an upright bobbin winder; this won't work on a machine where there is no space to fit the regular empty spool on the bobbin winder.) Here's the process:

- I place the empty bobbin on my sewing machine bobbin winder, positioned as if I'm going to wind a bobbin. I take a ball of poster putty and smoosh it into the end of an empty thread spool; I then push the putty end of the spool against the bobbin, making sure it is centered and secured.
- I hold a cone of serger thread in my left hand, wind a bit of the serger thread onto the empty spool, press the sewing machine pedal and begin winding—

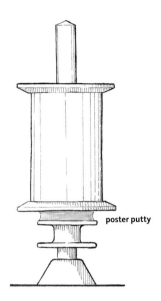

poster putty

using my right hand to gently guide the thread so it winds evenly onto the spool.
- Once the winding is done I remove filled spool, pull out the poster putty (to be used again) and I have an extra wound spool in the color I want to use in my serging.

*—utz*

## MEET THE SERGER THREADING CHALLENGE

**504** Here's my method for coaxing Woolly Nylon through the looper eye on my serger: Feed the Woolly Nylon through the thread guides up to the looper. Cut a 1' (30.5 cm) length of regular sewing thread. Tie one end of the sewing thread to the end of the Woolly Nylon in a square knot, and trim the tails close to the knot. Guide the sewing thread through the looper eye. With your fingers, put some tension on the Woolly Nylon so that it thins out behind the sewing thread as you pull the thread, the knot, and the Woolly Nylon through the eye. No heroics, no weeping, no problems. Works every time, and no contortions are necessary.

*—jan zita*

**505** When threading Woolly Nylon through loopers or needles, I use beeswax to coat the end of the thread. Pull about 3" (7.6 cm) at the end of the thread across a cake of beeswax, holding it tightly against the wax with your thumb. Sometimes you have to do that more than once. Now you can twirl, flatten, or otherwise shape the thread. I learned this trick in the factory where I sewed long johns and had to thread four needles and a looper on a big industrial machine with Woolly Nylon.

*—xenophea*

**506** When changing thread on a serger, lots of people use the method of cutting the last used thread near the cone, replacing the cone, tying the new thread to the end of the old, and then pulling the needle or looper end of the thread through most of the thread path. Most people think it necessary to cut off the knot and then rethread the needles manually. However, if you tie square knots in the needle threads, and cut the thread tails very short, it is usually possible for the knots to go right through the needle eye.

*—Shazza B*

**507** I was so confused by the term "hand-wound bobbin." I spent months holding the bobbin in one hand and winding the thread around and around and around and, as Yul Brynner used to say in *The King and I*, "Et cetera, et cetera, et cetera!" I finally realized I could get the same even effect by using my machine to hold the thread spool and the bobbin as usual, BUT, instead of feeding the thread through the tension guide on the machine, guiding it through my hand while running the machine slowly. I haven't had a problem with this method, which I have used for decorative ribbon and yarn for bobbin work as well as plain old thread.

—*Janie Viers*

**508** When hand-winding a bobbin, I used to slide it onto a pencil. But it always slipped off. So, I softened one end of a plastic drinking straw by holding it very briefly over the flame of a lighter and then inverted the softened end on a table, pressing it so it flared out a bit. Now I slide the bobbin onto this straw, holding the straight end in my hand; the bobbin won't drop off the flared end. The thread doesn't get caught on the straw either since the flare is flush with the bobbin.

—*Maria Hatfield*

**509** If you're fumble-fingered like me, you have trouble holding a bobbin while hand-winding thread such as Woolly Nylon onto it. Well, here's the solution I found: hold a chopstick in your left hand and slide the bobbin onto it; extend your thumb and forefinger so they cradle the bobbin. Wind the thread onto the bobbin with your right hand—you'll find your thumb and finger don't get in the way and the bobbin sits securely on the chopstick. If you're left-handed, reverse the process.

—*OP Gal*

**510** When I need to hand-wind a bobbin, I slide it onto a knitting needle, which already has a stop at one end that keeps the bobbin from sliding off.

—*Deepika*

## *Metallic thread know-how*

*Quilting (and sewing) with metallic thread can be an exercise in frustration.* **CharityAK** *has learned a few things that can lessen your frustration levels.*

**512** Use a metallic needle. You can also try a topstitching needle.

**513** Loosen the upper tension.

**514** Use a longer stitch length.

**515** Try running a line of Sewer's Aid (a lubricant) across your spool of thread. Put another drop at the top of your needle.

**516** Stitch at a slower rate of speed.

**517** Be careful not to put any strain on the needle. Do NOT pull at your fabric as it passes under the needle.

**518** You may have to use the metallic thread in your bobbin and quilt from the back of the piece.

**519** If all else fails, try couching the thread. Lay the metallic thread over your desired quilting lines and use a very narrow zigzag back and forth over it. You can use a clear thread or one that matches your fabric background.

## WOOLLY NYLON RULES

**511** On an overlock machine, use Woolly Nylon in the loopers only, not in the needles. On the sewing machine, use it in the bobbin when sewing with a twin-needle to allow the seam to stretch.

—*Mel.J*

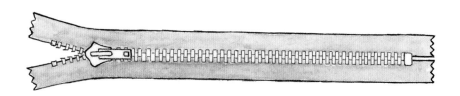

## EASY NEEDLE THREADING

**520** To make it easy to thread a twin needle, insert a wire needle threader through each needle eye BEFORE inserting the twin needle in the machine. Push the loops through from back to front and push them slightly apart if they want to overlap. Then install the needle in the shaft. Now thread each loop and pull it through, front to back. With this trick, you can hold the needle as close as needed to see the needle eyes while you insert the threaders.

*—homework*

**Deepika adds:** There is no reason to save this tip for a twin needle. Anyone who has trouble threading a single needle will appreciate it too.

**521** I was trying to thread my serger the other day, and for the life of me I couldn't find the tweezers that I need to grasp the thread. So what I did is this: I used a small bit of tape. If you can get the end of the thread through the needle, you can use the tape to pull it the rest of the way through. Just touch the tape to the thread where it exits the needle and pull towards the back of the machine.

*—SexiSadi*

**522** Invisible (clear monofilament) thread has many great uses, but can be a chore sometimes when it comes to threading a hand or machine needle. To make it easier to see what I'm doing, I mark the tip of invisible thread with a black Sharpie. You can put white paper behind or under the needle as you thread it for extra contrast if needed. Hope that helps!

*—tweedcurtain*

### Cut on an angle, dampen

*Water helps thread pass through the eye of a needle. Here are two takes on the process:*

**523** **Deepika's advice.** If you are ever struggling threading the small eye of a hand sewing needle, try this: Cut the thread on an angle with a sharp pair of scissors; then wet the end and pull the thread between your thumb and forefinger to make it even pointier. You'll see, cutting the thread on an angle creates a sharper point so threading becomes easier. Try it; it works!

**524** **PattiAnnSG's advice.** I would like to add a method similar to Deepika's that also includes machine needles. Cut the thread on an angle as Deepkia describes, but instead of moistening the thread, moisten the eye of the needle and the thread will wick through the eye like magic. I find this method very helpful when I thread the needles on my old thread-it-yourself serger.

**Deepika adds:** The needle type doesn't matter. Both techniques are helpful for threading any type of sewing needle. Moisten both and you will see water's cohesive properties work magic.

## NOVEL APPROACHES TO THREAD COLOR

**525** I frequently have the problem of not finding a topstitching thread that matches my fabric. However, I can usually find a matching construction thread. So for topstitching, I use two spools of the regular construction thread, passing the thread from each through the guides separately and then through the needle together. This is not quite as heavy as regular topstitching thread, but it does show better than just a single thread. Sometimes I am too much of a perfectionist and the color I want falls between two thread colors. So I use one of each for topstitching; they blend into the color I want once I stitch them on the garment.

*—MarilynB*

**526** When choosing thread for my garments I always choose an off-color thread for the bobbin—just a few shades off so that it's not distasteful on the finished garment. I do this so it's easy to see should I need to rip out a seam. I usually try to choose one or two shades lighter, not darker, than the fabric so it won't show on the finished garment. This is such an easy aid for that dreaded unpicking if you have to do it!

*—KarmenG*

## CREATIVE "SPOOL" HOLDERS

**527** I like to purchase large cones of thread for both my serger and embroidery machine. These machines, of course are set up to handle the large cones. But I wanted also to be able to use these cones on my sewing machine—especially when I do decorative stitching and want to use my embroidery thread. This is the solution I came up with:

- I cut a 5" (12.7 cm) length of ¾" (1.9 cm) dowel. I drilled a hole sized to fit the thread spindle on my machine into one end of it.
- I slipped it over the spindle, and it supports my thread cones.
- To further support the embroidery thread cones I also use the rubber four-prong base that came with my embroidery machine, but this isn't necessary for the serger thread cones.

*—ReneeSews*

**528** If you're using bobbins to supply thread to serger needles and the bobbins won't fit on the thread spindle—or if the thread doesn't feed smoothly when the bobbin gets about halfway empty, try this. Find a couple of tall drinking glasses. Put them behind the serger, drop a bobbin into each glass, and feed the thread through the guide "trees" as usual. The bobbins may jump around a bit in the glasses (adding an interesting counterpoint to your serger rattle), but the thread will feed smoothly!

*—Joey in Katy*

# Notions chat

*Stabilizers, fusibles, elastic, and closures are key to good structure and good fit (and buttons look cool, too). Here, from the resourceful members of PatternReview.com, are some smart ways to handle and apply them.*

## THIS & THAT ABOUT NOTIONS

**529** We all dislike the way Fray Check hardens as it dries. To counteract that, as soon as you apply it, press it dry with a steam iron. Don't let the iron sit on it; keep it moving as you steam, until you see the Fray Check is dry. Once the fabric is cool it will be soft to the touch.

—*PVA*

**530** Elastic may shrink when it is washed, so I always prewash and dry it before inserting it in my sewing projects. So that I always have elastic ready to go, I buy it in bulk, wind it loosely into a loop, tie it with string in several places to keep it from tangling, and wash and dry the whole amount.

—*Brine*

**531** You know those annoying ribbons that come in ready-to-wear blouses and dresses intended to keep the garment on a hanger: I never use them to hang the garment and they always end up hanging out of my neckline. So, like most, I cut them off. But I use them in my garments anywhere stay tape is needed, especially at the shoulder seam. The ribbon works really well and it's free. So, next time you cut out that ribbon, save it and use it in your next project.

—*SueV*

**532** You can use used dryer sheets as stabilizer. For making smaller templates, you can use the plastic insert from packages of bacon; just clean well.

—*comocosews*

**533** When I had trouble locating a suitable drawstring for a pair of pants I made for my daughter, I turned to the shoelace rack at the grocery store. I bought long oval athletic shoelaces, which come in an array of colors. Snip the little plastic ends off, and pull the "stuffing" out, and you wind up with two laces: the colored cover, and a soft white knit cord concealed inside. The navy cord was perfect for my daughter's pants, and the liner cord will be useful for travel shoe bags I'm making for gifts. I'm going to stock up on these laces!

—*Karla Kizer*

## STABILIZER HINTS

**534** Instead of staystitching, I use Glad Press'n Seal to stabilize neck and bias edges. It adheres very well to fabric and definitely stops it from stretching. I cut it into strips or to match a pattern contour, and press it firmly onto the fabric with my hands—or sometimes with a ruler. Then I pin and stitch the garment sections together in the normal way. Pinning and stitching through the Press'n Seal is no bother and it tears off easily along the stitching line. Another benefit is that it doesn't gum up the needle with sticky residue.

—*Vonnevo*

**535** Wash-A-Way Wonder Tape is a water-soluble, double-stick tape that can be used instead of pins or basting. It washes out in the laundry. However, it leaves a little bit of white residue behind (it's not the actual adhesive that stays around, just a kind of white lint). I've found that you can remove the residue by gently rubbing on it. I've found that subsequent washings won't remove this white stuff entirely; you really have to remove it by hand.

—*Debbie Lancaster*

**536** I've recently started using leftover scraps of pattern tissue as a starter and stabilizer for knits. I place the tissue on top of the seam, extending maybe ½" (1.3 cm) before the start of the seam. I start sewing right before the beginning of the seam and voilà, the knit doesn't get eaten by the feed dogs. The tissue paper also acts to reduce drag between the knit and the presser foot. This really helps to feed the layers evenly. I've also used the paper to act as a "slip" between the feed dogs and clear elastic—so that the clear elastic doesn't drag along the dogs.

—*Kim Winson*

**537** What to do if you can't get an invisible zip that matches your fabric? Obviously the only real problem is the zip pull/toggle as the rest of the zipper isn't seen. You can paint it with nail polish to the same color as the fabric, if you can get nail polish in the right color. The most readily available polish colors range from palest beige through all the pinks and reds to purples. However, I found blue-green that was an exact match to my fabric. So if you haven't had luck with finding the right color zip, you might be luckier with nail polish! Not cheap though. This solution is also good for eyelets/grommets.

—*KathleenS*

**538** My brother likes to make model cars. To paint them he uses Testors enamel paint, which comes in small bottles. You can paint zipper pulls, grommets, rivets, etc. with it—perfect when you can't find these in a color to match your fabric. Testors lasts better than nail polish, which scratches and chips easily, so if you want to wear something multiple times the Testors is a more permanent option. The bottles cost about $1.15. They also make paint pens for precision painting , about $3.

—*chick3y*

**539** I can't tell you the number of times I accidentally trimmed a coil zipper only to realize I had cut off the zipper slide. Well, it is possible to repair a slide-less zipper, though you must do it from the bottom, not the top, which means removing it from your garment if you've already sewn it in. You will need clippers or small scissors, a hemostat if you have one, and a pair of pliers.

• Separate the zipper at the bottom. With small scissors, clip the coil free from the bottom end of each piece of tape for about ¼" (6 mm).
• Use the hemostat to pull the freed coil ends nearly straight.
• Guide the zipper slide back onto one piece of zipper tape, inserting the straightened coil through the channel in the slide. Use the pliers to pull the coil and a bit of the tape through the slide, so that a bit of the tape extends below the slide.
• Now guide the coil on the other zipper tape into the other half of the slide. It may take a few tries to get the tape through evenly, so the tops align.

—*patsijean*

**Deepika adds:** Be sure to sew the tapes together at the bottom so the slide doesn't escape before you sew in the zipper. If you shortened the zipper at the top originally, there won't be any stops to align; just cut the tapes to be even and pin them at the top temporarily to keep the slide on.

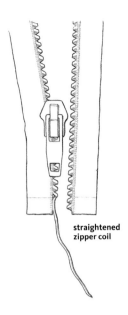

straightened zipper coil

**540** Metal zips are notorious for sticking and being difficult to zip/unzip. To unstick, rub the metal teeth with the tip of a pencil, then move the slide back and forth a couple of times. If the slide still doesn't run smoothly, just repeat the process until it does (a couple of attempts should be sufficient). Be careful not to get any of the graphite from the pencil tip onto the fabric.

—*Janine S*

**541** **Plastic canvas.** Most bag patterns tell you to put a piece of cardboard in the bottom of a bag to help retain the shape. I don't like this because it means you can never wash the bag, nor get caught in the rain with it. Instead I use a piece of plastic canvas. You can even stitch it into place by machine (without any special needle) to it so it does not "travel" around the bag. Plastic canvas is about 25 cents for a sheet about the size of letter paper, and can be found in craft stores near other needlework supplies.

—*candyo*

**542** **Plastic drop-ceiling panels.** Hardware stores carry 2' × 4' (61 × 123 cm) plastic panels for the kind of ceiling grid that covers fluorescent lights. They come in various designs and are flexible yet firm in small pieces. I used one cut to fit in the bottom of the purse so that the purse wouldn't collapse when I set it down. My original intent was to cover it in with my lining fabric, but since it is transparent, I left it as is. This seems to be working well and has much more body than the plastic canvas sheets I've seen recommended. Cutting the material is a little tricky—my husband used a Dremel wheel. The best part is that you can get LOTS of purse reinforcements for very little money.

—*Jan B.*

**543** **Nylon window screen.** If you are looking for a durable interfacing or interlining that adds body to fabric crafts such as purses, tote bags, Halloween costume hats, etc., try using non-metal replacement window screen. It is washable and lightweight, yet it has body, and won't get limp. It comes in nylon, polyamide, and polyester—each has a different stiffness. You can find it in rolls at the hardware store or Home Depot. Sometimes you can find a variety of mesh sizes too!

—*ShereeSews*

## RIVETING LESSON

**544** Often my spouse finds wonderful vintage jeans that don't quite fit. I had been afraid to attempt to remove the pocket rivets, as I wasn't sure if I could get them back on. I recently purchased a Dot Snapper Tool Kit on eBay, and it has been a dream tool. The tools I used to remove the rivets are simple household tools: A flathead screwdriver, a pair of pliers, and a hammer and awl to put in the new rivet hole.

- Insert the screwdriver in between the back of the rivet and tap the screwdriver once or twice with the hammer to loosen the rivet's grip.
- Use the pliers to pry the rivet top from the bottom. It doesn't take too much force. If either the top or the bottom of the rivet is warped, use the pliers to straighten it back out.
- After altering the jeans, place them on top of a phone book and then use the awl to poke a hole where you want to put in the rivet (tap it with the hammer).
- Insert the bottom rivet piece up through the hole; press the fabric around it with the screwdriver to make as much of the stem visible as possible. Place on a hard flat surface.
- Invert the top rivet piece on the rivet stem and cover with the Dot Snapper rivet tool. Hammer the rivet into place, making sure the fabric is held tight.

—*Jennifer.Huber*

## FUSIBLES SMARTS

**545** Cotton and linen (100%) are wonderful fabrics to sew and to wear, but they need to be ironed at high heat with lots of steam. That means that every part of your garment has to be able to "take the heat"—interfacings, trims, seam binding, any other fabrics you mix in. Most interfacings, including all those nonwoven fusible Pellon-types, contain polyester or nylon. If you iron them on high, they'll melt and shrink and ruin your garment. What if you don't know what's in an interfacing or trim? If you iron something on high, with steam, and it melts, feels sticky, or smells funny/oily, don't use it. I keep falling into this trap myself, so I thought it was worth bringing up.

—*Irene Q*

**546** I was unable to find a suitable medium-weight, sew-in interfacing recently so I improvised by applying a fusible interfacing to cotton batiste and then using it as a sew-in.

—*KarenP*

**547** I pink the edges of interfacing pieces fused under pockets and buttonholes, just to be sure it doesn't show through as a rectangle to the right side of my garment.

—*KarmenG*

## RESOURCEFUL WITH SEAM TAPE

**548** I'm using a lot of a particular stay tape, especially for shoulder seams, when sewing knits. I sewed the tape once with the wrong side up and believe me, it's quite itchy next to the skin. What I do now is brush the sides of the tape, one by one, against my lips. Your lip skin is so sensitive that you feel immediately which is the smoother, silkier side.

—*LauraLo*

**549** Sometimes I don't have or don't want to use purchased stay tape so I make my own from the selvage of the fashion fabric that I am sewing. Try it, I think you will like how well it works and best of all, it's free, and matches the fashion fabric!

—*PattiAnnSG*

**550** When I make a sleeve that has a ruffle at the wrist—the kind created by a casing with an elastic sewn a few inches above the hem—I use Seams Great to make a non-bulky casing. I keep various widths on hand. Patterns usually tell you to make a bias strip from the fashion fabric for the casing, but Seams Great makes a nice, soft, non-fraying substitute. Of course this also works for ruffled pant legs or at the neck of a peasant blouse—good to know if you make costumes.

—*Teri*

## BUTTON, BUTTON

**551** Here's a simple trick to help select the right button for your project: Find a scrap of your fabric and cut small slits in it that are about the length of the buttonhole you want to use. Space them approximately the distance apart that they will be on your garment. Take this with you to the button store. Slide any buttons you are considering (while still on the card) through the slit. It is much easier to imagine how they will look this way than just holding them near the fabric. Much more convenient than waiting until you have completed the button holes and taking the whole garment to the store. You might decide on a different size button so you don't want to do the buttonholes first anyway.

—*Ann Smith*

**552** When discarding worn-out clothing, always cut off the buttons for reuse. Run a thread through the holes and tie the thread—this keeps the buttons together so later you won't have to dig through a button box to find them.

—*Sarah J Doyle*

**553** Something to keep in mind when the thrift stores have their special colored-tag and $1 sales: check those dress, blouse, and suit racks for buttons. Even check the skirts—I found a denim button-front skirt with 20 buttons for $1. My latest find was a quarter-size button with an abalone outer ring and an intricate marcasite-like silver design in the center. A double benefit: You find some great buttons and support your local charitable organization!

—*Oopsy-Daisy!*

# Essentials of Sewing Fine Lace

Couture sewing expert Susan Khalje is renowned for her custom wedding gowns and evening apparel and passionate about sharing her skills. She established the Couture Sewing School in 1993 and teaches throughout the country and on PatternReview.com. Every year she takes a group to Paris for an insider's look at the couture arts. Visit susankhalje.com to learn more about Susan, her classes, Paris tour, and Web store. Says Susan about the subject of this master class: "Is there a lovelier group of fabrics than lace? I don't think so, and happily, fine lace is widely available these days. Even better, it's surprisingly cooperative to work with."

*"Couture garments often join fabrics in unorthodox ways and that was the inspiration for this cocktail dress. The body is a mohair/wool blend, and the lace is beaded Chantilly in a wonderful mushroom color (there's black silk organza under the lace, to strengthen it, but as it's transparent, it maintains the mystique of the lace). Two silk velvet bows tie the whole thing together. It's a simple design, but what I think makes it special is the unexpected combination of mohair and lace."*

# Working with Alençon lace

*Alençon is perhaps the lace with which we're most familiar. It's popular for its inherent beauty, of course, and its three-dimensional nature. The cording that outlines its motifs not only gives visual definition, it strengthens the lace and makes it easy to manipulate. Fine French Alençon lace is available in a variety of widths, from 36" (91.4 cm) at its widest, down to narrow borders.*

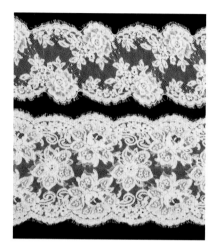

*Alençon is often found in galloon form (scalloped on both edges), in varying widths that are generally cut apart to form scalloped borders as on this bolero.*

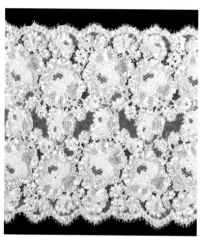

*When Alençon is embellished, it is even more spectacular.*

*Alençon lace makes an elegant bolero—especially when you plan the layout to take advantage of the motifs and borders.*

## PLAN AHEAD BEFORE STARTING

Alençon lace can be used on its own, or it can be worked with a layer of supporting fabric. An underlayer of silk organza would maintain the airy nature of the lace and give gentle, behind-the-scenes support. The sheen of silk satin would be beautiful through the net background, and its strength would make a very structured garment possible. The Alençon lace that I've chosen to make the bolero demonstrated in this class, though, with its firm cording and densely placed motifs, is sturdy enough to be used on its own. Decide which look is right for your garment.

I start any project by constructing and fitting a muslin. Once I'm happy with it, I dismantle it, press it, and use it for my pattern. This provides a full set of pattern pieces, which you need for the single layer

layout required. The pattern pieces have to be placed absolutely symmetrically; such careful placement would be impossible if the fabric were cut on the double. I remove the seam allowances from the muslin pattern pieces so that I can see and exactly mark the seamlines. Sometimes, the muslin pattern pieces can be slid *under* the lace during the layout process—then it's easy to see precisely where the internal motifs will fall.

The lace needs to be cut out with large seam allowances when possible. On the sample bolero, with the exception of the sleeves, the seams and darts will be overlapped and sewn by hand, so the more lace there is to work with the better, especially on the side seams. You'll see that in some cases, the seam allowances are small; hopefully there will be more room in the ones that they

match up with. And if all else fails, they can be patched. Lace isn't inexpensive, and tight layouts are the norm. Consider your seam allowance needs as you arrange the layout.

I generally sew the sleeve underarm seams by machine and set them in by machine too (be sure to stitch slowly; there's a lot of air in lace, and if you sew too quickly, your thread will snarl and might tear the lace). There's a lot of movement in the arms, and hand-sewn lace seams, even if carefully stitched, would abrade against the body and eventually weaken. I bind the seam allowances (together) with bias strips of flesh-colored silk organza or silk georgette so that they are all but invisible through the lace. Prepair some bias strips about 1¼" (3.2 cm) wide so you'll be ready for this step.

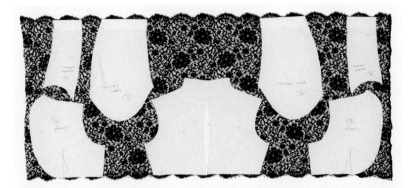

1. For my bolero (and most garments), it's essential to consider the placement of the borders; they're a critical part of the design, and unless an altogether different border is added once the garment is assembled, their placement is what drives the layout. In this case (and nearly always, in fact), there will have to be some piecing of the border because the curved center fronts need to be edged, but that's all right—you'll see how easily lace lends itself to that sort of manipulation.

2. Since standard seam allowances don't apply, the stitching lines (including any darts) need to be carefully and reliably marked—once the muslin has been removed, there isn't much to go on. The solution is to thread-trace the stitching lines. Since the seam allowances of the pattern pieces have been cut away it's easy— and accurate—to thread-trace the perimeter of each pattern piece.

## OVERLAPPED SEAMS

1. Using the thread-tracing as a guide, overlap the pieces at the side seams.

2. Before doing anything else, choose the layer that will be on top. Look for what I call the "leading edge": it should be the nicest edge, and the sturdiest, with pretty motifs, and nice firm cording along which you can stitch.

3. Neatly trim the excess net and any partial motifs from the leading edge.

4. Carefully pin the layers together along the leading edge.

5. Next, secure the overlapped seam with lots of small fell stitches—small stitches that are almost invisible from the top, with most of the thread on the wrong side of your work.

6. Finally, trim away the excess lace on the underlayer.

(continued)

7. Use the same process for the darts and the borders that go up the front of the bolero: choose the top layer, trim it, secure the seam with fell stitches, and then trim the underlayer. Sometimes, you'll want to shift the leading edge from layer to layer—one piece might start out on top, then partway through the seam, switch to the bottom.

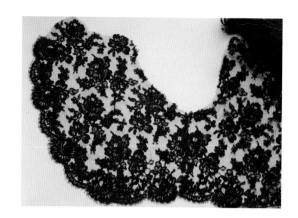

## BOUND SEAMS

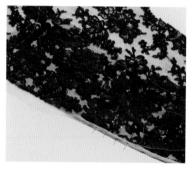

1. With the layers right sides together as usual, sew the seam by machine. As you do this, lay an organza strip along the seam, extending onto the allowance by ³/₈" (1 cm) and catch it in the stitching.

2. Press the organza strip toward the seam allowances.

3. Fold the strip over the extending seam allowances and then fold under its raw edge. Secure the strip to the allowances with fell stitches by hand.

4. While still slightly visible, the presence of the dark seam allowances is certainly muted by the organza binding. Use this process for seams that get a lot of stress.

### A FINAL PRESS

Once all the stitching is done, the lace needs a good pressing. Using steam and in this case, starch (the starch will be more effective if you let it absorb into the lace for a few minutes before pressing) and a silk organza pressing cloth, press the lace face-down into a thick terry towel to preserve its dimension. This final pressing is essential, and helps "set" the lace in place beautifully.

CHAPTER **FIVE**

# Layout, Cutting & Marking

> " *I enjoy sewing. I suppose it is the satisfaction of turning a flat piece of fabric into a three-dimensional garment that I like the most.* "
>
> —Talleymom

# Cut with confidence

*Accurate cutting gets your sewing off to a good start, so it's a process to be done with care. But smart planning and clever shortcuts make it easier, faster, and enjoyable—even for plaids and stripes.*

## MAKE LAYOUT AND CUTTING EFFICIENT

**554** Patterns with asymmetrical pieces (like pinwheel or swirl skirts) must be laid out on a single layer of fabric because cutting on folded fabric results in reversed pieces instead of identical ones. Here's a trick you can try if these pieces must be cut multiple times:

- First spread the fabric right side up on your table.
- Then, instead of laying out and cutting each piece individually, lay out half the pieces on it and mark them.
- Next cut all the way across the fabric to create a length with the marked pieces on it.
- Shift this length of marked fabric so it lies on top of the unmarked fabric (both are right side up); smooth the layers, match any print or stripe, and align the selvedges.
- Secure with pins or weights and then cut out both layers.
- If there are specific markings required, transfer them to the unmarked pieces.

*—belphebe*

**555** This might be one everyone in the world knows—but I sure didn't! I was making a tablecloth and needed to cut a 3 yard (2.75 m) piece of 88" (223.5 cm)-wide fabric in half lengthwise. I had the darnedest time the first time I tried: couldn't quite get the cutting line straight, couldn't see the fold line well enough to follow it. End result was very ragged and wavy. On tablecloth #2, instead of cutting along the middle for 3 yards (2.75 m), I made a 1" (2.5 cm) snip in the middle of one end of the cloth. I then grabbed the two sides of the cut and gently pulled them apart. The cloth tore neatly down the middle—it followed the grain perfectly. I was pretty jazzed when I figured this out.

*—Joey in Katy*

**556** I suppose it is my age that led me to this little tip. I was having trouble seeing the pattern piece numbers on a Burda skirt I was cutting out. Using a magnifier had become tiresome. I decided to scan and enlarge the cutting layout diagram to use as reference. I scanned it into my computer, and saved it as a PDF. I then printed it on standard letter paper. Not only was it larger, but having black lines on white paper made the diagram much easier to read.

*—Talleymom*

**557** There are advantages to cutting out paper patterns without seam allowances, for instance it's easier to fit pieces together to check the fit. Therefore, I advocate adding seam allowances at the time of fabric cutting. I also like to use different seam allowance widths for different types of seams. Here's my method for knowing which width to add where when I cut; adapt it to your seam allowance preferences:

- Trace and cut out all the paper pieces without seam allowances.
- Use a yellow highlighter along all edges needing 1" (2.5 cm) seam allowances: for me, that's all hems, side seams, and sleeve underarm seams. Leave the other edges unhighlighted to indicate a narrower allowance (for me, 3/8" [1 cm]).
- Lay out the pattern on the fabric with enough space between the pieces for seam allowances.
- Cut 3/8" (1 cm) away from the paper for all edges except the highlighted edges; for those, cut 1" (2.5 cm) away.

*—Seamingly Simple*

**558** This is such a simple thing, and it may be known to everyone, but my mom pointed this out to me only a couple of years ago. You can use fewer pins and have more accurately cut pieces if you cut with your pattern piece to the RIGHT of your scissors if you are right handed, or to the LEFT of your scissors if you are left handed because your fabric won't move away from your pattern. This technique is especially helpful if you are cutting slippery fabric.

*—Sew it seams*

**559** If you are cutting out more than one garment, use a strip of your fabric to tie up the pieces of each after rolling them up into a tight bundle. This is what we did when I worked for a French designer.

*—ryansmum*

**560** It's a pain to fold fabric for cutting when you don't want to fold it exactly in half. And it's a double pain when the fabric is slippery, like rayon challis or silk. So today I had a brainstorm: I spread the fabric flat on my table. I used a yardstick to measure twice the width of the widest part of the pattern piece I needed to cut double, plus an inch to account for the selvage, and marked this distance from the edge with chalk at several-inch intervals. Then I folded the fabric to the marks and adjusted it so the grain was straight along the fold. This goes a lot quicker than it sounds just reading it, and it much less stressful for me than my old trial and error method.

*—Debbie Lancaster*

## CHEATS FOR WHEN YOU'RE SHORT OF FABRIC

**561** I had a small piece of really cute *Finding Nemo* fabric. I thought it was enough to make my granddaughter a pair of shorts and little sleeveless top. Lo and behold, I was short. So, I found a piece of complementary material in my stash and used that for all of the shirt facings. YIPPEE: I had enough Nemo fabric for the rest. So don't pass up that cute piece of material; try something like this instead. It looks great.

—*Mary Stiefer*

**562** On my most recent pair of pants, I discovered I was just shy of having enough fabric. It finally occurred to me that I could piece the pants back at the crotch point. I cut the pants front as usual but cut the back with the pattern running right off the fabric edge at the upper inseam. I pulled a thread on each of the cropped edges, to get a perfectly straight-of-grain edge, and did the same with two scrap pieces. Then I sewed one scrap to each cropped edge and pressed the allowances toward the extension. I laid the pattern back in place and cut out the rest of the crotch point. Worked beautifully.

—*Lisa Laree*

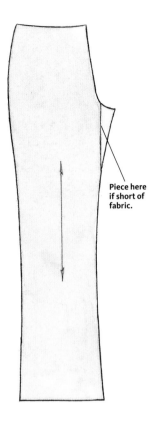

Piece here if short of fabric.

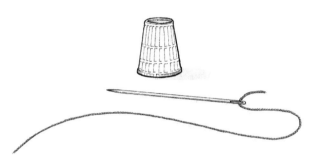

 *Put two necklines on one pattern piece*

*If you have a pattern where the front and back are the same except for the neckline, try these timesaving tips for pattern prep and cutting:*

**563** **leanmeansewingmachine's technique.** This is a tip for cutting out T-shirt style patterns for which the front and back are the same except for the necklines. You need a full pattern piece, not one that needs to be placed on a fold: Trace the front neckline onto the back pattern piece and cut along it, leaving a 1" (2.5 cm) section attached at the center front. Lay your fabric out folded double. Lay the back pattern piece on it and cut it out following the back neckline. Separate the cut-out pieces. Put the pattern back on one of them. Now cut out the front neckline, folding the neck area down where it's attached. The pattern remains in one piece for future use and you don't have to fuss with all that arranging in order to cut out the pieces on a single layer.

**564** **Deepika's method.** This is what I do when I use a single pattern piece with different necklines:

- Trace the top 10" to 12" (25.4 to 30.5 cm) of the back pattern piece onto a separate sheet of pattern paper.
- Place this piece on top of the front pattern piece aligning the shoulders. The only difference between the layers is the neckline. Tape the bottom edge of the back pattern piece onto the front pattern piece. You now have one pattern with a back neckline flap.
- Lay the pattern on your fabric. To cut the front, fold down the flap.

## BUTTONHOLE INTERFACING LAYOUT

**565** To reduce the possibility of stretched, baggy buttonholes, cut interfacing for the buttonhole area with the lengthwise grain oriented in the direction of the buttonhole. For vertical buttonholes, that would be the way that most patterns show to lay out the interfacing piece, parallel to the selvage. But for horizontal buttonholes, it would be perpendicular to the selvage, on the cross grain. I did them this way on my most recent shirt, and they seem to be holding up.

—*Diana M*

## DISCIPLINE UNSTABLE FABRIC

**566** When cutting a fabric that is slippery or unstable, I place sheets of inexpensive tissue paper (the gift wrapping kind) on the table and put my fabric on top of it. I pin the pattern to both the fabric and the tissue underneath and then cut both. This way, the fabric doesn't move much as I cut.

—*ladylola*

**Liana shares:** When working with silk chiffon, or any extremely lightweight fabric, one of the big problems is keeping the fabric grain line straight for layout and when cutting. These two tricks help me—they even make it possible to cut a double layer:

**567** Definitely use a rotary cutter and weights: the fabric won't shift once you begin, as it will with scissors

**568** Once you get the fabric laid on the cutting mat and generally in position, you can adjust it in very small increments by bending down to the edge of the table, and blowing on the fabric. Very lightweight fabric will shift when you do this, and yet it will shift smoothly across the width.

## MATCH THOSE STRIPES

**569** Here's a fast way to align pattern pieces when your fabric has a woven plaid or lengthwise stripe: Lay the fabric on your table. Fold each pattern piece along the grain line that's marked on it and crease from one end of the piece to the other. Now align the folded edge with a stripe in the fabric weave and pin the bottom portion of the pattern piece to the fabric. Then unfold the pattern and pin the rest.

—*Asa Hagstrom*

**570** When I work on fabric that has a plaid or stripe that must be matched, I position this pattern on the most important piece of the garment first. After cutting out the first piece, I lay the tissue pattern for the adjoining pieces over it with the seamlines aligned and draw the plaid or stripe onto the tissue at the seamline. Then I can safely cut this piece in fabric. For instance, I cut out the jacket fronts, lay the back pattern over the cut fabric and draw the plaid onto the seamline, and then continue in this manner for sleeves, pockets, etc.

—*Janie Viers*

**Deepika adds:** Make sure to keep each tissue piece on its proper lengthwise grain line when you use it; it's especially easy to go astray with horizontal stripes on pieces that taper from top to bottom.

**571** An easy way to perfectly match chevron stripes on identical pieces is to lay the pattern piece on the fabric on the bias (single layer), cut the first piece and remove the paper pattern. Invert the first piece on the fabric, matching the stripes perfectly, and pin together; on the edge to be joined, orient the pins ready for sewing. Cut the second piece; then go directly to your machine and sew the seam. The stripes will be perfectly matched.

—*Sew it seams*

## DON'T POINT OUT THE BUST

**572** When using print fabrics I strive to avoid the headlamps effect. D'ya know what I mean? It's when you get two big circles (flowers, faces, whatever) centered directly over the girls. It draws unwanted attention to the bust area—everybody who sees you can see the headlamps and nothing else. Here's a way to reduce this risk: When working with a fabric that has large motifs or distinctive colored patches, mark the location of your bust on your bodice pattern. Hold the bodice pattern against your body and draw a circle on the pattern around one breast. When you put the pattern piece on your fabric, you will be able to determine exactly where the motif will appear relative to your bust.

—*juliette2*

**573** When working with large or circular prints it can be important to place your bust point at a discreet place on the fabric. Although I mark bust points with a marker on the pattern piece, I sometimes have trouble seeing the fabric underneath the pattern piece. I've often used pins to mark a good spot on the fabric. However, I just realized that a coin, such as a quarter, works much better. It's heavy enough to not move and the right size. You can easily see a coin though tissue paper.

—*drsue*

## WAIT TO CUT PIECES THAT MIGHT NEED ALTERING

**574** If you routinely need to alter the armscye of your patterns and thus also alter the sleeve cap, as I do, it makes sense to hold off on cutting the sleeve until you've got the bodice fitting right. Sometimes I need to deepen the arm hole, sometimes I need to take in the shoulder, and the details depend on the nature of the pattern and its interaction with the specific fabric—they can't all be predicted ahead of time but each affects the sleeve cap. Another plus to altering and cutting the sleeve last is that I have become familiar with the fabric and have a better idea how much ease it "wants." The only drawback to this method is that you need more fabric as your pattern layout may not be as efficient.

*—drsue*

**575** Even with a "perfect" pants or skirt pattern, the fit will usually need to be tweaked a bit depending on the fabric used. I suggest laying out a waistband when you lay out the pattern, but not cutting it until you have the rest of the pants fitting just exactly like you want. This will ensure that you have enough fabric to cut it out, but save the frustration of it not being the right size after you've adjusted the pants—especially if you need to add some or if it's a shaped piece that needs to follow a curved arc exactly.

*—Diana M*

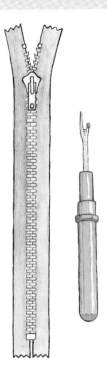

## LAYOUT ON PRINT FABRICS

**576** I was making a shirt out of a very busy print and wanted to match up the pockets. I tried the usual method of placing a transparent pocket pattern over the pocket placement lines but found the print was just too busy for me to trace. I solved the problem in the following way:

- First, I marked the pocket placement on the garment with tailor's tacks; then I laid a larger swatch of cloth over the pocket area on the right side, carefully matching the pattern, and basted it in place.
- Working from the wrong side I poked a pin through each of the tailor's tacks to mark the pocket edges on the swatch.
- I then removed the swatch and added my seam allowances, confident that my pocket would match when I stitched it on to the shirt.

*—Brine*

**577** I think the usual rule of thumb for large prints is to choose a garment with simple lines. However, as a very small person I don't find this works well for me. When I use large prints I use patterns that have many pieces. That way I can "edit" the fabric. This requires much more fabric than is usually called for and I have to lay the pieces out on a single layer of fabric, right side up. But I then can tell what part of the pattern will hit where. I can also usually completely eliminate parts of the fabric I don't like. Despite being tiny I have been able to successfully use large prints this way.

*—drsue*

**578** **Sue Wilson's advice** Using spray starch on slippery fabrics is a great way to make them more manageable for cutting and sewing. It adds enough body and stiffness to make the slinkiest rayons behave. Just make sure to test that it doesn't leave permanent marks on your fabric.

**579** **ryansmum adds:** I use "HEAVY" spray starch but have also used the concentrated form. Don't bother with regular starch or sizing. I will sometimes soak a piece of fabric in the watered down concentrate and then hang to dry overnight. Iron it after starching. If I am in a rush, I will spray over the fabric several times and get it pretty wet; then I will immediately iron it. Your fabric should be very stiff if done correctly. I actually starch most of my fabrics and bindings and zippers and encourage my students to do so as well.

## THIS & THAT ABOUT CUTTING VARIOUS FABRICS

**580** This sounds like a backward way of doing things, but may be useful at times. If you need simple shapes cut from quilted fabric, mark the shapes on the fabric and then overcast (zigzag) just inside the outline. Then cut carefully just outside the stitching/outline. The stitching presses the layers together, which makes it very much easier to cut the pieces, and there is no risk of the layers separating. I would also try this with fabrics that ravel a lot.

—Asa Hagstrom

**581** If you are not sure which way is "down" on napped fabric and you need to know before you lay out your pattern pieces, do this: Spread the fabric right side up on your table. Place a coin on the fabric and bang your fist on the table (not hard, you want to make the coin shift, not jump). The coin will shift in the "nap pointing down" direction.

—els

**582** It can be hard to get a smooth edge when cutting tulle, and if you're making a veil or other item for which the edge will be left unfinished, this is too bad. To smooth the jigs and jags left by scissors, run the edge of the cut tulle through an unthreaded serger.

—mamafitz

**583** Sometimes the sales associates at the fabric store do not do a great job when cutting faux fur; I suggest you recut when you get home. You must cut only the backing when doing this so that the fur isn't chopped off at the edge. I use a pair of stork scissors: Turn the fabric so that the backing is facing you. Slide the lower point of the scissors under the backing and then cut. These delicate scissors work like a charm.

—Mary Stiefer

## CUT NARROW STRIPS EASILY

**584** My rotary cutter, an Olfa ergonomic, can take a blade on either side of the handle, depending on whether you are right or left handed. If I put a blade on BOTH sides at the same time I can cut ¼" (6 mm) strips of fabric with one swipe! It works great for making your own strips of fusible web from yardage—much cheaper than buying by the roll. This is handy for narrow strips of bias interfacing to reinforce shoulder seams, also for tiny bias tape to finish seams, etc.

—Lizz

**585** Today I cut binding for a neckline using a rotary blade. However, I cut it too wide and when I tried to cut it down, it wouldn't allow me to (it was a very tight knit). I tried scissors and they didn't work either. I needed a very straight cut since the binding would be very obvious. So I folded the strip in half lengthwise and pressed it; then cut it with my unthreaded serger. The result was the most even piece imaginable, much narrower than I have cut before, and I ended up with a perfect bound neckline!!! What a thrill.

—ryansmum

**586** I was having problems making 2" (5.10 m)-wide bias strips. I couldn't seem to get them straight, and my fabric would shift all over the place. What a pain. So I made a 2" × 54" (5.1 cm × 1.4 m) template from heavy interfacing. I just pinned the strip of interfacing to the fabric and cut away. I didn't have any problems with it moving and shifting, so I had perfect strips when I was done.

—SexiSadi

**587** To cut bias strips or non-bias strips, use an unthreaded serger. Just run the fabric through using the measurement guideline to set the strip width. The cutting knife will do the work. I have found starching the fabric helps a lot too.

—ryansmum

**Deepika adds:** Remove the serger needles too so they don't mar your fabric.

### Help for grain line woes on knits

*The straight grain on knit fabrics is notoriously difficult to find and garments cut off-grain don't hang right. Here are two tips for overcoming the problem.*

**588** **Mary E Geauxtigers' marking method.** To find the grain on a knit, fold the fabric with selvages together, and at the fold, identify one rib and mark it with chalk or a pin in one place. Then unfold the fabric and lay it flat. Lay a long clear ruler next to the marked rib and make a chalk line along it. Try your best to follow this rib the length of the ruler, Do this all the way down the fabric and you will have as straight a grain as you can get.

**589** **Kris92833's cutting technique.** My first stab at knits was with a woman who taught me to make T-shirts and panties. She commented that some T-shirts became twisted with washing because they're not cut on the straight grain, which is not always parallel to the "selvage" of knits. She showed me this trick: Spread the fabric in a single layer; find and mark the straight grain. Lay your half-pattern on the fabric, aligning the pattern fold-line with the grain line. Cut the piece out except along the foldline. Now flip the pattern over and cut the other half. No more twisting.

# Marking smarts

*Can't tell the pieces apart? Can't find the dots? Wrong side/right side look the same? Buttonhole spacing refuses to be equal? PatternReview.com members have good solutions for these and other common marking challenges.*

## CLEVER MARKING METHODS

**590** I made my first zippered pocket recently when making a purse. I dreaded what for me had always been failure: marking and sewing this kind of opening with precision. Then the light bulb went on. What if I made a photocopy of the pattern piece with the markings on it, placed that where it belonged on the fabric, and sewed on the paper? Eureka!!! It worked like a charm. After sewing around the opening, I slashed the center along the lines printed on the paper. I then pulled the paper away, first from the outside and then the inside of the stitching. Perfect placement, perfect stitching, perfect cutting, without having to mark anything.

—*BillieJean*

**591** Try this if you need to transfer long straight lines from your pattern to the project pieces, especially if your fabric resists tailor's chalk: Use masking tape. First, fold the pattern along the marking line and position the pattern on the project piece. Then align the tape on the fabric, next to the pattern fold. Mark the tape to indicate which edge is the reference so you don't forget after the pattern has been removed. When you sew, be careful not to stitch the masking tape!

—*zoezmommy*

**592** The yardstick was MIA the other day when I wanted to mark the hem on a dress, and out of desperation, I reached for a retractable metal tape measure, the kind that winds up into a squarish metal case. Here's the good part: it can be locked into a particular length with the flip of a switch on the case. With the dress on the dress form, I established the distance above the floor to mark the hem, locked the tape to measure that amount, and placed the little beauty on the floor—it sat squarely with the extending metal tape perfectly upright. I had two hands free to use for smoothing, pinning and rearranging. No balancing the yardstick with one hand while trying to insert pins with my lips. Wish I'd discovered this forty—uh—a long time ago.

—*Karla Kizer*

**593** If you need to actually thread-trace a rib on a really fine jersey (to mark your lengthwise grain), use the largest hand sewing needle (length and eye) that you can without hurting the fabric. You'll just automatically take larger stitches and the job will go much faster. This may seem obvious, but it took me a while to figure it out, and it has made a big difference.

—*bunz*

**594** I suppose I'm not the only one who finds that the dot marking the clipping point for an inside corner always seems to be too far into the piece. I finally quit marking the dot from the pattern and now I do it this way:

- Set the machine to baste and, starting on one side about ½" (1.3 cm) from the corner, stitch exactly on the seamline into and about ½" (1.3 cm) through the corner (don't pivot).
- Now set the machine stitch to very short and turn the garment over. Coming at the corner from the other side now and stitching exactly on the seamline, begin about ½" (1.3 cm) away from the basting stitch and stitch right up to it. Stop with the needle down, pivot, and continue stitching for about ½" (1.3 cm).
- Remove as much of the original basting as possible (you may get all of it or it may be sewn into the stay stitching).

Now you have the corner precisely marked and reinforced for clipping.

—*Lisa Laree*

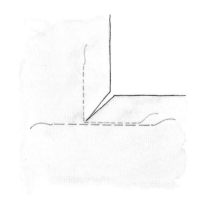

## CLEVER PLEAT MARKING

**595** If you're wanting a fast and easy way to make knife pleats without first marking the fabric, fold them into place with a table fork.

- Slide the fork prongs onto the fabric. The number of prongs placed on top of and under the fabric defines the width of the pleat.
- Now rotate the fork so that a pleat forms in the fabric.
- Carefully pull out the fork and secure the pleat with a pin.
- Now you can add a second pleat the same way. After rotating the fork, you can slide it to the side so the pleats abut. Or you can push in the fork, mark with a pin and then set the next pleat a fork-width away from the first one. Happy pleating!

—*Saskia*

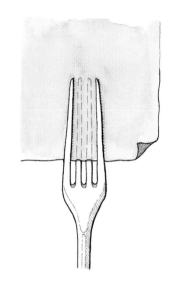

**596** Here's an easy way to get perfect, sharp pleats:

- First trace the pleating lines onto the dull side of a strip of freezer paper.
- Then iron the coated side of the paper onto the wrong side of your fabric.
- Now fold and press the pleats on the drawn lines. I like to crease them with a bone folder (you can also use a table knife or a ruler) and then set them with my iron and a wooden clapper.
- When you are ready to sew the pleated piece to your garment, peel back the freezer paper far enough to baste the pleats in place, then peel the rest of the paper off. It comes off easily and is ready to be used again.

—*tweedcurtain*

### Perforation tricks

*If you make a little hole in your pattern at each printed dot or notch, you can easily transfer them to your fabric. Here are ways to use this idea:*

**597** **ConnieLK says:** Here's one of the best ways I have found to mark darts, button placement, etc.: First use a hole punch to perforate the pattern at each place where you need to make a mark. Then you can make a dot with your chalk through the hole without ever shifting the pattern.

**598** **petra says:** When I am making a muslin (one that I am not planning to wear and only on woven material) I mark match points using the eyelet punch that came with my machine. It makes a tiny hole through the paper and both layers of fabric. This is easy to see on wovens (especially muslin!) and you can match up exactly with a pin or holding to the light. The hole in the pattern is useful in the future to pen-mark or tack through. Anything to save those extra seconds!!

## KEEP TRACK OF YOUR PROJECT PIECES

**599** I'm sewing a princess seam jacket that has almost 30 pieces, and that's just for the fashion fabric. With so many pieces it's essential to be systematic and organized. I've found it especially helpful to clearly mark the pattern piece number on every cut-out fabric piece. I also add an apostrophe (for example, 18') to each piece intended for the left side of the garment. As I cut and mark, I check the pieces off the list included in the pattern's direction sheet.

—*nancy2001*

**600** I write my measurements for quilt block pieces and strips on wooden clothespins—in pencil. When I have everything cut I clip the clothespins to each segment to keep everything organized. This has been a big help! I erase the measurements when I am done so the clothespins are ready for the next project.

—*quiltsick*

## IDENTIFY THE WRONG SIDE

**601** I've cut several of my scraps of brightly colored knit material into small squares and keep them in a little box. When working with fabric that has no obvious right or wrong side, I designate one side as the wrong side and then mark that side of each fabric piece as I cut it by pinning one of my small knit squares to it. These are more effective than adhesive dots that don't stick to all fabrics, tape that may leave residue, or chalk marks that rub off too soon.

—*jannw*

**602** I sometimes have a hard time figuring out what side is the right/wrong side of fabric. Once I decide, I stick transparent or invisible tape onto the wrong side. The tape also comes in handy if I want to label the pieces of my project—I just note the information on it with a ballpoint pen. You have to be careful to not iron over the tape, but it becomes obvious which side you're working with early in construction so you can remove the tape before you have a problem.

—*SexiSadi*

## NO-FUSS MARKING OF DOTS AND NOTCHES

**603** I am making a dress with a number of double-pointed darts, which means that the darts are in the middle of the piece of fabric. Here's a technique I came up with for marking them accurately: First make a template of the dart. Then, with the full pattern on the fabric, mark only the ends of each dart (use a pin or a chalk dot). Remove the pattern; position the template so its ends sit on the marks, and draw around it. If you have a TNT pattern with lots of darts, I think this will make it easier.

—AnneM

**Deepika adds:** This gives you a completely marked seamline for each dart and is especially useful for curved darts.

**604** I often use my computer-drafted patterns as printed, on letter paper, which is difficult to mark through with a tracing wheel. Today I had one of those EUREKA! moments: I realized that I could cut out the darts on the printed pattern and then line the pattern up on the fabric piece and trace the outline of the dart right onto it using a chalk marking tool. This worked beautifully.

—Linda L

**605** Patterns from the Big 4 companies indicate the top of a sleeve cap with a dot, but I think that mark is hard to find when pinning the eased sleeve into the armscye. Instead, I just cut a notch at the dot's location and line that up with the shoulder seam. This method is so much more helpful, and it takes less time than marking that silly dot. You could also just make one snip, but I find the notch easier to see.

—candyo

**606** I am working on a McCall's pattern and included in the directions was a great tip: If you snip the seam allowance to mark all notches, circles, squares, center fronts, pleat lines, fold lines, facing lines, and hemlines it sure does make marking much faster. In some cases you don't have to mark certain things. I'm working on the front of the blouse and where you would fold the facing in, if you use the snip marks at top and bottom the rest falls in place. This trick works great.

—Mary Stiefer

**607** When dealing with a complicated pattern and you need to keep straight which dots or notches match which, use tailor's tacks with different colored thread for each set; that way you only have to match, say, the red dots, then the green dots, then the yellow dots. If you have bobbins with odd colored thread left over from earlier projects, you can use that thread and empty the bobbins for future use.

—Lisa Laree

## Templates: homemade and improvised

*Janie Viers offers five more or less freebie template material tips.*

**608** I use a piece of stiff cardboard to make custom spacing guides for anything that is small and needs to be marked at a repeating interval. I cut notches at whatever interval I want and then I don't have to worry about remembering "are buttonholes 2⅞" (7.3 cm) apart or 2⅝" (6.7) apart?" I just use my handy dandy homemade spacer. I have used this for marking curtain pleats, skirt pleats, buttons, buttonholes, trim, and any other thing I need to mark multiple positions for.

**609** A dinner plate makes a perfect guide for drawing a rounded corner on any large item. I was going nuts with a tulle wedding veil and solved the problem by using a plate to guide my rotary cutter.

**610** I used a drinking glass and "ground" it into some fleece to leave marks so I could get a bunch of 3" (7.6 cm) circles. If you first dip the glass or a similar "marker" in ground chalk it will leave a chalk mark behind!

**611** I often use a box to make a template for pockets. I have used kiddie size shoeboxes and CD cases and VCR cases too!

**612** I use business cards to space buttonholes and even used my DH's crosscut saw to get a LONG ragged edge!

# CHAPTER SIX

# Fitting

" *Recently retired software engineer, with plenty of time to sew! Avid quilter, mostly my own pieced designs. Now I'm back into garment sewing after a long hiatus, thanks largely to finding this Web site. I've learned so much, especially about fitting, and I'm having a great time— thanks, everyone!!* "

—Irene Q

# Start with the right size

*Before you can sew, you must choose which size pattern to make, and very likely alter it in some way. Most sewing enthusiasts know that pattern sizes are not the same as ready-to-wear sizes. And most us have body measurements that vary from the standards anyway. Here are suggestions for how to judge the size you should use.*

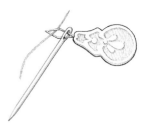

## MEASURE AND TEST TO DECIDE THE SIZE

**613** You can develop an eye for good fit by looking at how others dress and figuring out what works and what doesn't. If you're unsure of which pattern size to use and where to alter, here's a simple approach to getting it right. There are other ways of fitting but I think this one is easier than most:

- First use your measurements to purchase the correct size pattern. Base the size on your high bust measurement for tops and jackets. You primarily want shoulders and armhole to fit because you can make bust adjustments fairly easily. For bottoms, use your hip measurement to figure out what size; the waist can be easily adjusted.
- Next, rough cut your pattern pieces. Place them against your body and look in the mirror. Does it look like it will fit? Using a marker, outline what you think would be a good fit, keeping in mind how much ease you want.
- Once you have it somewhat figured out you can highlight the lines that work best for you and then add seam allowances if needed. You may blend in and out of different sizes. This will increase your chances of making a garment that actually fits.
- Make a test garment and then make corrections and transfer that information to your pattern.
- Sometimes it may take making a couple of tests, but that's what that fabric you now think is ugly is for.

—*ryansmum*

**614** We all have our favorite clothes to wear, why not take some measurements of them? Match those measurements in the clothes you make and you'll enjoy wearing what you sew! I measured many of my favorites and set up a spreadsheet for easy comparison to patterns; this in turn shows me at a glance what alterations might be needed.

—*Mollykat*

**615** When I have to make length adjustments on pants legs, I measure the inseam on my favorite pair to get the right length and make adjustments on the pattern accordingly. The inseam length will not change no matter where the garment's waistband sits—at your waist, hips, or high above. I've marked the length of my preferred inseam length on my measuring tape.

—*Kim Winson*

**Deepika adds:** This is true for the most part, but loose trousers may have a slightly longer rise (crotch depth) than tight ones, so leave yourself some wiggle room at the hem.

**616** I didn't realize that one of my legs is shorter than the other until I started to sew. But now that I've noted this, I know to hem one leg longer than the other. Now I don't have to keep pulling that side down: I have embraced my asymmetry.

—*Deepika*

**617** I see a frequent problem with garment shoulder width. For most people, it is WAY too wide, causing a very sloppy look. The armscye seam should sit on the crest of the shoulder. Find a top or cardigan that fits you well; measure the shoulder seam and record the length for future reference. (To be really accurate, measure all the way across the shoulders from armscye seam to armscye seam.) When adjusting a pattern, you can cut off the excess at the end of the shoulder seamline, tapering into the front and back armscye; just remember to leave a seam allowance. In most cases the sleeve will still fit but check by measuring the original armscye seamline to see if it changed length.

—*ryansmum*

## IT HELPS TO KNOW THE SIZE STANDARDS

**618** I discovered that the "Big Four" U.S. pattern companies have collaborated to produce a brochure, *Do You Really Know Your Pattern Size*; it's designed to help home sewers achieve a better fit using Simplicity, Vogue, Butterick, and McCall's patterns. You can view it online at their individual Web sites and may find it also at a local fabric store. It includes a lot of detailed information and I was pleased to see it tells you about "full bust vs. high bust."

—*chick3y*

**619** The European petite and tall size identification system used by Burda patterns can be confusing. The number that indicates the European size of their regular-length patterns is divided in half to indicate the equivalent petite size and doubled to indicate the tall size. For example, the petite version of Burda's size 36 is labeled size 18, and the tall version is labeled size 72. Burda's size chart is helpful but it doesn't make any reference to the sizing terms regular, tall, and petite.

—*Joan1954*

# The big picture on fitting

*Fitting is part art, part skill, and challenging to do for oneself. Logic, dress forms, experience, and diligent trying-on each play a role. But no need to be intimidated, with the tips that follow you can improve your understanding and technique.*

## TRICKS THAT MAKE FITTING EASIER

**620** I had the luxury recently of being home alone with time to sew all day long. I decided to close the blinds in my sewing room and sew in my underwear so I could easily try things on as I worked. It was great! I was much more motivated to try on every step of the way and things seemed to go a lot faster. If you can't follow this example, you can still make it easier to try things on: consider what item you're sewing and dress accordingly. If making a top, wear a blouse that buttons in the front. It's easy to slip on and off and you only need to close one button to keep your modesty till the next fitting. Meanwhile, your hair and makeup stay in place. If making bottoms, wear pull-on pants. Slip-on shoes are fine for this but barefoot is best IMHO.

—*jbrewer*

**621** I teach a fitting class and this is what I think is crucial: Fit as you sew. Do not just sew up a garment entirely and wish for the best as many of my sewing students do. You should be fitting at least three times while there is still time to make adjustments. Try on a garment right side out first to get an idea of how things are fitting. Then turn the garment inside out and start marking with pins where you need to make changes while you are wearing it. This makes it easier for you to alter.

—*ryansmum*

**Deepika adds:** When you are making changes with a garment inside out, be mindful that left and right sides are reversed.

**622** When pin-fitting a muslin, use safety pins. As you achieve a fit that you are pleased with, close the pins in that area. Your alterations will stay secure and you'll see at a glance which areas are fitted. In areas that need further tweaking, the pins remain open and ready to be easily changed. I feel much better about taking a muslin on and off many times when I know that the pins are secure and I'm not in danger of becoming a living pincushion!

—*Lizz*

**623** If you haven't had a trained bra fitter check your style and fit, it might be worth your time. I'm just beginning to learn about pattern fitting. So, on a whim, I went to the lingerie department at my local Nordstrom's and had the manager give me a bra fitting. I was stunned at how far off I was on size, shape, and type. The positive change in my appearance and the increased comfort is remarkable. Now I know where my bust should be, so I can take my measurements, plus I know what to look for when purchasing a bra. Just make sure the fitter has been trained and is not simply a salesperson.

—*Patzee*

**624** Whenever I am making a garment for which there may be a lingerie-exposure problem (plunging front or back neckline or boat neck, for example), I put my existing lingerie on my dress form while I'm fitting. This lets me know whether 1) I need to change the fit of the garment or 2) I need to buy new lingerie! When I sew for brides, I always have them bring their foundation garments and shoes—I'm not sure why it took me so long to make the connection to do this with my dummy for my own sewing.

—*Robie Kentspeth*

## Check it and check it off

*Be methodical when you fit. Make a list of things to check—standard points like hem length as well as any "issues" that are problematic for you.*

**625** **Helen near Sydney shares her system.** Here are two checklists I follow when sewing a top. I don't have a 3-way mirror so I take lots of self-timer photos when I do this. After checking, I make all of the fit changes on the paper pattern. I don't generally record the style changes since these decisions change with each garment.

Fitting checklist:

• Upper bust: too loose/too tight?
• Full bust: enough room for the girls?
• Waist: need extra for a full tummy?
• Back width OK?
• Center back length: folds (too long) or pulling (too short)?
• Length/side seams: shape ok? straight fall to hem?

• Hemline: is it even?
• Darts: do they point to the bust? is the uptake enough? are the darts the right length?
• Sleeve: does the shoulder seam sit on your shoulder point? is there room to move? is the length good?
• Collar and collar stand: check the notch position, point spread, length, and roll

Style checklist:

• Hem shape: what suits you best? Mine is a gentle curve.
• Darts: should any be unsewn?
• Sleeve: check for shape and cuff.
• Collar: is it a good shape?
• Other style features: does it need side splits, pockets, embroidery?

**626** For skirts, alter at the hipline; if you want the skirt hemline wider or narrower to be in proportion with the length change, then you can alter beneath the hip but above the knee and redraw the side seams or gores to increase or reduce the amount of taper or flare.

—*els*

**Deepika adds:** Here are six tips for adjusting the length of pattern pieces:

**627** The lines on which you shorten or lengthen must be at a right angle to the lengthwise grain, otherwise the balance will be wrong.

**628** For a dress, jacket, blouse, and coat, shorten or lengthen the pattern halfway up the armhole, and halfway between the armhole and waist.

**629** When you're lengthening or shortening a pattern at several points—not just at the hem—make sure you don't add or subtract too much at once. Doing so might distort the proportions. I never alter by more than 1" (2.5 cm) at a single point.

**630** For pants, shorten or lengthen halfway up the crotch, halfway between the crotch and knee, and halfway between the knee and hemline.

**631** The sleeve has to be altered too, because it has to fit in the new armhole: For flat sleeve caps, narrow or widen the sleeve cap at both underarm edges by the amount of change made to the armhole depth and then taper the new underarm seam to the wrist/hemline. For a high sleeve cap, draw a line across the cap and then shorten or lengthen to correspond to the amount of change made in the armhole depth.

**632** For all these adjustments, you first need to know the amount by which you wish to lengthen or shorten and then divide that amount by the number of places at which you make the alteration.

**633** Use a center back zip when making a muslin for a skirt, even when the pattern is for a side zip. This will allow you to check the fit and make any necessary adjustments to both side seams without a zipper in the way. Then make the final garment with the zipper on the side if you wish.

—*Diahn*

**634** I use different fabrics for the front and back pieces when making a test muslin. This makes it MUCH easier to discern which issues are 'front' and which are 'back'.

—*MaryLynn in Long Beach*

**635** I have a bag of knit fabric that's left over from various projects. Because of the layout of many of the patterns and the 60" (158 cm) width, there seems to be too much to just throw away but not enough to make something (except maybe for kids' outfits.) I realize I can mix them together to make a fitting muslin when I want to test a knit garment. Obviously this won't be a "wearable muslin," but it will give me a good feel for the fit without having to cut my good fabric.

—*RobinMCPA*

**636** As I've posted reviews on PatternReview.com, I realized a photo of a garment on a body can show tugs and folds much more clearly than I can see them in the mirror, especially the rear view. My dress form can be useful, but it doesn't have a swayback! And if I'm near a mirror, I've also found I stand up straighter than I do in "real life" when my posture shifts once I am no longer studying myself. So I take digital photos of myself wearing garment, front and back, during first baste-together, and look at them in the camera. I've found digital photographs are especially helpful with tailored garments.

—*redsquid*

**637** Here's a way to take a picture of yourself without having to use a mirror. Assuming that you have an ironing board that has adjustable height and a camera with a timer, use the ironing board as a tripod, adjusting it to the right height for the camera to capture the correct information. Set up the camera on the board, aiming the lens in the right direction and set the timer. Then make your million dollar pose, and voilà, you have picture of yourself.

—*Kim Winson*

**638** I found a mini tripod in my local camera store. It cost about $8 and is 6" (15.2 cm) tall. The legs are bendable and allow a camera to be placed solidly on almost all surfaces. It screws right into the bottom of my plain Jane digital camera and with the delay on the camera, I can take pictures of myself in my sewing projects when there is no one around to help.

—*touran*

**639** If there is nobody around to help you with a fitting, use a video camera as a helper. Set it on automatic and place it at a height where it can capture you as you walk, revolve to show all sides, and raise your arms. Then watch the video and when you see fitting problems, push the pause button, analyze the problems, and make the necessary alterations.

—*els*

## CUSTOMIZE YOUR DRESS FORM

**640** When the chest circumference of your dress form does not correspond with your own size you can supplement it with shoulder pads. The size of the shoulder pads depends on the amount you need to add.

—els

**641** In my quest to find a good, sturdy dress form that closely mimicked my body, I really struggled. So I decided to buy a commercial form that was smaller than I am; I got it on eBay. I just love it (still, one year later), especially since I padded her out to look like me. Here's the skinny (that term is figurative, of course) for doing the same:

Supplies:

- A sleeveless fitting shell or sloper, made from a commercial pattern and fitted to your body with no ease at all. Use a woven fabric that doesn't stretch. I used a poly-cotton linen look-alike and bound the edges with packaged seam binding.
- A bra, of the type you wear.
- Polyester quilt batting, both high- and low-loft.
- Sturdy, flat-head straight pins.

What I did:

- I put the bra on the dress form and firmly filled the cups with batting. Then I measured her chest and back. My form was narrower across the back than I, so I put some layers of batting under the bra straps, measuring and padding till it looked like me. By putting the batting UNDER the bra, she even has those pesky little fat "bumps" like I do (sigh).
- I continued to layer batting over the form, affixing it with pins, until it had my contours. The whole process is nothing more than pad and measure, pad and measure. And look in the mirror. And be honest (but NOT overly critical!). Accuracy is key. I set up a full-length mirror near where I was working and checked it often, from every angle. Where there were curves, I put curves.
- Then I put my finished fitting shell over the padding. You want the cover stuffed pretty firmly. Otherwise, it'll squish around and change shape pretty quickly and inserted pins won't stay put. I opted for a non-permanent closure so that if I need to tweak her fluff, alter her measurements, etc., I can do so easily.

—EveS

## A TEST YOU CAN WEAR

**642** Making a wearable muslin allows you to fit and test a pattern yet have something you can wear too. So the first time you make up a pattern, make the no-frills version. Make it up in its simplest form without embellishment. This lets you test the style and fit without spending a stack of time on it. If it's a great pattern you can embellish to your heart's content next time, knowing it will work. If it isn't great, well, you haven't wasted too much time and energy on it. Here's my process:

- First make your usual paper pattern adjustments: Bust, sloping shoulders, whatever.
- Choose the view that lets you test the most complex version of the pattern (sleeves, not sleeveless).
- Choose a fabric that is easy to handle and presses well, doesn't require pattern matching, and doesn't ravel.
- Don't spend time adding special details like pockets, trim, topstitching.
- Analyze the results according to your own requirements.

—Helen near Sydney

## TRYING IT ON IS A MUST

**643** Few garments have ever been ruined by too much trying on while you are making them, and this is just a reminder to try things on as you sew. Probably many times if it's the first time you've made a particular pattern. This is true even when you've done the flat-pattern measuring, altering, etc. Those are a great start, but each fabric is going to be a little different, and will usually benefit from at least some minor individual tweaking. It's so easy to get so caught up in the excitement of the actual sewing that you skip the fittings needed to see whether you like the garment as is, or if you need to make changes. Changes are always easier to make before you have to rip back to do them.

—Liana

**644** Proper fitting saves time and money. It's best if you have a sewing buddy who can help you though. You can fit yourself but it's more of a challenge. I fit myself and struggle . . .

—ryansmum

**645** Find a fitting buddy on the PatternReview.com forums. There are many regional groups that you can join.

—Deepika

**646** Since I dislike setting-in sleeves, on a recent muslin I just sewed the underarm seam, slipped the sleeve over my arm, and decided that it fit. Me, not the garment. Although the sleeve on the final version fit into the garment well, it really changed the whole fit of the upper body in a way that was not comfortable or flattering. Now I will cut and sew in both sleeves for any mockup I try.

—Ann B.

**647** I use my dress form for preliminary test fittings (tissue or garment) all the time, try out fabric pattern positions (no boob blossoms, thank you very much), experiment w/ trim, etc. I find her quite invaluable to the whole process and I think I use her on almost every garment I make at some point. I would like to point out, however, that this is NOT a substitute for testing a garment out on your body for accurate fittings. The dress form helps me with early-stage fittings, but is never a replacement for flat pattern measurements, muslins, and fittings on my body. I still do all of the above.

—EveS

# Your body, your challenge

*How dare they make the pattern shape different from your body contours? Take comfort; you're not alone. Here are solutions to common specific fit problems.*

## THIS AND THAT ABOUT FITTING A TOP

**648** Don't cut your sleeves out until you have basted your bodice together at the shoulders and side seams. So often the shoulder seam is way too long and must be shortened. If it's only a small amount you don't have to alter the sleeve cap. But if it must be adjusted more than a tad, you need to re-cut the armscye to fit, measure it, and compare your sleeve cap to the circumference—remember to measure at the seamline, not the cutting line. If your fabric is a woven, there should be at least ½" (1.3 cm) of ease in the sleeve cap. I've noticed that most of my sewing students don't take the time to make this crucial adjustment; it makes a big difference when they do!

—*ryansmum*

**649** I was confused for a long time about where my shoulder point is. I posted a question about it on the boards and found that some other people were having the same problem. I Googled "shoulder anatomy" and found some useful info that I thought I'd share:

- The shoulder point in pattern making is actually the AC joint (acromioclavicular joint). This is the joint between the collarbone (clavical) and the tip of the shoulder blade bone (acromion). I was mistakenly marking the joint where the head of the arm (humerus) enters the shoulder socket!
- I found my AC joint by running my fingers along the top of my collarbone until I felt a little dent. I'm pretty confident that I've got the right spot now, even though I still don't see that 'dimple' at the hinge point that I keep reading about!
- If you Google "AC joint" there are some helpful images.

—*ladybegood*

**650** Sometimes I get strange wrinkles and folds radiating from the armscye to the shoulder front and back. After doing some research, I learned this is because the armscye is not deep enough for me. To fix this, I drew a line from the notch straight down to about 2" (5.1 cm) below the bottom of the armscye and then across to the side seam, cut that out and moved it down about ½" (1.3 cm)—on both the front and back bodice pieces. I then slashed and added about ½" (1.3 cm) to the sleeve cap height just under the notch, so that the adjusted areas were basically matching (see below). I did not think that adding this length above the notch would work, as that would put too much extra length in the upper chest for me. Well, no more wrinkles, pulls, folds or otherwise. The side seam hangs smoothly; there are no buckles or bulges.

—*Deb Fox*

**Deepika adds:** To make the armscye smaller, you can do the same in reverse (raise your cutout section and shorten the sleeve cap). Note that these alteration do not affect the fit at the bust so if you need a full bust adjustment, you can do that too.

**651** I tried something new to make a better fit over my sway back in a lined jacket. After sewing the center back seam I pressed the seam allowances open and ironed a 1" (2.5 cm)-wide strip of fusible interfacing over them to give this area more body. This did what I wanted it to do: it keeps the back "crisp" so it doesn't collapse over my sway back or hang up on my high hips.

—*redsquid*

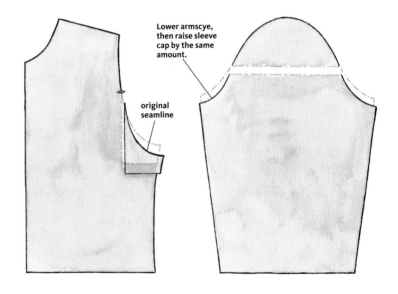

Lower armscye, then raise sleeve cap by the same amount.

original seamline

**652** The usual way to adjust for narrow shoulders is simply to inset the armscye, but if you are making a top with a wide neckline, you can't do this because there will be nothing left of the shoulder seam. Instead, you have to shift the whole shoulder closer to the neck. Here's how I do it:

- I start with a multi-size pattern where the sizes are lined up on the centerline. Trace the smallest size neckline with shoulder and armscye down to the notch, and cut out to use as a template.
- Place the template on the pattern, shifting its shoulder to the shoulder level of the size you need to make but keeping the center front aligned.
- Redraw the neckline, shoulder, and top of the armscye following the template, then blend the armsceye into the larger size below the notch.
- Do a tissue or muslin fitting to check the new shape.

*—wood turtle*

**Deepika adds:** It's much easier to see what you're doing when making this adjustment if your pattern has no seam allowances.

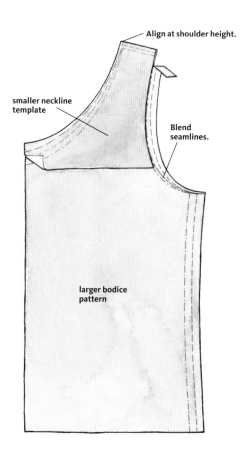

Align at shoulder height.

smaller neckline template

Blend seamlines.

larger bodice pattern

---

## THE EVER-POPULAR CLOWN-BUTT ADJUSTMENT

**653** For those of us who consistently need to add length to the center back seam of pants and at the same time shorten the inseam, here's a technique that accomplishes both alterations at the same time:

- Slash the pattern horizontally at about the middle of the CB seam and also on the inseam 3" to 4" (7.6 to 10.2 cm) below the crotch. The slashes need extend only a few inches into the pattern.
- Now connect these slashes by cutting parallel to the grain line. You are detaching the lower crotch/upper thigh portion of the pattern.

- Now slide the separated area down the back leg and overlap it by ¾" (1.9 cm) on the pattern.
- This gap thus created in the pattern above the crotch level lengthens the CB seam; the overlap shortens the inseam. To finish your pattern, patch with tissue paper and then redraw the interrupted outlines.
- When you sew the inseam, ease the front onto the now shorter back.

*—Karla Kizer*

## GET THE CROTCH CURVE RIGHT

**654** I just bought a flexible curve ruler. I immediately grabbed the two people I sew for and used the ruler to determine their front and back crotch contours. As soon as I was done bending the ruler to fit the front or back crotch, I laid it on a manila file folder and transferred the shape to the folder with a pen, identifying the location of the inseam and waist ends. I labeled each with the client's name and "front" or "back"; then cut the folders into templates I can use for pattern alteration. I punched a hole in one corner of each and hung them on a hook in my sewing area.

*—MaryLynn in Long Beach*

## MODESTY MATTERS

**655** A wide and low neckline will not hug your body unless the garment is tight fitting, and while it can show off your cleavage, it may invite some unwanted looks from others when your bend forward. To prevent gaping on tops that aren't tight, you can affix one end of a short piece of covered boning to the neck edge and tuck the other end into your bra. Cover the boning with a tube of the fabric used for the top; sew both ends shut, or if you want to remove the boning for laundering, use a snap at the bottom. Snap or sew the boning to the inside of the center front neckline, or at the left side of the facing behind the button marking if your garment has a front closure.

—els

**Deepika adds:** Try on the top to find the best place for the bone. Experiment, depending on the neckline and your figure, a bone on each side might work better than one in the middle.

**656** This is my technique to eliminate gaposis and pulling on wrap-style T-shirts.

- Cut the underwrap side about 3" (7.6 cm) shorter than the overwrap side and finish the edges. (This eliminates bulk at the bottom edge, not gaposis.)
- Sew the shoulder seams.
- Fold over ⅝" (1.6 cm) all along the neckline edge.
- Slip a length of ¼" (6 mm) elastic under the folded allowance on each front and anchor at the shoulder seams.
- Baste along neckline to form a casing over the elastic pieces.
- Overlap the fronts and baste the front to back at the side seams, but don't stitch through the elastic ends.
- Try on the top; adjust elastic to fit snugly against your body, but without pulling at sides. Pin the elastic ends in place.
- Remove the side-seam basting. Secure the elastic ends and stitch the casing (I use a coverstitch or twin needle hem). Then complete the top.

—Sue Wilson

**657** It's challenging to get a wrap skirt to fit neatly without revealing all when you move. Here's a way to solve the exposure problem that doesn't affect the wearing ease:

Sew a ½" (1.3 cm) button on the inside of the underneath layer near the edge, at or just above knee level. Sew another ½" (1.3 cm) button at the same level to the side seam allowance of the top layer. Lay the skirt flat, inside out, so that both buttons are visible. Cut a piece of buttonhole elastic long enough to secure to both buttons and lie flat without stretching, and slip it onto the buttons.

—Lizzy

## WHEN THE PANTS SAG BEHIND

**658** If you find baggy saggy horizontal folds at the top of the back thigh on pants, you can easily remove some of the excess fabric that causes them by taking a tuck in your back pattern piece. Slash the pattern below the crotch from the inseam to the side seam, leaving a hinge at the side seam. Overlap the slash edges at the inseam to remove up to ¾" (1.9 cm). Redraw the inseam. When you sew the inseam, ease the front onto the now shorter back. This is fast, simple, and easy, and really does make a difference in the way the back of your pants fit.

—Diane E

**659** Here's a technique that might help if you've nearly finished making a pair of pants, and find the butt is saggy (on the garment, can't do anything about the body, sigh).

- Pinch out the excess at the back of the thigh till the folds disappear and measure the amount you've pinched. Lower the back waist by the pinched out amount, tapering to the side seams.
- Of course, this'll probably create a wedgie, so you'll also have to scoop out the crotch in the back. Do a little bit at a time. It may not be the "perfect" fitting pants, there's only so much you can do at this stage. But they should be presentable enough for everyday wear.

—Dale C

## NO-FAULT WAISTBANDS

**660** Everyone has her own idea of how tight or loose a well-fitting waistband should be. Here's a way to be sure yours will fit as you wish:

- Cut the waistband the length of your waist measurement plus overlap (and underlap if you like), plus seam allowances, plus a little extra. Interface the band and fold in half lengthwise. If you use both over and underlap, future alterations are so much easier.
- When it is time to apply the waistband, try on the garment and place the band around your waist, pinning closed when it is comfortable. Mark the center front, center back, and side seam lines as they correspond with the garment.
- Remove the waistband and take off the garment. Pin and sew them together as usual; there should be a bit of ease in the band.

—Liana

**661** Tiny alterations make a huge difference on a bra, yet it's practically impossible to tissue fit or make a meaningful muslin for one. I have sewn bras from commercial patterns and from a pattern I cloned from a RTW bra. Both methods have their strengths and weaknesses. Cloning a well-fitting RTW bra means you start with a good pattern. On the other hand, there are no instructions on how to make it and no advice about appropriate fabrics. I recommend making a cloned pattern for the shape and using the instructions from a commercial pattern that is similar to put it together.

—juliette2

**662** On most swimsuit patterns, adjustments to the lower torso length are usually indicated to be made to the front and back equally. Well, that may work for someone who is perfectly proportioned, but if the major reason for a size difference is a large derriere, you can end up with a suit that is too long in the front and still not long enough in the back. Here's how I adjust the patterns to add 1" (2.5 cm) length to the back only:

• First I make the back ½" (1.3 cm) longer than the front, adding length all the way across.

• Then I slash the back pattern from the center back to the bottom of the side seam, leaving a hinge at the side seam. I pivot the lower portion to add ½" (1.3 cm) at the center back.

• Then, to make the front side seam the same length as the altered back side seam, I slash the front pattern piece from the side seam to the highest point of the front leg opening, leaving a hinge, and pivot the lower portion to add ½" (1.3 cm) at the side seamline.

—rhoda bicycle

**Deepika adds:** This works for briefs too.

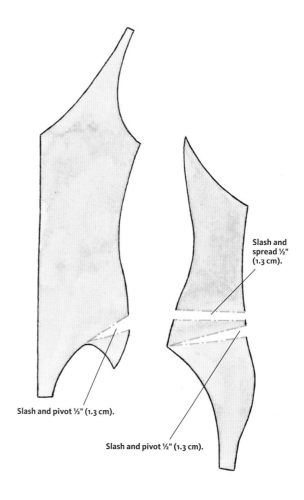

Slash and spread ½" (1.3 cm).

Slash and pivot ½" (1.3 cm).

Slash and pivot ½" (1.3 cm).

# Sew Lamé Fabrics Like a Pro

Kenneth D. King is a master of the ornate and intriguing garment. He relishes structural challenges that result in effects that look spontaneous, and is known for combining modern materials with traditional techniques. He's the proprietor of Kenneth D. King Design, a small haute couture house. Kenneth is a generous teacher who is happy to help others master the craft of haute couture patternmaking and construction. Visit www.kennethdking. com for information about his books and classes—many of which appear on PatternReview.com.

*" I often create what I call a hybrid fabric, and this toreador jacket is a good example: I layered and quilted lamé lace on top of a sheer green organza and then embellished it with chain-stitch embroidery and jet beading. The basic methods for handling lamé fabrics are explained in this lesson, and they also apply when using lamé fabrics that are more complex and decorative. Once you are familiar with them, you'll understand that this little jacket, which appears quite complex to execute, isn't difficult. "*

## Lamé fabric at a glance

Lamé is the French word for "blade," and under magnification, lamé yarn looks like a very tiny strip of tape. Lamé fabrics are regarded by some as too difficult to work with for any but the most experienced. This isn't true—with a little information, and a little practice on the scraps of the fabric you are working with, you will get polished results.

I refer to these fabrics as lamé fabrics, instead of metallic fabrics, because the appearance of the yarns varies—they don't necessarily look metallic. For the look of metal, the yarns can be made from actual metal, or of man-made materials. Metal yarns have a richer luster, but they are difficult to work with, and may tarnish or darken over time. Man-made yarns vary more in appearance; some have a pearl finish, some a holographic finish, some just a high-gloss color, some look like metal. An assortment of lamés is shown here.

In this class all the examples are made from man-made fibers, as these present fewer challenges. Working with real metal lamé is like working with metal foil—the effect of crushing is permanent. You can press the creases out somewhat, but there will always be a shadow of the creases left behind, which makes these fabrics look old and tired before their time. All the fabrics shown are woven with the lamé yarns in the crosswise grain and either silk or other man-made fibers in the lengthwise

When planning a project using lamé fabrics, know that you need to use a "with nap" layout. These fabrics do have a subtle nap, which may not show up until you finish the piece and get a good look at it in evening light.

*houndstooth, black jacquard, and silver matelassé*

*metal tissue*

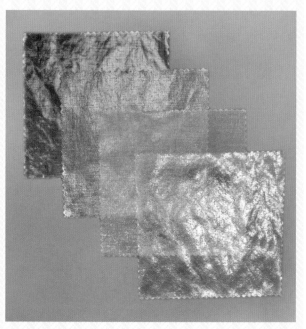

*man-made tissue*

# Things you need

*Having the right supplies and knowing how to use them gets working with lamé fabrics off to a smooth start.*

## CUTTING TOOLS

Aside from good sharp pins and a good sharp rotary cutter, a pair of serrated blade scissors is helpful. The serrated blade keeps the lamé fabric from "jumping ahead" along the blade when cutting, and so provides a more accurate cut.

For man-made-fiber lamé, a stencil burner, sheet of glass, and palette knife are essential cutting gear. The stencil burner heat-seals the cut edges of the fabric, preventing any of the fraying that normally occurs. You may use the burner to actually cut out your pieces, or, if you cut with scissors or a rotary cutter, use the burner to seal the edges of

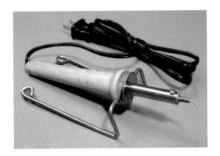

*Stencil burner*

*Palette knife*

each piece. This tool is available from the quilting section of your local fabric store—the quilters use them with acetate sheets, to create quilting stencils.

Place a sheet of ¼" (6 mm) plate glass under the fabric to serve as the cutting mat for the stencil burner. Use as large a sheet as you can manage. Mine measures 16" x 20" (40 x 50 cm)—large enough to cut a proper armhole and side seam on a bodice, but not so large as to be unmanageable.

The palette knife is a tool from the art supply store, but its size, length, and shape of blade make it an ideal guide for the stencil cutter. You want a metal guide as opposed to a plastic ruler—plastic melts.

### Stencil burner safety

This tool is HOT!
- Don't rest it on the cutting table—have a separate small table, or high stool, where you sit the stencil burner when you aren't cutting—this will prevent your fabric from straying onto the hot tool, which would burn holes in it. Also, rest the stencil burner on a heat-resistant plate or trivet to protect the surface of the table from burns.
- Watch your hands when using the tool—the point is narrow, but the shaft of the burner gets hot as well. Grip it only by the handle.
- Unplug it after use—even if you think you're going away for just a moment.

## THREAD

Use a good-quality polyester thread that matches the color of the fabric. If you don't want the thread to show when making a machine rolled hem, a fine monofilament nylon thread is a good substitute.

To prevent either type of thread from stretching when winding it onto the bobbin, do two things: wind the bobbin slowly, and bypass the bobbin tension disc and hold the thread loosely to put just enough tension on the thread to get it to wind evenly. Stretched

thread will snap back to its original length a day or so after you sew the seam, and the seam will always pucker.

When sewing with monofilament thread, loosen the top tension almost to zero—this will keep the thread from stretching and drawing up the seam later. Sew slowly, as the friction of the take-up lever will heat up the nylon thread, and make it break.

*Monofilament thread*

## MARKING GEAR

Avoid wax chalk, or tracing carbon, and most importantly, don't use a toothed tracing wheel if you do need to mark with carbon—the teeth will snag the lamé yarns and damage the surface of the fabric.

## NEEDLES

For polyester thread, use either a universal 70/10, or a "jeans" 70/10HJ needle. For nylon monofilament thread, you may need to use a finer needle, like a universal 60/8. Some lamé yarns will dull the needles on your machine, so change needles frequently to preclude snags and runs in the fabric.

## CASH REGISTER TAPE

Also known as adding machine tape, this paper tape makes a great temporary stabilizer that makes the needle less likely to force the yarns of the fabric through the throat plate on the machine. It is thin, so it is easy to tear away later.

# Working with lamé fabrics

*Master the four basic processes of cutting, sewing straight and curved seams, and creating a fine rolled hem by machine, and you'll find lamé fabrics are fun and rewarding.*

## CUTTING

When cutting out the pieces with a stencil burner, use a single layer layout (if you fold the fabric, you'll weld the two layers together as you cut). However, it's also a good idea to divide up the fabric into sections that are a little larger than the piece to be cut—these sections are easier to manage than wrestling with the entire length of fabric.

Pin your pattern to the fabric, lay the fabric on the glass, and, using the palette knife as a guide, cut out the piece with the stencil cutter.

If you have a steady hand, you can cut freehand. Make sure to pull the fabric taut with your index finger and thumb to get a smooth cut.

## STRAIGHT SEAM

1. To prepare a basic seam for sewing, place the lamé fabric pieces right-sides together as usual. Place a strip of cash register paper under them, aligning the edge of the paper with the cut edge of the seam allowances, and pin together.

2. When sewing the seam, pull it tight—this prevents puckers.

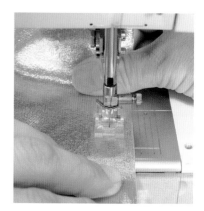

3. To prep the paper for removal, turn the work paper-side up. Fold the paper over along the stitching, onto the seam allowance, and crease with your thumbnail to make tearing easier (rotate the work as feels comfortable while you do this).

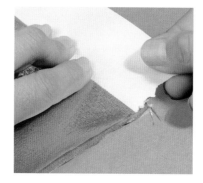

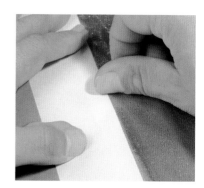

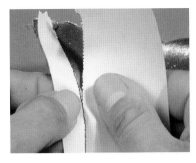

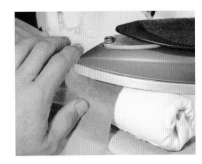

4. Tear the paper as shown, removing each section individually.

5. Press the seam open on a rigid seam roll, using the synthetic setting on your iron. If you have a temperature setting on your iron, set it to 275-290 degrees Fahrenheit.

6. And here we have the finished basic straight seam.

## CURVED SEAM

1. If the seam joins opposing curves, pin the flatter of the two, right side up, to short strips of paper tape; don't worry about aligning the edges. Staystitch ⅛" (3 mm) from the seamline, inside the allowance,

through the paper tape. Clip the curve. Position the other piece right side down on top, aligning the cut edges. Pin the seam allowances together, onto the paper tape.

2. Cut off any paper extending beyond the cut edge of the seam allowances.

3. Sew the seam through the paper. It will look like this from the back.

## MACHINE ROLLED HEM

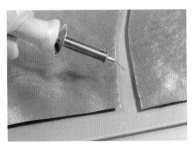

1. Begin by trimming the seam allowance on the edge to be hemmed to ¼" to ⅜" (6 to 10 mm), cutting with the stencil burner.

2. Pin a strip of the cash register tape to the right side of the fabric, along the edge to be hemmed. If the edge is curved, extend the paper over the edge.

3. Turn the work over, and cut the paper to match the cut edge of the fabric.

(continued)

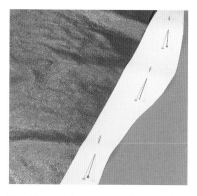

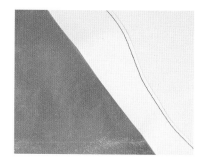

4. Turn the work back over, so the paper is uppermost before sewing.

5. With a straight stitch, sew through the paper and fabric, ⅛" (3 mm) in from the cut edge.

6. Take the work to your pressing table. This is what the work looks like after sewing.

7. Place the work wrong side up on your pressing table. Fold the paper over, onto the wrong side, rolling the fabric over the cut edge of the paper as you do this. Press the hem flat.

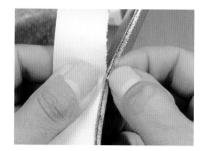

8. Edge stitch the hem though all layers, stitching very close to the exposed paper.

9. This is what the finished work looks like.

10. Tear the paper away from the work, as shown. The paper caught in the roll of the hem will remain there.

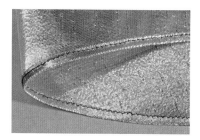

11. The result: a lovely, neat, tiny rolled hem.

## Sheer lamé rolled hem

If you are working with a translucent lamé, you don't want to see the paper left in the rolled hem. So, make the following substitutions to the preceding rolled hem method:

- Instead of the cash register tape, use strips of water-soluble stabilizer (Sulky Fabri-Solvy is a good choice).

- When sewing, use the fine monofilament thread for all steps. Once the sewing is finished, dissolve the stabilizer, and press dry—you will have a sheer hem!

## CHAPTER **SEVEN**

# Sewing

> " *Sewing is my therapy. It's the only thing over which I have complete control from beginning to end. I enjoy every step of the process. After spending many hours doing something I really enjoy, I have a new outfit! What's better than that?* "
>
> —Elaray

# Good strategies for easier sewing

*Love to sew, but pressed for time and have no patience for small irritants that get in the way of sewing pleasures. Sound familiar? Passionate sewists like you have figured the way to get the most and the best from their time.*

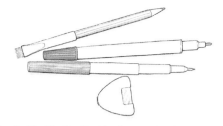

## TIMESAVING STRATEGIES LET YOU SEW MORE

**663** I am a "rusher" at times. I want an outfit made so I can wear it that same day! I used to avoid cutting bias garments as the skirts or dresses technically need to hang some hours before you hem or finish. Who has 24 hours to wait? Well here's what I came up with: I cut my garment out the night before I need it. I make sure it's too late to actually make the garment. I pin the pieces (loosely) on my dress dummy and go to bed. The next morning voilà! The bias is set—not to mention the garment is cut out! I sew the side seams and put in the hem first (with a long stitch, just in case) and then finish the rest of my construction. Sewn in one day so you get that "last minute high"!

—*anncie1*

**664** I tell all of my students and friends who sew this important thing: When you are tired your judgment is not good, your patience is short, and your project will more than likely end up in the circular file or the "hell freezes over" pile. We are all junkies, so here is what you do: Get to a good stopping point, put the project down, don't clean up, and get some rest. Your project will be there when you return to it. Eat some food and get the blood sugar up, read a magazine or the paper. After that you will be refreshed and ready to attack the finish line. The better you feel the better your project will be.

—*anncie1*

**665** Refilling bobbins and changing thread colors really cuts into the limited amount of time I can put toward a project. I have a small worktable with a machine on each end. If I'm about to sew something for which I need lots of thread (or two thread colors), I thread both machines and I also fill about six bobbins for each. Then when I'm sewing, rather than rethreading if I run out of thread or need to change color, I just go to the other end of the table and use the other machine. In this manner I can get more done without wasting time. When a bobbin runs out, I just grab a loaded one.

—*Coot*

**666** I have limited time in which to sew. So I wake up ten minutes earlier than I would otherwise, and spend those minutes in the sewing room before I head for the shower. At first I thought this was a waste of time: what could I get done in ten minutes? I was amazed to find I can make a knit top in five ten-minute sessions. I can sew and press two seams, or set in a sleeve, or cut out a pair of pants—all in ten-minute sessions!! I get many garments finished this way because I'm not waiting for a big chunk of time to sew. Give it a try!

—*featherweight48*

**Deepika adds:** Most of my projects are done in smaller increments too. It's only recently that I've allowed myself more than two sessions per garment, and I am really enjoying it!

**667** I used to try to finish the step I was doing before packing my sewing away for the day. But I always found it slow going the next time I started: Finding my place in the instructions, figuring out which steps I'd done, which one to start. Now I do the exact opposite. I stop halfway through the step I'm doing so I can start with something familiar next time, something quick and easy. For example, I'll pin a side seam but won't sew it. Or sew a seam but not press and topstitch it. That way, when I get started again I get straight into the swing of it and after that, well, it just seems to flow a bit more easily.

—*Helen near Sydney*

**668** When you need to repeat a sewing action on piece after piece (like stay stitching), instead of finishing one piece, cutting the thread, then starting another piece anew, stitch your first one but instead of cutting the thread, just push the next piece through right behind the first, leaving a little thread space between them for clipping and separating the pieces later. You'll be amazed how such a little step can streamline your sewing!

—*Nancy Anne*

**669** When I try a pattern for the first time, and I am not sure how it will turn out, I often leave out the time-consuming details like belt loops and patch pockets. If the garment turns out to be a wadder, then I have not wasted precious time on those little details. If I like the finished product and I decide to make it again, then I go all out to add all the details that will make it special.

—*SandraB*

**Deepika adds:** Don't forget to check PatternReview.com to see if someone has written a review of the pattern.

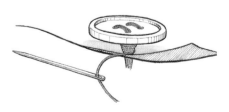

**670** The first time I gathered something, I needed my mom to hold both ends while I made the piece the right length and spread the fullness evenly. This isn't very practical if you are alone or the gathered fabric is too long to hold. So I learned to insert a pin at each end of the gathers and wrap the threads around it in a figure-eight. Once the gathered area is the right length, you can easily put it on a table and shift the fullness so it's evenly distributed. And if you need to adjust the length of the gathered section, you can just unwrap the thread, loosen or tighten, and rewrap.

—*Saya*

**671** This method is perfect for gathering miles and miles of ruffles: Instead of running two or three rows of basting stitches, set your machine for the widest, longest zigzag stitch. Lay pearl cotton or another lightweight cord over the seamline and sew, so that the zigzag stitch forms a "casing" over the cord. I use a presser foot that has an opening in the front, this helps keep the cord in place as I sew. Then just slide the zigzag stitches together over the cord to form the gathers.

—*anetjay*

**672** If a pattern calls for gathering or ruching, I find it easier to sew this step first, and then measure and cut the length needed. Gathering is not an exact science, as the weight of fabric, length of stitch, and needle thread tension can all play a role in determining the ratio of gathers to flat fabric to get a desired final size. So I cut an extra-long strip, gather it to the effect I like, and then trim off what is not needed. This works when gathering with a gathering foot, a serger, or a ruffler attachment.

—*tweedcurtain*

**673** I just completed my first project that has gathers. The way the pattern was configured, there were two rows of gathering threads, a row of basting, and another row of stitching. I was sewing with thread that matched my fabric and was really confused as to which threads to pull for the gathers. Long story short, I messed things up. When I redid the gathers, I used a different colored thread. It was easy to tell which they were.

—*shesflipped*

**674** When I'm pinning a ruffle onto a garment, I used red-headed pins to mark the midpoint, quarter, and eighth dividers. I don't use them anywhere else. That way, when it comes time to even out the gathers, I know which pins need to stay put: red pins mean "STOP: Don't move me!"

—*Diana M*

## Let your serger do the gathering

*Sergers make speedy work of gathering. Here's how:*

**675** **hongkongshopper gathers one layer of fabric.** A serger makes it really fast to gather large amounts of fabric. The following settings work for me, but you may need to fiddle around to see what's best on your machine (or check your manual): stitch length 5; needle thread tension 6 to 9; upper looper tension 3 to 4; lower looper tension 3 to 4. Now serge away! Keep reasonable lengths (tails) of chain at the beginning and the end so that if you need to reduce the gathers you have enough thread so it does not unravel.

**676** **Seamingly Simple gathers one piece onto another.** While making a set of knit tops in which the bust area is gathered into the side seams, I found I could form the gathers at the same time I serged the seams. This does away with the need to get out the sewing machine to run a line of basting stitches and then fiddling to space the gathers evenly. Here's how to do it:

• With the fabric right sides together and the shirt back on top, pin the side seam at the top and bottom as well as at the notch that marks the bottom of the gathered area. Put the pins far enough away from the edge that they won't get nicked by the serger knife.

• Feed the seam into the serger with back on top so that the edge to be gathered (the front) will be against the bed of the serger.

• Set the stitch length at 3 to 3.5 and the differential feed at its usual setting (I use 1.2 on knits and 1.0 on wovens) except in the gathered area. In the gathered area, crank the differential feed up to 2.0 to 2.2. The front will be lightly gathered onto the back. This works for light gathers; for more heavily gathered areas, increasing the stitch length may be required.

**677** I saved the pattern review template on my computer. Each time I sew a pattern, I print one out and keep it handy with the pattern instruction sheets. I fill in information as I go along, so I don't forget anything I came across that I wanted to mention in the review. It saves time posting the review when the project's completed, not having to compose everything again.

—*HeyJane*

**Deepika adds:** You can also start a WIP (work in progress) review and keep updating it online. You can make it either private or public—the latter allows others to follow your progress too.

**678** I admit to a passion for Far Side cartoons, and each year someone in my family makes sure I get the page-a-day tear-off version for Christmas. I've started using the back of the individual pages to make notes of pattern alterations and adjustments. They're plentiful (365 of 'em, to be exact), they fit into the pattern envelope very nicely, and they serve as a preprinted reminder of the approximate date I attempted to alter a pattern and sewed a muslin. And this is also a way to surprise myself with a cartoon I've forgotten about; since it always pains me to discard the good ones, now I can claim that I'm recycling. They look much better in the pattern envelope than all over the refrigerator.

—*Karla Kizer*

**679** Oh, this is so simple, but it took me three years of sewing to think of it. Get a pack of file cards or other small, stiff paper that won't get crunched up in an overstuffed pattern envelope. When you finish a project, write down any changes you'd like to make or tips for the next time you sew it and then pop the card into the envelope. In the past, I've altered the tissue pattern right after sewing, and then I never bothered to make it again. Or I relied on memory for the next version, but I'd forget. Or I would promise myself to try on the first model before making a second, and that rascally project was always in the wash when I wanted to cut out a new one. The annotated card saves you from all of that hassle.

—*Katharine in BXL*

**680** My PDA is the other half of my brain; I use it for everything. But for some reason, it just wasn't cutting it for keeping track of my sewing projects. I found it was easier to just use plain old paper and pencil. I've always been a fan of Paperblanks brand journals and sketchbooks. They are sturdy, have acid-free paper (lined or unlined), a satin ribbon bookmark, some have a magnetic or other type of closure, and most have an accordion file pocket for loose items. They come in a variety of elegant covers—the most recent ones are reproductions of antique books and textiles. Here's the way I put them to work:

- The accordion file is perfect for carrying swatches.
- When I get an idea of a project I want to do, I sketch it out and record the pattern and view number. On the opposite page, I list the notions I need and things I already have that I might want to use. I write any notes I want to remember while I make the project. I also jot down notes after the project in case I want to make the same thing in the future but can improve on it.
- Not only do the journals make shopping for projects easier, I end up with a beautiful log of all my work. I've just now thought each would be a nice heirloom, so I'm also going to start recording fabric names and dates completed.

—*khrome*

**681** I write notes (especially my mistakes) about a project or a particular fabric on the direction sheet for the pattern. I tend to remember my notes by project so it's easy for me to organize them and "look them up" by pattern.

—*Kim Winson*

**682** My pattern pieces become great places to make notes. I'll write the pattern number and size on each piece, of course. But then I'll add the date and fabric I used each time; how much bias I needed to cut to finish armholes, necklines, etc.; also amount of elastic used and number of spools/bobbins of thread. It's not just a pattern anymore, but a historical document!

—*Oopsy-Daisy!*

**683** If like me you have those senior moments, when techniques you've done a zillion times or the latest brilliant tip from PatternReview.com eludes you, and you remember it after you've messed up one time, this may be of interest: I've started writing notes for the best technique to use (say zip insertion), and any tips, (say fuse down back waistband before stitch in ditch) on a main pattern piece. That way, it hits me in the eye as I cut out, and is always available as long as the pattern is. Much quicker than unpicking.

—*petro*

**684** Sewing for children? In a small notebook write down:
1) Garment sewn. 2) Fabric used. 3) Pattern used. 4) Size used. 5) Any alterations made to width, length or size. 6) Date sewn. I did this when I sewed for my children. I often passed the clothes down to younger siblings, and when I wanted to make another garment I could easily decide which size to make and tell if the garment needed to be larger than the last one I made for that child, etc. I was reminded of this yesterday talking to my daughter, who asked me to make some clothes for my grandson with tops the same size as last time and pants 2" (5.1 cm) longer. I have to work out what I made before—I guess I will have to start a notebook for the grandchildren.

—*LiZ*

**685** One of the things that I love about sewing is that it isn't full of bureaucratic details, like filing things everyday or writing reports. But I do want to revisit some of the decisions I made in sewing particular items. The memory blurs: "What DID I do in that pattern?" "Why did I do it?" I love my notebook with printouts of the envelopes of my patterns organized by garment type. Aha! The glimmer of an idea emerged: I printed out my PatternReview.com reviews and put them in a (very small) binder so that they are easy to consult. Some of the reviews are already saved as digital files but this will be much easier to keep near the sewing machine and save me wracking my brain trying to remember helpful details.

—*Patti B*

## GAMES FOR BETTER SEWING

**686** Here is a little game I play when I do my projects. It helps me focus—I pay close attention to the details before I start sewing; I don't rush; I check my machine. It also makes me mark and draft better. Here's my challenge:

I count the number of times I use my seam ripper for the project I'm working on—let's say six times. When I start my next project I am only allowed to use my ripper five times. Next project four times, and so on. If you go over your previous number (shame on you ☺) continue to try to beat your personal best. I got all the way down to one once! If you hate picking out seams as much as I do, this is the tip for you.

—*anncie1*

**687** I'm helping a young neighbor learn to sew, and this tip I learned from who-knows-where popped up in my brain: When sewing something new or challenging, whether it be a new kind of seam, seam finish, a new technique of any kind, focus only on the next 3" (7.6 cm) to sew. Assuming that you've properly prepared the seam for sewing with basting or pinning or whatever it requires, this reduces tremendous amounts of anxiety!

—*Diana M*

## MASTERING THOSE INSTRUCTION SHEETS

**688** I always intend to read the instructions from go to woe but somehow about halfway through my eyes glaze over and hey presto, I've failed the first step already! A better system, I find, is to speed read the sheet and highlight just the main bits: e.g., 'View A' and the list of all its pattern pieces; 'View A' wherever it's written in the instructions; and all the diagrams relating to View A get circled with the highlighter. Obviously this doesn't keep the instructions in pristine condition so you have to be okay with that. But it does give you an overview of what's involved.

—*Helen near Sydney*

**689** This seems like such a no-brainer tip, but I have been sewing for two years and just figured it out. If you have a pattern, and you seem to always struggle with the instructions, you can write yourself better instructions right on the instruction sheet. For example, I have been learning how to make my husband's dress shirts. It seems as if I always get caught up on one of the collar steps. THIS time I'm going to write myself better instructions so I won't have to sit there every time I make this shirt wondering how I got it right the last time.

—*SexiSadi*

## BANISH TANGLED DANGLING THREADS

**690** We all know about pressing as we sew, but here's something simple that I've been doing lately that has been very helpful. I tend to forget to clip the threads at the start and finish of my stitching lines, resulting in jungles of threads dangling from my project. Now, I keep my thread clippers on my ironing board so I'm always reminded to clip threads as I press the seams.

—*sewgirl*

**691** I just learned a great way to prevent thread from hanging up at the end of a seam. I assumed that it was poor backstitching technique on my part that accounted for the occasional need to YANK the material away from the machine in order to trim the thread after finishing a seam. Actually I was sometimes not finishing a stitch, resulting in thread remaining across the bobbin. The solution: when you finish stitching, make sure you turn the hand wheel toward you so that the thread take-up lever is all the way up.

—*Eme*

## BASTING AND PINNING HINTS

**692** Whether you machine-baste or hand-baste, it is much easier to pull out your basting thread if you use a color that is obvious on your material rather than one that matches. I am working on a black blouse and for basting, it is much easier to see a white thread. Hope this helps; it has certainly made my sewing life much easier.

—*Mary Stiefer*

**693** If you want to machine-baste using a contrasting thread that will stand out for removal later, just change the bobbin thread. It is a lot easier to change than the top thread, so saves you time. It also makes only one side of the basting-thread-removal absolutely necessary, in case some of your basting stitches have been stitched-over and are difficult to remove.

—*Nancy Anne*

**694** On delicate fabrics I like to baste with silk thread in a contrasting color. Not only is it easier to see—because of its sheen—it's even easier to pull out.

—*Deepika*

**695** I've found it takes a lot of steam to adhere fusible thread, depending on the fabric; a damp, clean tea towel helps a lot.

—*ValerieJ*

**696** When pinning to sew, I direct the pin toward the body of the project, leaving the pin head extending past the outer edge. That way, no matter which side is up, the pin is accessible to remove or adjust as you sew the seam. 'Tis a habit that took some conscious thought to develop, but it's worth it to me.

—*Diana M*

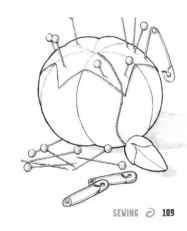

# Press as you go

*If you sew a lot, you know you spend as much time with your iron as with your machine. Here are insights on the best ways to press your fabric, press your work-in-progress, and press the finished garment.*

## THIS & THAT ABOUT PRESSING

**697** To avoid damage or shine from an iron when pressing a seam in knit fabric, steam the seam with an iron and then press it with a clapper. I've been happy with the results doing this.

*—Beezer*

**698** Use a hardwood (not fir or plywood) kitchen cutting board instead of an ironing board when pressing small pieces. The idea came after reading a chat on PatternReview.com with David Page Coffin. David says padded surfaces like those on most ironing boards are way too soft for good pressing results. This is a good tip, thanks David! Here is the link to that chat:
http://sewing.patternreview.com/cgi-bin/archive.pl?var=chat&id=dpc_dec_19

*—j222b*

**699** When working on a wool jacket, I was having trouble getting the seam allowances to stay flat pressed open. I would press them, but five minutes later they'd be springing back up again. I asked my tailoring tutor about it, and she said to press the allowances open with steam, then switch the steam off, cover the seam with a press cloth to prevent it from burning and press with the dry iron until the seam dries out—it's the moisture that makes wool spring back. And it worked!

*—cakehole*

**700** I just finished making my granddaughter of pair of slacks and used a sleeve board to press the legs, which were too small to fit over a regular ironing board. I know this is a simple tip but I thought some fellow grandmothers or mothers who sew for children could use this info.

*—Mary Stiefer*

**701** The secret to keeping pleats set is to not move your fabric until it's dry and cool. If you want a center crease or pleats to stay, it pays to press and cool, press and cool. I also use a wooden block to "pound" creases if I want them super sharp; again, pound when hot and steamy and then let cool. You can also leave the wooden pounding block resting on the area till it cools. The wooden block holds in steam and heat so that the garment cools more slowly, which enables a better crease.

*—Janie Viers*

**702** I have a little basket near my sewing table in which I keep clean, rolled, press cloths. I find that I go through a lot of press cloths, especially when I'm doing a lot of fusing or working with colored fabrics that bleed. I like a fresh cloth for each new project, so I cut leftover muslin into useful pieces with my rotary cutter, roll them up individually, and place them in my basket. It takes less than five minutes and I have a good supply on hand whenever I need one!

*—jen_e*

**703** For some reason, this didn't dawn on me until today, when I had the ironing board up to press (as you should) as I sewed: I use a chair on rollers at my machine, so I would sew, turn my chair around, stand up, go to the iron (a few steps), iron, step back, sit down and sew. How silly is this???? I realized that if I lowered my ironing board I could rotate my chair away from the machine, scoot it a bit to the board, iron, and scoot back.

*—Mary Stiefer*

**704** Today, when pressing a considerable length of cotton fabric I had pre-shrunk, I draped the unpressed portion over my shoulder. It worked! It did not drag on the floor.

*—Jennifer shaw*

## *Six pressing tips to remember*

***Sarah J Doyle*** *says: Many of us have been sewing for so many years that the various aspects of the process are second nature to us. However, because I ran into a small problem while pressing a garment I was working on, I thought it might be time to actually think about what I was doing, and not just let the hands move while the brain is someplace else. So I've put together a few "pressing" tips that I'm sure most people know but are easy to forget when a job is being done in a hurry.*

**705** The hint for my current problem is: if in doubt of how pressing will affect the fabric you're working with, make sure to ALWAYS press it on the wrong side.

**706** Speaking of clean, once worn, NEVER press or iron or "touch up" a garment for a second wearing. Any stains or soil, even if you can't see it, will be ironed in permanently.

**707** Always try on a garment BEFORE pressing in sharp creases, such as pleats, zipper laps, etc., in case you have to make a change.

**708** You can make press cloths out of pieces of an old sheet, old diapers, or clean linen dish towels.

**709** Always press hems with an up and down motion—not "around" the hem—this will help eliminate the ripples in the hem.

**710** And check out this last tip! Did you know that if you press or iron when you're angry it will cause you to have a "heavy" hand and perhaps cause damage to some garments you're ironing?

With that in mind, I think I'll check my ironing basket and get busy while I'm in a good mood and having a great day!

**711** As I remove the tissue when cutting a garment, I look for any hemline, waist casing, or similar folds and press them in the fabric pieces. It's easier to do this before joining the pieces and it gives me "memory lines" that will be helpful later in the sewing process. I then unfold all the pressed areas and construct the item per the instructions. The pressed memory lines are easy to use when I'm ready to complete the hem or casing and tend to increase the accuracy of my work. This simple step early in the project actually will save you time during construction.

*—jbsew*

**712** When I make a shirt with a collar, I always find it a challenge to press the neck area. The collar/neck seam can be pressed over a tailor's ham, but I've found that if I position the shirt with the shoulders flat on the ironing board and the collar sticking straight up, it makes it easier to press those facings around the collar area. (I also do this when I iron shirts and blouses.)

*—Irene Q*

**713** Here is advice for how to press open seams in little corners that are seemingly impossible to press into, for example, at the ends of a waistband.

• First press the piece flat as sewn, wrong side out.
• With the piece still flat, lift the seam allowances on both edges of the corner on the top layer, fold them back along the stitching, and press.
• Turn the piece over and do the same with the allowances on the other layer.
• Trim the allowances and turn the piece right side out. Dampen your fingers and "work" the fabric away from the seams, pressing with the iron as you go.

*—Mahler*

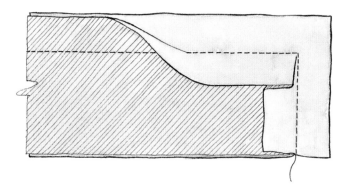

# Successful seams

*It's just sewing and the machine does the work, right? Truth is, good seams make the garment and they don't just happen: they benefit from sensitive handling. Get yourself on the right track with savvy suggestions from those in the know at PatternReview.com.*

**714** Recently my son was doing some sewing and it was a big "aha" moment for him when I told him this: To sew straight, don't watch the needle; use the guidelines on the throat plate or the presser foot to keep the fabric properly aligned. If you look at your presser foot, there is a marking on the center front that indicates where the needle will sew. Match this with the line you want to sew on. If you're appliquéing one piece onto another, this is where the center of your zigzag stitch will be.

*—Dale C*

**715** On my older machine I can use only the narrow twin needles. I usually have problems with the fabric tunneling and wanted a wider space between the lines of stitches, so I experimented with presser feet to find another method to get parallel lines of topstitching. For the first line of topstitching, I use the edge stitch foot with the blade resting against the well of the seam and the needle set to the far left. For the second line of stitching, I use the quilter's ¼" (6 mm) foot, which has a longer guide that aligns on the edge of the fabric; I set the needle as far left of center as the foot will allow. Using these two feet gives me two really straight lines of topstitching that are spaced correctly for jeans or jackets.

*—elizajo*

**716** I've found that when topstitching, it is much easier to keep the lines straight if, in addition to choosing the straight stitch setting, I have the straight stitch foot and straight stitch throat plate on my machine. So, if you are having trouble edge stitching, stitching in the ditch, or sewing another fine straight stitch application, try replacing your zigzag foot and throat plate! (the straight stitch throat plate has only a tiny hole for the needle as it doesn't have to allow for the needle to move left or right.) WARNING: Remember not to put the machine on zigzag until you change the foot and throat plate back. You will not totally ruin your machine, but that needle most certainly will break!

*—Janie Viers*

## CLEVER STITCH APPLICATIONS

**717** The 3-step (or multi-step) zigzag found on most machines (its icon is a zigzag symbol where each zig and zag is made up of three short dashes) makes sturdy bar tacks that are good to secure pocket or fly openings or to attach belt loops. Simply disengage the feed dogs so that the fabric is not fed forward (I suppose you could also set the stitch length to zero). Then just place the fabric under the needle, lower the presser foot (not a straight-stitch foot, mind you!) and let the needle sew back and forth a few times. Remember that the bar tack will form left-to-right. In most cases, you'll want the widest possible stitch on your machine, but try a few widths to see which you like best.

*—Asa Hagstrom*

**718** Every now and then I come across some really tightly knitted fabrics that bunch up on my sewing machine if I sew them with a simple zigzag stitch. I also have problems with skipped stitches. But the 3-step zigzag stitch works like a charm. It makes a stretchy and very strong hem too. I use the default setting on my machine although I've shortened the stitch width for doing edgestitching on some tops. When you try this, as always, do some samples to get a feel for the stitch and decide which setting looks the best. I hardly ever used this stitch before but now its one of my favorite stitches.

*—Deepika*

**719** When you must sew around a tight curve such as a rounded pocket edge or a scallop or a shaped tie, if you reduce your stitch length to a very small stitch, it will be SO much easier to get a smoother curve. You don't struggle to make that turn.

*—ryansmum*

**720** When I need to understitch I usually make a test to see if I like the traditional ⅛" (3 mm) straight stitch or if I prefer the wider 3-step zigzag. More often than not I like the way the 3-step zigzag controls the fabric. I especially like it on knit fabrics.

*—jbsew*

**721** I love the look of cover-stitched seams, but there won't be a coverstitch machine in my life any time soon, so in one of those light bulb moments that change your life, I came up with this. First I serge the seam with the pieces wrong sides together (so the serged seam allowance is on the right side of the garment). Then I separate the layers, press the protruding allowance to one side, and topstitch it down with matching thread as closely as possible to the loose edge. It's very quick, easy and neat, and looks great on sporty garments and fabrics (see below).

*—Judy Williment*

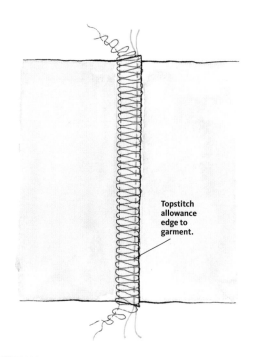

Topstitch allowance edge to garment.

**722** Sewing to a point, as when setting a godet into a skirt, is intimidating and a little difficult, but not as bad as it first seems. The trick is to give yourself a little guide. Now that I've figured this out, in fact, I really like sewing in godets!

- First mark the seamline on the skirt at the top of the godet. I like to baste it.
- Place the skirt and godet right sides together and, with the godet against the feed dogs, sew from the hem edge to the point; this way you can see the marking thread when you get to the point. Use small stitches at the point, and stop just before you get to your marking thread. Backstitch once, remove the work from the machine.
- Then sew the other side of the godet, again starting from the hem. This time the godet will be on top, but you now have the stitches from the first side to let you know when you reach the point. Stop just before you get to those stitches—you never want the stitches to overlap because the point will not sit correctly.

*–AnneM*

**723** Here's a way to get a great point on a godet or gusset that is to be set into a slash in the garment (rather than into a seam that joins two pieces):

- Mark the seamlines on the garment.
- Stitch along the marked lines, stitching up one side to the point. Then with needle down, lift presser foot and pivot the piece; take ONE stitch across top of point; pivot again and stitch back down other side.
- Slash the fabric between the stitched lines, cutting right up to the point. Sew in the godet as instructed in your pattern but pivot in the same way. That blunt point at the top will give you a much better finished godet than pivoting once for a sharp point does.

*—Marji*

**724** Ever since I discovered fusible tapes I stabilize all seams that tend to be weak or stretch:

- Crotch seam: Fuse bias fusible tapes to the crotch curve on the stitching line before sewing.
- Neckline and armhole: Prevent gaping by fusing bias tape to these as well.
- Waistline: Fuse straight tape on the stitching line. The waist will NOT stretch out of shape.
- Zippers: Fuse straight tape on the stitching line. This stabilizes the fabric where the zipper goes for perfect, non-ripply results. This is especially effective for side-seam zippers.

*—Deepika*

**725** Stay stitching works best when it is the first thing you do. I've noticed on several of my patterns that this step is shown on the neckline after the shoulder seams are done. This is way too late. By then you have moved the garment around a lot and the neckline has already been stressed. It's best to stay stitch immediately after transferring any markings. My tricks:

- Stitch from shoulder to center back or front on each side.
- Place the stay stitching near the edge so it can be trimmed off when the neckline is finished and you want the stretch back.
- Use a walking foot to stay stitch knits (see below).

*—beginagain*

**726** On my most recent knit top, the directions specified to use clear elastic to stabilize the neckline. Well, I found myself to be fresh out of clear elastic, but found that I had a package of nylon/Lycra seam binding. I cut a strip to length, trimmed it to ½" (1.3 cm) wide and used it in place of the clear elastic. Not only did it work great, but it was MUCH easier to handle than the clear elastic. I don't think you could use the Lycra as a substitute in every case, but as a stretchy stabilizer it will be my choice over clear elastic from now on.

*—Lisa Laree*

**727** To prevent the neck of a knit top with a collar from stretching out of shape over time, I add clear elastic to the collar seam. Clear elastic has a tendency to stick to the presser foot and the application process itself can stretch out the neckline if you aren't super careful, but Wash-A-Way Wonder Tape solves both problems beautifully: Apply the ¼" (6 mm) Wonder Tape about ⅛" (3 mm) from the fabric edge around the entire neckline. Then adhere ¼" (6 mm) clear elastic onto the Wonder Tape. Now sew on your collar, using a ¼" (6 mm) seam allowance to catch the clear elastic and sewing with the elastic against the feed dog so there is no drag on the presser foot. After the first washing, the Wonder Tape's "stabilizing" effect is gone and the collar will stretch nicely to fit over your head while the clear elastic ensures good recovery.

*—andrearn9*

**728** I bought a RTW top and decided to lift the shoulders a bit (the neck was too low). I discovered on undoing the neckband at each shoulder (just the usual type band on a knitted top) that threaded through loose was clear elastic! It was not stitched anywhere except at its ends, but worked to stabilize the neckline anyway. The shoulder seams were stabilized with the clear elastic too, serged into the seam.

*—Winifred*

**729** The weight of jersey can cause shoulder seams to stretch during wearing, dragging the sleeve seam down onto the arm and in general looking sloppy. Tape the shoulder seam to prevent stretching there: Use a ¼" (6 mm) stay tape or soft twill tape and cut a length 1" (2.5 cm) longer than your shoulder. Turn under ½" (1.3 cm) each end, then use a straight stitch to sew it to the shoulder seam allowance, or stitch in the ditch of the seam. Make sure to use the straight grain stay tape, not bias. (A selvage cut from silk organza will work too.)

*—Marji*

**730** In the throes of sewing up a wrap top I discovered that it gapped at the center front where the two layers met. To stabilize the neckline, I sewed stay tape on the seamline. In order to make the fit a bit snug, I cut the tape ⅛" (3 mm) shorter than the seamline and eased the fabric onto it. Unfortunately for all you Steam-A-Seam fans, this only works with sew-in tape. I found that the two layers fit snug against my chest and did not gape open. I guess the technique would work to slightly shrink any bias edge.

*—Lorna C. Newman*

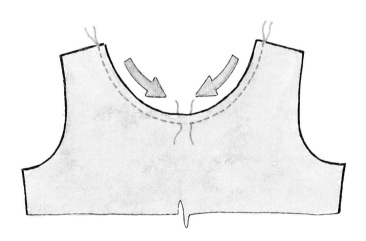

**731** I needed to stabilize a curved armhole edge on a sheer red fabric and, because fusible tape comes only in black or white, I decided to do it with homemade red fusible bias tape. Here's what I did:

- Started with packaged plain bias tape, which I pressed open and cut into ½" (1.3 cm)-wide strips using my rotary cutter. I made each strip the length of the armhole plus about 1" (2.5 cm).
- I sprayed the underside of the strips with temporary spray fabric adhesive.
- I positioned the tape on the wrong side of the fabric ¼" (6 mm) from the raw edge, pulling the tape snug (but not too taut) as I eased it into place. The temporary adhesive allowed lifting and repositioning the tape until it was placed as I wished.
- I stitched it in place ½" (1.3 cm) from the raw edge, using a stitch length of 2.2 mm and then cut off the excess tape.
- When the lining was attached with a ⅝" (1.6 cm) seam allowance, the bias tape held the shape nicely. I clipped the curve to the seamline (including part of the width of the bias tape), turned and pressed. The resulting armhole has lovely shape and doesn't sag! I'll do it this way again.

*—Seamingly Simple*

**732** A French seam is really not difficult to make and gives a beautiful finish. Here are the steps:

- Pin fabric wrong sides together
- Sew seam with a scant ¼" (6 mm) allowance and press—first flat, then open.
- Turn the fabric right sides together and press the seamed edge.
- Stitch ⅜" (1 cm) away from the seamed edge, enclosing the raw edge.
- Press seam flat, then to one side. Ta-daa! You have a beautiful French seam.

*—Nancywin*

**733** When I first started doing Hong Kong seam finishes (for which you bind the edge of each seam allowance), I was a little confused by the process and had read several different methods. This is the one that works best for me.

- Calculate how many finishing strips you will need by counting the seam allowances and measuring the length of each. You will need one strip for each allowance (in other words, two for each seam), one for the hem, and one for each facing. Cut as many 1½" (3.8 cm)-wide bias strips as you will need for the total length just figured.
- Sew each seam with a ⅝" (1.6 cm) seam allowance and press the allowances open.
- Turn your garment so that only one seam allowance is extended, with the allowance right side up. Lay one of your finishing strips face down on the allowance, matching the raw edges.

- Sew the finishing strip to the seam allowance using the edge of your presser foot as a guide or, my preference, a ⅜" (1 cm) allowance.
- Fold the finishing strip up along this seam, and press it to extend over the seam allowance edge.
- At your machine, extend the seam allowance right side up again and fold the finishing strip over it, to enclose the raw edge; stitch in the ditch of seam that attached the strip. I use my left hand to guide the fabric and my right hand to wrap the strip under as I sew. This is much faster than using pins and just as effective in my opinion.
- Trim close to the stitching on the underside of the seam allowance, removing any excess finishing strip.
- Repeat for each seam allowance. Then press open the seam allowances again, and you should have a beautiful Hong Kong finish.

*—Nancywin*

**Deepika adds:** Bias edges won't fray, so it doesn't matter that the binding has a raw edge on the underside of the allowance.

**TEST TO CHOOSE STITCH SETTINGS**

**734** Whenever I try a new technique on my serger and am happy with the results, I attach samples labeled with the settings to my notebook for later reference. I still test on a scrap the next time I use a technique, but this saves me lots of setup time.

*—Deepika*

**735** While you are cutting out your pattern, cut a couple of strips or swatches of the fabric on which to test stitches, thread, needles, and practice buttonholes. My students often ask what stitch length, or how far away topstitching should be from the seam or what color thread to use and I constantly remind them to do test outs and find out the answer from their results.

*—ryansmum*

**736** When I fuse the cut-out pieces of fashion fabric and interfacing together, sometimes there's stray interfacing sticking out around the edges. Instead of using a pair of scissors to trim it, I use my unthreaded serger; it gives a quick nice clean line.

*—els*

**737** I use the chisel-type buttonhole cutter to clip into seam allowances when I want them to lie flat. You never have to worry about clipping too far, or too little (which is a very common cause of curves that won't lie flat.) It is also the best tool for cutting the little angle cuts at the ends of bound buttonholes. Again, you will never cut too much or too little. I use it in any situation where I need a small, precise cut. It's perfect for buttonholes of course.

*—Liana*

**738** When I clip a seam allowance, I fold the fabric perpendicular to the stitching line and then I clip OUTward, toward the cut edge of the seam allowance. That way there is never a danger of clipping too far. You get a nice notch with one snip plus eliminate the danger of clipping through the stitching!

*—Janie Viers*

**739** When I trim various seams, I frequently use my pinking shears rather than straight shears to remove the excess fabric. This method softens the edges and eliminates a hard, straight impression should you over-press or if your fabric is somewhat sheer. Another benefit is the zigzag edge allows you to spread a piece along a curve without making all those little clips, which I think sometimes show through to the right side. Pinking shears are made to cut one layer only (or they will go out of alignment) so be sure to follow that rule. Try this method, I think you will like it!

*—KarmenG*

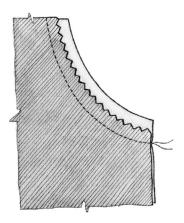

**740** When you serge the seams of a garment and then turn up the hem, the hem will be bulky where the seam allowance is doubled. If you clip the seam allowance at the hem fold line, you can then orient the allowance in opposite directions above and below the clip, and this will make a flatter hem. This is especially helpful when using a coverstitch because a bulky seam often gets hung up under the presser foot.

*—LoriB*

## Sew seams with perfectly matched patterns

*When you pin a seam prior to stitching, it's tricky to secure the pieces so stripes and other fabric patterns stay perfectly matched when you sew. Two PatternReview.com members offer variations on a way to match and secure from the right side, then sew as usual. Use the techniques whenever you want to keep the layers from shifting on straight and moderately contoured seams.*

**741** **Ann D Chafin uses an adhesive.** Wonder Tape is good for matching stripes or other fabric patterns at seams: Press under the seam allowance of one piece of fabric; attach the tape on the allowance, right on the edge of the fold. Lap that piece over the adjacent piece (both right side up), matching the fabric pattern, and press it in place. Then unfold the top piece so the two are right sides together as usual for sewing, and stitch right on the fold line. Voilà! A perfectly matched seam.

**742** **Kay Y uses a temporary zigzag stitch.** I was making a jacket out of fabric that has a teeny woven grid pattern. The repeat is so small (less than ¼" [6 mm]) that I didn't even attempt to match when cutting, but then discovered that it was hard to pin and sew the seams conventionally so that the pattern matched across the seams. Here is how I resolved the problem:

• On each long seam I pressed the seam allowance under on one of the pieces. I lapped that piece over the other one, matching cut edges and the pattern, and pinned through all three layers.

• I then temporarily sewed the two pieces together from the right side, centering a long, narrow contrasting-color zigzag stitch over the fold. Sewing from the right side meant I could see the pattern as I went.

• Then I unfolded the top piece so the two were right sides together as usual for sewing. The contrast zigzag stitches were visible on the wrong side; I stitched over them to make the real seam and then removed them.

## TROUBLE-FREE DARTS

**743** Have you ever had the problem where your dart tip looks too sharp, causing an unflattering point right over your chest (or butt, depending on what you're darting)? It's probably because your seam isn't perfectly straight. To combat that problem, align a strip of masking tape on your dart seamline and sew from the garment edge to the dart point, stitching right next to the tape. Knot the thread ends and remove the tape—you should have a perfectly shaped dart. You can use low-tack painter's tape for more delicate fabrics.

*—alysonwonderlan*

**744** I was having trouble sewing a dart that had one straight and one curved leg. I found it tedious to do if I folded the dart before basting it (particularly since the curved leg was longer than the straight one). It finally dawned on me that an easier way to get the dart legs to meet is to lay the fabric flat and baste loosely, keeping the bars between the stitches parallel. When I reach the end of the dart I pull the basting stitches taut and close it.

*—Brine*

**745** I have finally found the best way to start and finish darts! I place a small piece of tracing paper under each end of the dart. I sew from the garment edge to the dart point: I start sewing on the tracing paper using a tiny stitch and continue onto the dart for about ½" (1.3 cm). I then change to a regular stitch length. At the dart point, I change to the tiny stitch length again and make several stitches along the fold and then stitch onto the tissue paper. The advantages of doing this method are: no puckers at the end of the dart; no backstitching; when you tear off the tissue, stitches form their own knot; the dart looks neat and lies flat; and it works great on even the sheerest of fabrics. Give it a try, you'll be hooked!

*—Nancywin*

**746** To sew darts in sheer fabric you can feed the bobbin thread into the needle so you sew with only one thread and the dart tip doesn't need backstitching or knotted thread ends. Here's how:

- Fold and pin the dart as usual.
- Remove the top thread from the needle eye but leave it in the guides. Pull out some thread from the bobbin and feed it into the needle eye from back to front; then tie it to the end of the top thread in a square knot. Carefully draw the bobbin thread up through all thread guides until the knot reaches the spool. (For extra-long darts draw up even more thread.)
- Sew the dart from the point to the garment edge. Cut the threads.
- Repeat to rethread the machine for each dart you need to sew. This may seem like a lot of work but it surely is worth the effort.

*—els*

## HIDING THREAD TAILS

**747** Someone recently remarked to me that they do not use the automatic thread cutter when machine quilting as they wish to "bury" all threads for a clean finish as is done in hand quilting. The thread cutter does not eliminate this option, although you should use a few tiny machine stitches to secure the threads before cutting. Then, when all done quilting, remove the work from the machine and use a "tired eyes" or "self-threading" needle (the kind with a slit frame at the eye) to pull the thread ends under. The secret is to stick the needle half way in just where the thread tails come out of the backing and then slip the threads into the eye through the notch (with the help of a tweezers if they are too short) and run them under the backing.

*—Astrostitcher*

**748** There is a double eye needle that in my opinion is a must have for securing serger thread chain tails if you use a serger. Run one end of the needle back under the looper threads on the seam, thread the loose thread tail into the other end of the needle eye and pull the thread tail back under. Works great!

*—Heidi H*

**Deepika adds:** A blunt-tipped yarn needle works well for this too.

**749** When sewing the side seam on a knit top, you are sometimes left with a serger chain that needs to be enclosed in the hem. To make it easier to lose: Sew from bottom to top; hold the chain in your left hand as you begin the seam. After two or three stitches, swing the chain around from the left through nine o'clock to six o'clock so the chain is being stitched into the seam. After an inch or so of stitching, swing the remainder of the chain to three o'clock and let it be cut off by the cutter. Voila! chain secured without glue or a knot!

*—Shazza B*

# Who makes mistakes?!

*We all do. Maintain a sense of humor, forget blame, and keep your eye on the gorgeous garments that result when you take the time to set things right if they've gone awry. Here are tips from those who've shared your pain.*

## THIS & THAT ABOUT FIXING SEAM MISHAPS

**750** Have you ever been dissatisfied with some portion of the seam when topstitching? This is an easy way of repairing your stitching without having to remove all of your work; it can be used for a double needle as well as single:

- Clip the top thread in the middle of the area that you're unhappy with, and with your seam ripper, work enough of the thread free in both directions to be able to pull the ends to the wrong side (tug the bobbin thread to pull the top thread through).
- Then insert your needle exactly into the end of the stitching that remains and topstitch over the removed section, ending precisely where the previous stitching begins again.
- Tug on your new bobbin thread and pull your new threads to the back. Tie the group of threads together at each end.

*—Sew it seams*

**751** This just happened to me so I thought I would share what I did. I matched the thread to the fabric so well for a recent project that it caused me a little problem. I had to rip part of a seam and found the thread matched so well that I couldn't find the stitches. My solution was to rub a bit of contrasting chalk over the seamline area; this highlighted the stitches.

*—Mary Stiefer*

**752** I just had a big ripping job to do and it left a huge mess of thread bits still anchored on the fabric, which even the adhesive-tape-type lint roller didn't pick up. Picking the thread out by hand was a pain, and slow, and my fingers just weren't doing that good a job anyway. So I rubbed the seam with a clean eraser (in this case, one of those retractable erasers called a Clic Eraser). The eraser pulled up the threads and then the lint remover was able to swipe them away. I imagine one of the stubby Pink Pearl erasers would work, and maybe dishwashing gloves would also do the trick—at any rate, something that has "grip" is going to work way better than your fingers!

*—Debbie Lancaster*

**753** If you are working with a napped fabric and find the presser foot leaves a white mark, try this: Take a piece of the same fabric, wet it with water, wring out and then dab it in some vinegar. Rub onto the white area of the fabric and it let dry. The white may be gone when it dries. This worked for me on a brushed twill when I had to reposition pockets that had been topstitched with two rows of thread.

*—Mary E Geauxtigers*

**Deepika adds:** Try this to remove creases on wool too.

**754** I don't know about the rest of you, but there are times that I have to rip out a seam. This leaves me with all those little threads that need to be picked out. The easiest and fastest way that I know to do this is to smooth a piece of masking tape over the threads; when I pull the tape up most of the threads come with it. Sometimes I may do this two or three times, but it is still faster for me than trying to pick them out.

*—Mary Stiefer*

**755** I have a tendency to end up hunched over sewing work, especially when it requires close attention, like removing basting stitches. I started picking out some stitches last night, and realized it was bothering my upper back and shoulders, so I took it into a bathroom where we have a high hook on top of a door for hanging laundry and robes. Hanging the garment there allowed me to work standing up straight, and as a bonus, the light was better. No shoulder ache afterward. This may become my preferred way to tackle this tedious task.

*—kkkkaty*

## QUICK WAYS TO RIP A SERGED SEAM

**756** I was recently faced with undoing some LONG serged seams. After sweating about this for a little, I thought of an easy way to do it: With your seam ripper, carefully pick out the needle thread(s) from the end of the seam (they will be more accessible from one side than the other). When you have enough to grip, pull them out—just as you would pull out basting stitches. Once this is done, the looper threads easily pull out. For a really long seam, do this process in sections.

*—AnneM*

**757** Unpicking a 4-thread serged seam can be time consuming. After many years I finally worked out the secret:

- From the top side of the seam, run the seam ripper under the upper looper threads, cutting them along the entire length of the seam. It is VERY important that you only cut the upper looper thread and not the lower looper thread as well.

- Flip your garment over, and from underside of the seam, pull on the lower looper thread. It will unravel as one long thread. Pull the entire seam undone.
- Flip your garment back over and now pull on the two needle threads. Again they will unravel as two long threads.
- Now run your fingernail along the seam edge to remove any remaining bits of the cut upper looper threads.

*—Sew4Fun*

# Elastic chat

*When you need a fast finish or comfortable stretch, elastic is your friend. PatternReview.com members have great tips for handling it well. (For elasticized waistbands, read the waistband section, beginning on page 120).*

## CONTROLLING SEW-ON ELASTIC

**758** This may seem obvious, but as I have been quartering and sewing a lot of elastic I am prompted to note: If you tack down both ends of the elastic before stitching, it won't slip out of your hand when you get to the end.

—*Sewshable1*

**759** Just a quick trick I use when applying elastic: I measure the elastic per the instructions and mark with washable marker leaving 1" (2.5 cm) tails on either end. The length is then 2" (5.1 cm) longer than needed. Having the tails makes it so much easier to sew the ends securely at the casing edge. Simply line up the mark with the end of the casing, sew, and then trim. The tail gives you just enough to hang on to, making it easy to position everything under your needle.

—*jbsew*

**760** The function of elastic on the leg opening of a swimsuit or similar garment is to hold the garment to your body while you move, hopefully without cutting into your skin. In truth, the elastic needs to be tight only in the lower crotch area, between your legs—tight elastic on your butt or thigh cuts into the flesh making your suit look too small or you look too big no matter what size you are. I've found a good way to get this right. Like most techniques it requires a little practice but it really pays off. To attach the elastic you can use a serger (good for speed) or zigzag (good for control).

- Use ³⁄₈" (1 cm) polyester elastic: it's cheap, strong, and lasts.
- Always exercise the elastic before applying, stretching it out at least three or four times.
- I mark on my suit about 2" (5.1 cm) on either side of the bottom crotch seam, you will need to experiment to determine how much to mark since we all have different dimensions.

- Start sewing the elastic outside this area stretching it just slightly as you sew. If you leave a small lip of fabric on the edge of the elastic the stitching will tend to curl that fabric up over the edge creating a very nice finished look when you turn it under and top stitch.
- For better elastic recovery, I set the zigzag width so that only the left edge of the elastic is pierced, on the right swing of the stitch the needle pierces the fabric only.
- When you approach your mark give the elastic a good tug—I usually stretch it to the maximum so this area really cinches in. Keep it taut until you reach the other mark; then resume the light tension.
- When you've sewn the elastic all the way around, cut it so that ends butt (no overlap). Zigzag the ends together; this makes a flat join that won't create a lump on the outside.
- Turn the elastic under and topstitch while stretching as necessary. I like to stitch from the wrong side so I can sew exactly on the edge of the elastic.

—*BrianSews*

## SHIRRING WITH ELASTIC THREAD

**761** I use elastic thread all the time to make shirred clothes such as sundresses for my daughter. Here are the basics:

- Hand wind the elastic thread onto the bobbin without pulling it. Use regular thread for your top thread.
- Set the stitch to the longest length; I usually set the tension around 3 to 4.
- Cut your fabric with at least a 2:1 ratio for the size you need. Hem the top of the piece (or the edge along which you'll shirr) before shirring because it's difficult to do when it is all bunched up.
- Sew straight parallel rows. You can mark guidelines if you want or just go slowly. I space the rows three stitches apart. Go slowly and pull the shirred fabric semi-flat to sew subsequent rows. When you are done sewing, tie the top and bobbin threads together at each end; you can't use an anchoring stitch with the elastic thread.

- If the fabric didn't shirr enough while you were sewing, you can use a steam iron to shrink it into shape. It usually shirrs more when I put the outfit in the dryer too.

—*StacyCK*

**Deepika adds:** Some PatternReview.com members remarked that not every machine will do this successfully; some seem to apply the elastic so tightly it has no recovery or stretch left.

**762** Fold-over elastic makes a quick, neat binding. I find this way of applying it faster and neater than trying to fold it over the edge before sewing it on. Try it:

- Quarter-mark your elastic on the wrong side and your fabric on the right side.
- Place your elastic wrong side up under the presser foot. Place your fabric right side up on the elastic, aligning the fabric edge with the fold line of the elastic and matching a quarter mark.
- Stitch using a small zigzag stitch; stretch as needed to match the other quarter marks.
- Fold the elastic over the edge of the fabric. Stitch from the right side using a straight stitch.

*—Liana*

**PixieCat says:** Fold-over elastic gives a beautiful finish and it comes in such a variety of colors. It's a welcome change from ribbing or self-fabric binding. However, as a newbie sewer, I found it not-so-easy to apply until I discovered these eight tricks:

**763** Once you're done stitching, a light burst or two of steam from the iron should snug up the elastic nicely.

**764** A regular presser foot kept slipping off of the elastic but a roller foot worked perfectly and stayed right where I wanted it. I used a stretch needle and a fabric glue stick to hold the fabric in place on the curves.

**765** Slide the fabric edge into the folded elastic, right side up, so the elastic sandwiches the fabric. I quickly learned to be sure the fabric is in far enough that both the zig and the zag catch it.

**766** It's easier to apply the elastic to an open curve—for example, leave one shoulder open for a neckline binding. Cut the elastic longer than you need (or don't cut it until you're finished sewing).

**767** Colored thread, even white thread on white elastic, highlighted any inconsistencies in my zigzag stitching. So now I always use lingerie thread, which is clear.

**768** Before positioning the elastic on the garment, fold it in half lengthwise, on its fold line, and sew it closed at the end, stitching down the middle for about an inch using a medium-wide zigzag. Stop with the needle down and raise the presser foot. The needle anchors the elastic while raising the foot, which creates room to slip the fabric in.

**769** Sew the elastic to the garment; be careful not to stretch the fabric, but hold the elastic taut, stretching it just a very little bit. You'll need to adjust the fabric or elastic position frequently to keep the elastic where it belongs.

**770** It's difficult to keep the curved-edge of the fabric far enough inside the elastic sandwich for both the zig and zag to catch it. To solve this problem, I put a light swipe of the fabric glue stick on the right and wrong side of the fabric before I slipped it into the elastic, inserted it, and then pressed for a few seconds with my fingers.

## Clear elastic is something to love

**771** **Deepika offers this overview of clear elastic:** What is it? It's a "clear rubbery" sort of narrow elastic. When to use it? For KNITS!!! When you are making things out of knits with no Lycra in them, you can be sure that bias and curved edges like necklines, armholes, and shoulder seams will stretch out. So stabilize these areas with clear elastic (henceforth CE). It is especially helpful in low V-necks and wrap tops; helps "hug" the neckline close to the body. Here's how to use it; this may seem a long procedure but trust me, when you get used to using this stuff you'll be putting it everywhere:

- First, before you begin, recognize there's one shortcoming to CE: You can't use steam with it. I ruined a top doing that!
- VERY IMPORTANT! Before cutting the CE, stretch it a few times to loosen it, otherwise you'll find that it's too long when you sew it. Measure the seamline you want to stabilize (measure from the paper pattern not the fabric). Cut the elastic the same length as the measurement.
- Using a Teflon foot on your sewing machine (I found mine on eBay cheap) prevents the CE from sticking to the foot. Always sew CE to the wrong side of your fabric.
- To attach to your garment, place the elastic on the wrong side of the fabric on the seamline and sew it in place. This stitching will be permanent so use a matching thread. For shoulders you can sew it while sewing the two edges together on your serger, in which case you'll have two layers of fabric and CE on top (or bottom). For necklines, after sewing the CE to the stitching line, fold over the hem allowance and topstitch with a zigzag or a stretch stitch.
- If you'd like to bind the neckline and use CE too, do this: Place the fabric right side up, place the binding right side down on top, matching the edges. Then place the CE on top of the binding. Stitch together with your serger or sewing machine. Then fold the binding over the edge and topstitch.
- When using my serger to attach CE, I like to position the CE under the fabric, next to the serger bed. I leave extra CE extending at the beginning of the seam so it doesn't get trapped in the feed dogs. Line up the fabric and elastic close to the edge of the serger bed and serge. It works. Try it a few times just to practice.
- That's it!

# Successful waistbands

*Fabric, ribbon, elastic—each has a role to play at the waist. Whether you choose sleek or stretch, visible or not, you'll find clever techniques for the top edge of your skirts and pants here.*

## GOOD TRICKS FOR CASINGS & DRAWSTRINGS

**772** I heard about this awhile back and it's become my favorite method to join elastic when using it in a casing. Instead of overlapping the elastic ends to join, butt the ends together, with a piece of ribbon or something non-stretchy placed perpendicular behind the joining area. Zigzag the elastic ends together, sewing through the ribbon. Then trim the ribbon ends even with the top and bottom edges of the elastic. You have less bulk with this than with the overlap.
—khurtdvm

**773** If you wish, you can distribute the fabric a bit along the elastic, so there is more at the back and the front is flatter. To secure the fullness and keep the elastic from rolling, I stitch in the ditch at the side seams and center front seam.
—mamamaia

**774** For a drawstring used in casual clothing, instead of making a long turned tube, cut the drawstring piece along the selvage. Then fold the selvage over the opposite edge and stitch, folding in the raw ends. I did this when I made a drawstring on some cotton pants and it worked great.
—LoriB

**775** Yesterday I made a pair of pants and I was in such a hurry I did not pay attention while cutting the waistband. I sewed one edge of the band to the pants waist and found the band was too narrow for the elastic it was going to cover. I wanted to finish the pants and did not want to rip off the whole band and cut a wider one, so I made it wider by sewing a matching color satin bias tape that was in my stash to the free edge. This gave me just the extra I needed.
—els

**776** My favorite "yard work" pants' elastic waistband had given out. I briefly thought about removing the elastic and reinserting a new piece in the folded over waistband, but found it to be entirely too much trouble to unpick the tiny stitches I had used. Instead I cut off the entire band and added a strip of brightly colored calico in its place. I then folded the calico over new elastic and stitched down. I think I like the rejuvenated pants better than the original.
—Brine

**Deepika adds:** If your pants aren't long enough in the crotch to give you seam allowance at the waist for this, make the elastic looser than before so the new waistband sits just below your waist.

### Use a loop turner as a bodkin

*Threading elastic through a narrow casing is always a challenge. PatternReview.com members discovered that a loop turner (a slender metal tool with a latch hook at one end) makes a great guide:*

**777** **Kit Kat explains the method:** For years I would always use a safety pin at one end of the elastic to thread it through a long casing. Then I came up with this method: Slip a loop turner all the way through the casing. Attach the elastic to the turner when it exits the far end; make sure the latch is closed. Then gently pull the elastic through the casing. Get the longest loop turner you can find.

**778** **kkkkaty adds:** I sew a lengthwise bar tack on the elastic and slip the hook through this tack. I don't like this tool for turning loops, but it's great for this application.

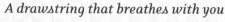

### A drawstring that breathes with you

*Two PatternReview.com members note that a little elastic makes a nicer drawstring.*

**779** **katharin's discovery.** I went window shopping last weekend. When I tried on an expensive pair of drawstring pants, I noticed that it was unusually comfortable. I examined the pants and finally understood that a part of the drawstring, at the back, was replaced with elastic. That results in a softer waist than only string and can easily be copied.

**780** **newlywedws figured it out.** It's easy to make an "adjust-able" elastic waist—make a drawstring with an elastic section that will breathe with you after it's tied. Make two buttonholes near the center front in the casing before you fold it over. Make your drawstring as usual, but in two sections. Then sew an 8" (20.3 cm) length of elastic in between the sections. Thread the drawstring through the casing, extending the ends through the buttonholes.

## EASY SEW-ON ELASTIC WAISTBANDS

**781** This is my favorite way to make an elastic waistband, especially for lightweight knit skirts. I use ½" (1.3 cm)-wide lingerie elastic, which has pretty scalloped edges and a brushed side that is soft (which goes next to my skin once this band is finished).

- Cut the elastic to the correct length, overlap the ends and sew to make a circle. Mark the quarter points on both the elastic and the garment waistline.
- With the brushed side out and the scallop edge pointing above the waistline, place the elastic on the seam allowance on the right side of the garment. Match the quarter points and pin.
- With the elastic facing up and stretching it between the pins, sew together close to the waist seamline.
- Fold the elastic to the inside and iron into place.
- From the right side of the garment, secure the elastic with one to three rows of topstitching.

—*Helen near Sydney*

**782** I copied this from a light floaty skirt I saw in a shop and think it's a great finish. I love the comfort of an elastic waist but hate the bunchiness at the high hip that comes with a skirt large enough to pull on. With this technique, you cut out a slim skirt as usual, insert the zip and sew up the side seams, but don't bother to sew the darts. Then try on the skirt and pin a length of ½" (1.3 cm)-wide elastic over the waistline seam allowance, adjusting the skirt fullness under the elastic to look good. Take off the skirt; cut the elastic to end just short of the zipper, and stitch the elastic in place close to the waist seamline. Trim the excess seam allowance under the elastic; then fold the elastic to the inside and sew with a 3-step zigzag stitch from the right side of the garment, making sure that the ends of the zipper are turned in and finished. Finish with a hook and eye. I think this is a really nice, light lingerie-style finish perfect for a summer skirt.

—*Jennie Pakula*

**783** I was trying to replace the elastic in a nylon tricot half slip in the usual manner, by quartering the elastic and waist, matching the quarter marks, and stitching the elastic to the top edge. Even though I stretched only the elastic and not the tricot, the edge of the tricot kept curling. I found that if I marked the waistline a bit lower down (in this case I made a line about ¾" [1.9 cm] down from the edge) and placed the elastic at the line I was able to avoid the problem caused by the cut edge curling. I simply zigzagged the stretched elastic and trimmed the excess fabric above after stitching.

—*Brine*

**784** This is something I learned quite a while ago and I routinely do it on all the waistbands that have the elastic sewn to the fabric (as opposed to threaded through a casing). Most pattern guides state to quarter-mark the elastic and the garment, then match them and sew the elastic, stretching as you go. I've found that basting vertically through the elastic and the garment at the quarter marks really helps keep the elastic from shifting. I even baste again after I've turned the elastic to the wrong side—this just keeps everything lined up well.

—*Lisa Laree*

## ELASTIC-INTO-CASING MADE EASY

**785** If you want to fold down the waistline edge to make a casing for elastic, first stitch the edge of each intersecting seam allowance to the outer layer of the garment. Then fold down the fabric and sew the casing. When you thread elastic through, it will go over the seam allowances easily since there are no loose edges for it to catch on.

—*LiZ*

**786** I usually use a bodkin to insert elastic in a waistband, but it sometimes slips off the elastic. Today as I was getting ready to put the elastic in my pants, I noticed an extra large pin in one of my desk drawers. It's the kind you would use on a wrap skirt. I decided to give it a try—I simply pinned the elastic to it and poked it through. It worked great! This is what I will use from now on.

—*BJ1400*

**787** I was trying to run a relatively short piece of ¼" (6 mm) elastic through a narrow, very long casing at the top of a gathered bodice. I threaded the elastic through the eye of a yarn needle and tied the threaded end in a secure knot just under the eye so it wouldn't slip out. Then, to keep from losing the elastic as I pulled it though the casing, I tied about a yard of sturdy yarn to the free end. I was able to run the elastic through the casing in a matter of minutes—with no worries about having to fetch a lost end!
P.S. Since the ends of the elastic may get a bit gnarly when you tie them to the needle and yarn, cut it extra-long.

—*Joan1954*

**788** Threading elastic through a casing is often frustrating. Rather than cutting the elastic to size before inserting, I mark the beginning and end of the length needed on a very long piece of elastic. I find that with the extra length I don't lose the end inside the casing. Once it is pulled all the way through I cut off the excess. (I make both marks on the same side so I don't inadvertently sew it together twisted later.)

—*ryansmum*

**789** Grosgrain ribbon makes a great waistline facing when you're using a heavy fabric and don't want the added bulk of a self-fabric facing or are too short on fabric to cut facings. Acrylic grosgrain works better than polyester, but I've had good luck with polyester too. Here's what to do:

- Use a wide grosgrain ribbon (1½" [38 mm]). Cut it slightly longer than the finished waist edge so you can turn under the ends. Lay it on your ironing board and use the tip of your steam iron to shape it into a curve.
- Lay the ribbon on the right side of the waistline seam allowance, with the smaller curved edge just above the seamline and the longer curved edge extending beyond the cut edge of the allowance. Topstitch in place along the edge nearest the seamline; then trim the seam allowance, fold the ribbon to the inside, and press the fold over a ham.
- From the right side, stitch in the ditch of vertical seams and darts so your facing will never flop out or roll.

—*Katharine in BXL*

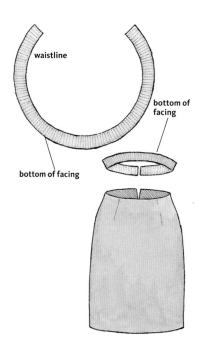

waistline

bottom of facing

bottom of facing

**790** I was given a beautifully constructed skirt that unfortunately didn't fit in the waist. When I started to unpick the waistband I discovered a new way to make a perfect narrow waistband.

- Cut your waistband 2½" (6.4 cm) wide (I interfaced with a very lightweight iron-on material).
- Sew one long edge of the band to the fashion fabric layer of your skirt with a ⁵⁄₈" (1.6 cm) wide seam allowance and then sew the other edge of the band to the skirt lining, using the same seam allowance.
- Trim the seam allowance on the lining edge of the band, but on the fashion fabric side, press the allowances onto the inside of the band to provide more support.
- Fold the band in half and, from the right side, sew the fashion fabric to the lining in the ditch of the band seam. You end up with a beautiful narrow waistband with the lining attached and no hand sewing.

—*JenniferBee*

## Neat fold-over elasticized waist

*If you sew the edge of the elastic to the edge of the casing before folding the casing over to the inside, you can make a nice, concealed-elastic waistband without the hassle of threading elastic through the casing or having to worry about it twisting.*

**791** **Meggie LuLu explains:** Here's a nice way to make an elasticized fold-over waistband. Before starting, cut your elastic 2" to 3" (5.1 to 7.6 cm) smaller than the waist measurement and sew the ends together.

- Mark the quarter points of the elastic and waistband. Place the elastic inside the garment on the casing area, aligning the edges and matching the quarter points; pin at the quarter points.
- Use a zigzag stitch to sew the elastic and casing together along the edge; stretch the elastic to fit the casing edge.
- Fold the casing and elastic to the inside of the garment so the loose edge of the elastic is at the top of the folded casing; pin through all layers at several places.
- With a straight stitch, sew through all layers along the bottom of the casing, over the zigzag stitches; stretch the elastic as before.

**792** **PixieCat adds:** This technique creates even gathers throughout the waistband that won't shift out of place. It's comfortable too! I like to use it for sew-through elastic, especially if I'm making pajamas. When you sew the bottom (zigzagged) edge of the elasticized casing to the outer layer, stop every few inches to push on the edge of the elastic to make sure it lies snug against the top fold. And if you find the elastic has relaxed from the stitching, try a few bursts of steam to shrink it back down.

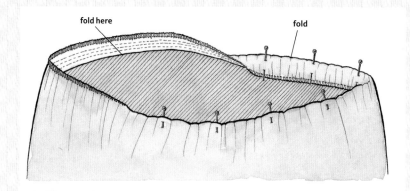

fold here

fold

## ADJUSTABLE ELASTIC WAIST

**793** Using buttonhole elastic in a casing on a child's garment is a nice way to make the waist size adjustable. Before starting you need to cut a piece of buttonhole elastic that goes around the child's waist. You also need two small flat buttons. Here's what you do:

- Make two buttonholes perpendicular to the waistline in the casing on the front or back of the garment, spacing each 3" to 4" (7.6 to 10.2 cm) from a side seam. (Make sure they will be on the inside when the casing is folded down.)
- Sew a button next to each buttonhole, on the side closest to the center front (or center back).
- Complete the casing and the garment. Thread the elastic through the casing

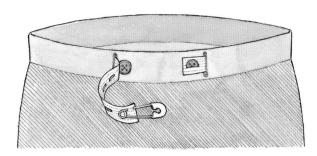

(use a safety pin as a guide), inserting it through one buttonhole, passing around the garment and bringing out at the other buttonhole. Secure the elastic by slipping a buttonhole at each end over one of the buttons.

- Have the child try on the garment and adjust the elastic to fit. If there is a lot of extra sticking out, slip the loose end over the other button. Loosen the elastic as the child grows.

—Meggie LuLu

# Zipper chat

*Zippers are easy to love and easy to puzzle over too. Check out these clever techniques for inserting them and troubleshooting common problems.*

## EASY CENTERED ZIPPERS

**794** A centered zipper application is the easiest of all in my opinion, closely followed by an invisible zipper. But sewing a ripple-free centered zipper on a side seam (on the hip curve) has always been a challenge for me. With trial and error I came up with this foolproof method and so far it hasn't failed me. It's almost as invisible as an invisible zipper application.

- Sew the side seam, basting the zipper area. Turn the garment inside out and press the seam allowances open over a ham.
- Adhere Steam A Seam to the right side of the zipper tape (on both sides of the coil).
- Center the closed zipper face down over the side seam, making sure the coil is on the seam, and press into place.
- Turn the garment right side out and topstitch along both sides of the seam to attach the zipper; use your zipper foot and sew from the bottom of the zipper to the waist on both sides. Stop every inch or so to smooth any wrinkles if you need to

—Deepika

**795** I think this is the easiest way to center a zipper on the seam: First baste the seam in which the zipper will be placed and press the seam allowances open. Then open the zipper and align one side of the coil with the seam. Baste this side of the zipper to the garment by machine, stitching as close to the outer edge of the zipper tape as possible; you don't need to pin, just use your eyes to keep the coil on the seamline. Now close the zipper and from the right side of the garment, topstitch it in place; first sew the side that has the basting and then sew the other side. Remove all the basting. Perfectly centered and so easy!

—drsue

**796** Once the zipper is pinned or basted in, take ½" (1.3 cm)-wide blue painter's tape and center it over the seam (over the zipper coil) on right side of the fabric. Then sew along the edge of the tape with a zipper foot. Remove the tape and your topstitching will be ¼" (6 mm) from the center of the zipper.

—Rosemaryschild

## ATTACHING A LINING TO AN INVISIBLE ZIP

**797** This is the procedure I use to get everything looking neat when making a sleeveless dress with an invisible zipper and a lining. First sew any darts in both dress and lining and sew the shoulder seams of each. Then sew the lining to the dress at the neck and armscyes; turn right side out and press:

- Install the invisible zipper in the dress fabric only. Leave lining free and do not finish the bottom of the seam yet.
- With the zipper open, on one side, flip the lining back over the neck edge of the garment so that right sides are together and the zipper is covered with the lining.
- Sew the edge of the lining to the dress seam allowance and zipper tape using a zipper foot. Go the full length of the zipper and then stop. Flip the lining back over so that you now have a clean finish next to that side of the zipper. Repeat on the other side.
- Now sew the remainder of the seam on the dress. Then, starting about 3" (7.6 cm) below the zipper, sew the remainder of the seam on the lining.
- Finish your dress as usual.

—Nancywin

**Deepika adds:** You can use this for a dress with sleeves too, just don't stitch the armscye seams before installing the zipper.

**798** It can be difficult to open and close a zipper in hairy fabric like fleece or faux fur. You can get around this by inserting a piece of fabric tape between the zipper and the hairy fabric. I like to use satin bias tape (pressed in half with the cut edges even), but you can use any sort of fabric tape or a strip of lining fabric folded in half. This works for real fur too.

—els

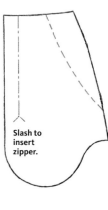

**799** I have more control when I install a zipper if I use my regular zigzag foot instead of a zipper foot. It's wider and provides a more stable grip. The only reason for using a zipper foot is the regular foot can't stitch past the zipper pull. SOLUTION: Get the zipper several inches longer than you need and sew it in with the pull well above the garment edge. Then unzip the zipper and do a satin stitch where you want the new stop to be, and cut off the excess. Other plusses to using too long zippers: you always have the right length available and the metal top stop isn't hidden to nick your needle when you finish the neckline (and cause extra bulk). I have put in more than a hundred zippers with this method.

—Janie Viers

**800** Ideally, you want to have at least a 1" (2.5 cm) seam allowance when sewing a lapped zipper—anything less makes it difficult to get a nice, wide lip on the overlapping edge because the seam allowance would not be caught in the stitching. However, I usually don't remember to do this when cutting out my patterns. In order to correct this, I create a "facing" for the overlapping edge: I cut a 2" (5.1 cm)-wide strip of fabric somewhat lighter weight than the fashion fabric and about 1" (2.5 cm) longer than the zipper. I clean finish all but one long edge (I usually serge it, but you could stitch and pink for a flatter finish). I sew the unfinished edge to the seam allowance with a ¼" (6 mm) seam allowance. I then insert the zipper as usual (I use a piece of adhesive tape as a guide for the final topstitching).

—Nancywin

**801** I first saw the zipper concealed in a pocket on a pair of Liz Claiborne pants about 20 years ago and thought it was really cool, but could not find a pattern to describe how to do it. Just this past winter it hit me that the zipper is in the pocket—who cares if it looks really elegant or not? The next time I made pants with slant front pockets, I stitched a zipper-length rectangle about $3/8$" (1 cm) wide on the left pocket yoke piece (that's the piece that forms the side of the pocket closest to the body; the one you see when you look at the pants). I slashed to about 1" (2.5 cm) from the bottom of this rectangle, then cut into each corner (making a little triangle). I pressed the raw edges to the wrong side, zigzagged them down, positioned the zipper in the opening with double-sided basting tape and topstitched it in place as shown below. From that point on, the pocket is made in the normal fashion. One end of the waistband is at the top of the slanted edge of the pocket, the other is at the zipper, so plan your overlap accordingly.

—Lisa Laree

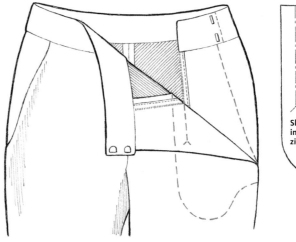

Slash to insert zipper.

### Invisible zipper know-how

*PatternReview.com members have clever and sometimes conflicting advice for inserting those nearly invisible closures and sewing the seam below them. Try these to see which is best for you.*

**802 elizajo's technique.** I don't have an invisible zipper foot. Instead, I use a pintuck foot that has three grooves. I use the left groove and my needle position knob to do all the work: Basting is still important so I can check the position of the zipper and hold it firmly in place; for this so I use larger stitches and position the needle closer to the edge of the zipper tape. Then I change the needle position to the far left side and use a smaller stitch for final stitching. And thanks to Els, I now sew the seam below the zipper before inserting it. This is contrary to many pattern instructions, but I get much better results—no bubbles below the zipper.

**803 regine's system.** I am a great fan of invisible zips and use the plastic foot to insert them. There was only one problem and that is often after inserting the zip there was a little fold where the seam and the zip come together. This problem is easily solved if one inserts the zip before sewing up the seam. If, for example, you are using the zip at the back of a skirt insert the zip and then sew up the back seam; it works like a charm.

**804 Linda L's method.** Here's my preferred method for sewing the seam after inserting an invisible zipper; I have eliminated the little bump at the bottom of the zipper using this technique: Change from zipper foot to regular foot and sew the seam from the bottom of the garment up to the end of the zipper stitching. It is easier to see the stitching at the bottom of the zipper this way and you can easily move the remaining zipper tape out of your way as you approach it. I then stitch down the remaining zipper tape to the seam allowances.

## TOPSTITCHING GUIDES FOR FLY ZIPPER

**805** Fly fronts are intimidating to me because of the topstitching. But recently I discovered that the package of a basic Coats & Clark zipper has a curved flap on the back that can serve as a fly-front guide. Just position it in place (using double-sided tape if necessary) and stitch next to the cardboard. This use isn't mentioned anywhere on the package—to think I've just been throwing those away and then struggling.

—*PixieCat*

**806** I decided to make a fly-front zipper guide: I cut a piece of cardboard to be 1¼" (3.2cm) wide and then rounded off one side on one end, the way a fly should be stitched, and then I laminated it. I made it long enough for any length fly; I can just raise it to shorten. And if I need it left handed, I can just flip it over. To secure it for tracing around, I either use double-sided sticky tape or just press it down, depending on the fabric.

—*Teeavilnor*

**807** If you like the contour of the fly topstitching on a pair of ready-to-wear pants or jeans, trace it and transfer it to cardboard for a template.

—*Deepika*

# Piping, binding & tube chat

*These techniques play different roles but are closely related. Here are shortcuts and smart advice that will help you fall in love with all three.*

### GOOD TO KNOW FOR BINDINGS

**808** I was having trouble getting my self-fabric bindings the right length on some of my knit tees as all the knits had different degrees of stretch. Now I have started cutting a strip that is longer than my neck opening rather than measuring. Then I simply pin it in place, stretching slightly as I go around the curves. If the binding needs to be seamed into a ring, I mark the seamlines and unpin enough to be able to sew the ends together. Since I started doing this I have not had a binding roll to the outside from being too long or pucker from being too tight.

—*mssewcrazy*

**809** I use fusible thread to apply double fold binding. This is not a couture technique by any means, but it'll save you all those pin pokes!

- With fusible thread in the bobbin and the binding wrong side up and unfolded in your machine, sew a basting line ⅛" (3 mm) from the fold on the cut edge that ultimately will be turned to the inside of the item to be bound.
- With the right sides together and using regular thread in the bobbin, sew the other cut edge of the binding to the edge of your project (in other words, sew on the binding as usual).
- Fold the binding over the edge of the project, turning under the edge with the fusible thread. Press with an iron to melt the thread and fuse the binding in place. No need for pins!
- To permanently secure the binding to the inside of the project, topstitch on the right side of the binding.

—*Leslie in Austin*

**810** If you make your own double-fold binding you can make the "inside half" a bit wider so you can "stitch in the ditch" to secure it.

—*Deepika*

## SUCCESS WITH TUBE TURNING GADGETS

**811** If you have one of those tube turners that is a long wire with a latch hook on one end and a loop "handle" on the other, put the loop over the thread spindle of your sewing machine when you turn a tube. That way you can keep constant, even tension on the tube using both hands as you turn it (and it won't unlatch half way, which I've had happen more than once!). The tubes turn in seconds.

*—Judy Williment*

**812** The Fasturn notion is great for more than turning tiny spaghetti straps or stuffing tubes of fabric for purse handles or other craft projects. The gadget once again earned its keep when I used it to turn the lined narrow shoulders of a halter dress. Sure, I could have used a chopstick or knitting needle, but the Fasturn was, well, faster. Much faster.

*—lisaquilts*

**Deepika adds:** This cool 2-piece device features a metal cylinder that slides inside your wrong-side-out fabric tube and a long wire "turner" with a twisted point; you insert the turner through the cylinder, twist the point into the end of your fabric tube, and pull it back out, turning the tube right side out as you pull it through the cylinder.

## PIPING MADE EASY

**813** If you are making piping or cording and hate that sometimes the basting you use on the piping shows in the finished garment, I have a solution for you. Plus you can do this without your sewing machine!

- Place the piping cover strip wrong side up on your ironing board. Then place a strip of fusible web along one long edge. Lay the filler cord in the middle and fold the plain edge over to match to the one with the web.
- Iron along the edge so that the fusible web secures the fabric around the filler. This way you never have to worry about any basting stitches showing.

*—Janie Viers*

**814** I have an obsession with flat piping. Lately, I put it on everything. Well, not everything, but anything that suggests itself. I hate to make bias strips. I don't even like making a continuous bias strip from a constructed tube of fabric. So I have been experimenting with knit fabric for piping. I usually cut a 2" (5.1 cm)-wide strip of cotton/Lycra knit, fold it in half, right side out, and press. Then I attach this strip as I would any piping and the result is beautiful flat piping that works even on the most curved edges. I have a lot of knit scraps so it has been 'free' as well! This is just too easy.

*—maryfrana*

**815** This is my own self-discovered tip. One of the hardest parts of making your own piping is trimming the seam allowance to an exact width. Try this: If you own two rotary cutting mats, butt them up against each other. Now spread them apart slightly and push your piping in between them, so the cord is sitting in the groove between the mats. Place a transparent-grid quilting ruler over the top of the piping and cut to an exact width with a rotary cutter.

*—Sew4Fun*

**816** Use an unthreaded serger to cut an even flange when you make your own piping. First make the piping with a flange a bit wider than you need. Then decide how wide you want the flange to be (the seam allowance width for whatever you are making), and run it through the unthreaded serger to trim it to that width. This discovery is going to make sewing piping SO much easier for me and I only wish this tip had been posted YEARS ago for me, as I have suffered immeasurably from making a mess of piped projects.

*—ryansmum*

 *Turn tubes quickly over ribbon*

*It's common practice to turn a narrow tube over a cord, but two PatternReview.com members prefer to use ribbon:*

**817** **Melissa S explains.** I have tried many methods to turn narrow tubes of fabric. The one that has worked best for me with the least amount of fabric distortion/bruising is to use a ribbon basted to the short end of the tube. The job is made easier if the ribbon is just a bit narrower than the tube; in other words, use a wider ribbon for wider tubes:

- Cut a length of ribbon that is a few inches longer than the tube you wish to turn.
- Fold the fabric in half, right side together, so that the long edges meet; tuck the ribbon inside the layers against the fold and baste together at one end.

- Stitch the fabric layers closed on the open long edge, being careful not to catch the ribbon.
- Pull the loose end of the ribbon through the open end of the tube, thus turning the tube right side out.
- Remove the basting threads that secured the ribbon. The ribbon will easily pull out.

**818** **gail1 adds.** I didn't have the cotton cord that my pattern instructions called for to sew and turn a teeny-tiny neck loop, but I did have a length of ¼" (6 mm)-wide silk ribbon leftover from some embroidery in the drawer. It worked great—thin, strong, and really slippery for pulling the loop through on itself. I'll be using it for loops from now on.

## Knit fabric makes a great binding

*Bound edges give a neat finish and they're easy to do with knit fabric. Two PatternReview.com members share the how and why:*

**819** **cabinbaby's method** I have been using a narrow strip of knit fabric to bind the edge of my facings. This looks better than serging, adds no bulk, and is easy to do. Here's my process:

- Assemble the facing if it has more than one piece, so it's ready to attach to the garment.
- Cut a strip of lightweight jersey at least 1" (2.5 cm) wide and about ½" (1.3 cm) shorter than the edge to be bound. Be sure to cut on the cross grain, so the direction of stretch is on the length of the strip.
- Next, place the knit and facing right sides together. Use a ¼" (6 mm) seam to attach the knit to the facing; stretch the knit a little so it fits the facing.
- Wrap the binding over the edge of the facing; pin or press in place.

- Place the facing right side up in your machine and "stitch in the ditch" of the first seam to secure the loose edge of the binding.
- Turn the piece over and trim any excess binding fabric close to the stitching. All done.

**Deepika elaborates:** I used to be a fan of the turn-under-and-topstitch finish until I started doing a bound edge. Now I am a total convert to the latter. I especially like to bind necks and armholes, which means the binding is visible on the outside of the finished garment, so I choose the same or a complementary knit for the binding.

- As cabinbaby suggests, cut the binding shorter than the edge to be bound, but don't forget to include seam allowances if the edge is a closed loop like an armhole.

- If the edge is a closed loop, sew the ends of the binding together. I like to do this on my sewing machine—much less bulk because you can press the allowances open. But you could certainly use a serger and press the seam allowances to one side.
- Attach the binding as cabinbaby explained. I fold both the binding and the edge to which it's being attached in quarters and mark the folds; then match the quarter marks and pin. I usually just use a tiny straight stitch to sew on the binding, and when I press, I support the piece on a curved surface like a ham. I use an edgestitching foot as a guide when I "stitch in the ditch."

# Successful hems

*Deep, narrow, straight, curved, invisible, or totally decorative: Whichever hem effect is right for your garment, PatternReview.com members have mastered the process and are glad to share their techniques.*

## CONVENTIONAL OR SERGER BLINDSTITCH TRICKS

**820** Here's blind-hem technique for a sewing machine that is the equivalent of a hand picked hem; it can be used on the finest of fabric and doesn't show on the right side. I've even tried it with a contrast thread and even then most of the time it's not visible. Install your blind hem foot on your machine and select the blind hem stitch, choosing width of 2, length of 1.5 to 2, needle position halfway to the right (I can't give you an exact position as it depends on your machine).

- Turn up and press a narrow margin at the raw edge, then turn up the depth of the hem and press. (For sheer fabric the first fold should be the same depth as the hem.) Then fold the entire hem under, toward the right side of the garment, so the top fold of the hem just peeks out beyond the folded edge of the garment fold.

- Place the garment under the foot exactly as usual for a blind hem. Sew the blind hem making sure that the zigzag stitch catches both folds while the straight stitches fall off the edge and form a chain in the air, along the upper edge of the hem.

*—MareeAlison*

**joann says:** I have had a blind hemming foot for my serger for years and finally tried it out today on seven knit shirts that needed shortening. If you've had trouble getting perfect results doing this, you may be interested in two things I learned:

**821** I discovered that when I guided the fold of the fabric next to the guide on the foot, per the instructions, I sometimes did not catch the fold. However, when I ran the edge of the fold directly UNDER the guide the fold was always caught and there were no unstitched gaps. The difference is probably ¹⁄₁₆" (1.6 mm) but the change worked beautifully.

**822** I also found having the right hand needle tension set one number below the usual and the upper looper set one number over the usual produced a nearly invisible stitch on the right side and was very flat. I used 3 threads as I don't have 2-thread capability.

**823** I just made a dress with miles of chiffon flounces. In order to make hemming them easier (or even possible) I used a liquid fabric stabilizer. After cutting out the flounces I spread them on a waterproof surface. Then I used a foam paintbrush dipped in the stabilizer to paint a margin about 1½" (3.8 cm) deep along the edges. I let them dry (running a fan makes it go faster). It was SOOO much easier to make rolled hems with my serger once the chiffon was stabilized. I used my washer to wash out the stabilizer afterwards, although if you had a small project you could rinse it out by hand. Of course, your fabric has to be washable to do this.

—*Mandolin82*

**824** When a sheer fabric is so fragile that a rolled hem tends to break away from the body, I reinforce the hem with a narrow strip of the same fabric, feeding both layers through the serger together. When I'm done, if any excess of the strip peeks out, I simply trim it away.

—*Deepika*

**825** Starting a rolled hem is a challenge on very sheer or slippery fabric, as the fabric tends to shimmy away from the needle after it goes under the cutter, resulting in the first ½" (1.3 cm) or so of the fabric not being wrapped by the thread. I was able to correct this by placing a 3" (7.6 cm) square Post-it note at the top of the fabric. This held the fabric in place and kept it straight so it couldn't get away form the machine:

- Position the Post-it right at the starting end of the hem with the sticky strip parallel to the edge to be serged and about ³/₈" to ½" (1 to 1.3 cm) to the left of it.
- Lift the presser foot and place the fabric underneath, right up against the cutter. Lower the presser foot, and start serging. Place your left hand firmly over the Post-it and give some gentle pressure to help the fabric start moving through the machine. I made 14 scarves, each with all four edges serged, and this worked every time!

—*jimsgurl*

**826** While attempting a rolled hem in a sheer fabric, I kept having problems with the stitches perforating the fabric and the roll breaking away. I tried a variety of stitch lengths and density, but the problem continued. So I laid the hem along a length of fusible web tape as I serged, placing it adhesive side up and aligned so that about half the tape was cut away and the other half lay under the hem. The stitches grabbed the tape and the hem no longer pulled away from the skirt. I then pressed the hem (low setting) and the web fused the hem even more securely.

—*CharityAK*

**827** I use this technique whenever I need a hem on a sheer garment: Fold and press ¼" (6 mm) to the RIGHT side of the garment. Yes, the right side! Now fold and press ¼" (6 mm) again to the right side. Stitch this right down the middle of the folded allowance. Now turn the allowance to the wrong side along the stitching; it will make a tiny mock piping on the edge of the garment. Press well. I like to use my clapper to get a hard press on the hem edge. This technique also helps the garment stand out a very tiny bit which I think is pretty on a sheer.

—*solosmocker*

## LETTUCE EDGE, WITH OR WITHOUT A SERGER

**828** I experimented with two ways to make a lettuce hem on knit fabric using my serger. Here's what I did and how it worked out:

I used a stretch needle in the right position only, regular thread for the needle and Woolly Nylon in both loopers. I changed the tension guides for the loopers to D for decorative thread. For both techniques, the stitch finger needs to be in the R position (it moves out of the way so the thread rolls directly onto the fabric).

- I used these settings: Cutting width: normal; stitch length: 1 mm; RN tension; normal; UL: 1 (if using Woolly Nylon, otherwise set at normal); LL: 6.
- Technique 1: Without using differential feed, I stretched the fabric in front of and behind the presser foot while serging. When the tension on the fabric was released, the tightly stitched edge created a ripple.
- Technique 2: I dropped the differential feed to the lowest level (mine goes to .05). This way I didn't have to stretch the fabric, just guide it under the foot. The DF creates the ripple and, I believe, it's a much nicer look that is more wavy and flowing than the other. This is a fun and very easy way to finish an edge.

—*PixieCat*

**Jackie M says:** You don't need a serger to make a lettuce edge on knits. All you need is a scrap of your fabric and a few minutes to practice.

**829** I set my zigzag stitch to the widest width and almost the shortest length. Then position your fabric so that the hem allowance is about 1.25 times the width of your zigzag. This extra is for the edge that will be forced to "fold over" when you sew—you need this little fold of fabric to achieve a good lettuce edge. Then stitch along the edge, stretching the fabric both in front of and behind the presser foot. Some tips:

**830** You'll probably need a second pass of zigzags. For the second pass, I narrow my stitch width to about two-thirds the width of the first pass. Then stitch again, this time stretching the fabric only from behind the presser foot.

**831** You may need to slightly angle the fabric a little to the right as it passes under the presser foot to achieve the "fold over."

**832** This technique may need to be fine-tuned, depending on your fabric and machine; you may need to stretch from both behind and in front of the presser foot on both passes, etc.

**833** My arthritis has been acting up and I was getting so cramped up as I was making a rolled hem on a blouse cuff. The contortions I go through to keep the material tightly rolled as it feeds through the foot! I had an "aha" moment and turned my machine on the table so that the end of the head was facing me. OMG! No hand cramp and wrist dislocation! No leaning over to the left to get a better view of the material coming through the foot. Dang, I just wish I had figured this out when I was making my daughter's prom dress last spring.

—svetlana

**Deepika adds:** Don't' wait till your arthritis acts up to try this; it makes the fabric feed through the rolled hem foot better anyway. Works well with both straight stitch and zigzag rolled hems.

### Unconventional feet for narrow hems

*While it seems there's a presser foot for every task, there are times when a smart PatternReview.com member does the machine manufacturers one better. Consider these inventive ideas:*

**836 loohoo44 prefers a blind-hem foot for baby hems.** I use my blind-hem foot to facilitate making a knife-edge baby hem. I know there are different styles of feet so I don't know if this will work for other types, but it did a great job on my Janome. It held the fabric very flat while I stitched close to the edge after folding once, and it served as a perfect guide when I stitched again, after folding the second time. I was a chicken when doing this project, so my hem is wider than it could have been. The foot held everything so perfectly I could have sewed a lot closer to the edges.

**837 Summerlea finds the flat-fell foot does a great rolled hem.** I have a ¼" (6 mm) flat felling foot that's great for making a rolled hem. I roll the hem to ¼" (6 mm) wide to match the groove in the foot and sew the first few stitches. Then I wrap the fabric up around the foot and continue sewing as for a rolled hem with the rolled hem foot.

**834** I came about this by accident when I needed to finish the armhole, neckline, and hem on a thin, uncooperative knit. I tried a narrow rolled edge, but it rippled and then stayed straight in some areas. I folded it under ½" (1.3 cm) and did another rolled edge on the fold, almost like a tuck. It drew up the fold enough to pull in the first rolled edge. Some areas did still curl, but since it was the right side showing, it looked nice and like I had planned it. It gave it a fun mock-layered look. I may try this again, perhaps using contrasting thread.

—Oopsy-Daisy!

### FOOLPROOF COVER STITCH HEM

**838** Here's my "aha" solution for making sure that my cover stitch hems catch the hem allowance when I sew from the right side of the garment: With bobbin thread in an easily seen color (often the end of bobbins wound for some other project), I machine baste the top of the hem from the wrong side of the garment. When I position the hem right side up in my serger, I center the colored basting thread between the two needles. The thread from the looper always lies across the hem edge when I sew and the basting thread is easy to remove afterward. No additional fine-tuning (fixing missed sections) is needed.

—Sew Sew Sandi

**835** My past experience with serging an edge and then turning it under to hem has not always been very good. Sometimes the hem stays in place well enough to topstitch or even coverstitch, but most times not. I decided to put fusible thread in the lower looper of the serger and serge finish the neck, sleeve, and hem of a top as instructed. I then turned under and pinned the hems, and fused each with the iron. This worked great and held the fabric well enough to topstitch. If experienced enough in turning and pressing, you can probably eliminate the pinning part.

—Linda L

**Deepika adds:** If the fusible thread is in the lower looper, be sure to serge the edge with the fabric right side up.

### TAME AN UNSTABLE HEM

**839** I was making up a simple top from some rayon in my stash. When I was topstitching the hem at the bottom, I discovered that the machine wanted to "eat" the fabric as I started from the edge. So folded a scrap of Solvy in quarters and placed it under the fabric edge. I allowed about half of it to stick out beyond the starting end of the hem. The topstitching went very smoothly because the machine no longer began the stitching by eating the fabric. After completing the hems, I just trimmed off the excess and wet the Solvy to dissolve it. I will definitely use this technique again!

—nanflan

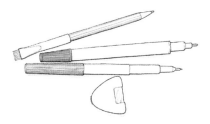

**840**  Here's an easy way to get a smooth hemline on a circle skirt. Start with a narrow hem allowance:

- Serge the raw edge of the hem allowance. With a conventional machine and medium-length straight stitch, sew around the skirt at a distance just slightly less than the hem depth.
- Turn up and press the hem; the stay-stitching should be visible on the hem allowance.
- Set up your machine with a twin needle and thread both needles with matching thread. Position the garment right side up in the machine so that the needles will stitch just below the serged edge or in the middle of it (feel the hem position with your fingers)—the idea is for the serging to support the zigzag of the bobbin thread and prevent the fabric from tunneling when you stitch. Begin stitching at a seam and sew around skirt. Press the hem from right side.
- If you don't want to use a twin needle, sew with the garment wrong side up, stitching along the center of the serging.

—*katlew03*

**841**  I've never been satisfied with a rolled hem, as it doesn't start or end well, and it's often uneven in width. Today I finished a shirt for my husband, and the single-fold hem from the pattern directions worked beautifully: overcast the bottom edge of the shirt, fold a narrow hem to the inside and stitch close to the inner edge. I did the overcast on my regular sewing machine and pressed the narrow edge up before stitching. The beginning and end (faced and interfaced edges) and the shirttail curves were perfect, and definitely looked professional. Even after laundering, that hem is still beautiful.

—*Annie- oh*

**842**  Any time you are hemming something that is curved you must realize that the turned up allowance must be eased to fit the smaller curve to which it will be attached. The fastest way to do this is to put the hem allowance next to the feed dogs and the outside of the item next to the foot. The feed dogs naturally want to pull the bottom layer a tiny bit faster than the top layer. I have gotten quite good at "feeling" the edge of the hem from the top of the fabric, and this method usually makes it cup under naturally. PRESS BEFORE TOPSTITCHING: sorry, just wanted to make sure you remembered that step, too!

—*Janie Viers*

**843**  I like shirts with shaped hems, but it's always so difficult to get those hems to lie flat along the curves. I stumbled on the idea of binding the edge instead of folding it for a hem when making my last shirt. Cut self-fabric bias strips just as you would for binding any edge. When you sew them to the bottom edge, be careful on the outside curves. They're harder to do than the inside curves and are more likely to stretch. After the binding is finished, gently press again to eliminate any wrinkles, especially on the outside curves.

—*xenophea*

**844**  I am making several summer tops from a pattern that has a shirttail hem. I finally figured out that pressing the curve up over a template gives a much smoother finish. You can make the template from a file folder: trace the curve of the pattern onto it and cut out. Place the garment wrong side up on the ironing board, position the template on the hemline, and then fold and press the fabric over it. There will be little folds/gathers on the curved part. Be certain to press well and let dry. You will have a lovely smooth curve!

—*ryansmum*

**845**  A narrower hem is better for curved edges, but even so, these hems are difficult to turn up and press as they are wider at the outside fold than where the stitching will go. Try this: Mark the fold line with chalk. Stay stitch just below the line, in the hem allowance. Turn up and press the hem; the stay stitching should be visible on the hem allowance. The stay stitching will pull the hem in almost automatically making the rest of the allowance lie flat.

—*Kirstenw*

## Differential feed eases curved hem allowance

*Hems with convex curves are always tricky because the perimeter of the hem allowance is bigger than the area to which it must be sewn. Two PatternReview.com members use the differential feed on their sergers to ease it prior to folding up.*

**846**  **Brine explains:** Here is my quick- and-dirty method of prepping a shirttail hem: serge just below the hem line using a differential feed setting of 0 until you get to a convex curve, increase the differential feed to stitch the curved section, and then return it to zero. Turn up the hem allowance and press; you'll see that on the convex curves the allowance has been drawn in to fit.

**847**  **redsquid adds:** Using the differential feed is quick when you've already planned to clean-finish the edge by serging. And it looks neat as there is no bubbling—a little careful pressing to prep and the hem is very flat! I set the differential at 1.2 to 2 (2 around stretchy bias curves) and either topstitch or hand sew the hem, depending on the garment and fabric.

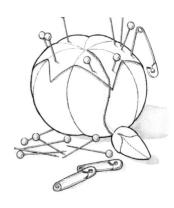

## ACCURATE PREP WHEN THE HEM DEPTH IS SET

**848** I hate measuring and pinning a hem. It's tedious, takes forever, and doesn't always result in a smooth line. Try this method; it's simple but effective. For example, say you need to turn up a 2" (5.1 cm)-deep hem:

- Place a strip of colored tape on your sewing machine bed, parallel with the needle plate and 2" (5.1 cm) from the needle.
- Thread your machine with a contrast color and baste all the way around your garment, keeping the raw edge of the fabric lined up with the tape.
- Finish the raw edge as usual (fold, zigzag, or serge). It doesn't matter if this is a bit wonky because you've already accurately marked the hem fold.
- Fold the hem up on the basting line and press it. You're ready to sew the hem.

—*Helen near Sydney*

**849** I needed to mark up a 2" (5.1 cm) deep hem. I measured a small yellow sticky-type note and found it to be exactly 2" (5.1 cm), so I measured with it, folded up the hem, and pinned.

—*sewinghappy*

**850** I've never gotten the hang of using tag board templates for marking and pressing up hems. Instead, what I do is mark twice the hem depth on the wrong side of the garment with chalk. I fold up the cut edge to the mark and press. Then I fold under the raw edge. I don't use a seam gauge to mark. What I've found works best is a 6" (15.2 cm)-square ruler (made, I think, for quilting). I place it over the inside of the garment, matching the raw edge with the grid line for twice the hem depth, then use chalk to make a continuous mark. Because you can see the marks (you aren't turning the fabric over them), I find this technique easy and very quick to do. And none of the marks will show on the right side of the garment.

—*Debbie Lancaster*

## HEMS TO THE OUTSIDE

**851** I decided to turn the neck edge, hems, and casings to the right side on a pair of fleece PJs; I wanted to show off the wrong side of my fabric but this also made the garments extremely comfortable since there are no edges on the inside. To use my technique you must have fabric with an attractive wrong side and you must construct the garment with flatlocked seams so there's no projecting seam allowance. Use matching or contrasting thread as you wish; experiment to see the effect:

- I used pearl crown rayon thread in the upper looper and finished the neck, hem, and casing edges with the wrong facing side up.
- Then I folded the neck edge and the hem and casing allowances to the right side and stitched each down along the top of the decorative serged edge.

—*drsue*

**852** Turning a hem to the outside can be a nice detail if your fabric looks the same on both sides, or if the wrong side makes a nice contrast. The problem is, how to keep an intersecting seam from showing on the outside? This is a technique I came up with to hide that seam, explained using a sleeve hem as an example:

- Before sewing the sleeve seam, press the hem up to the outside. Mark a spot on the seamline about ¼" to ½" (6 mm to 1.3 cm) below where the top of the finished hem will be. With WRONG sides together, sew the seam from the bottom to this spot; then clip the seam right to the stitching.
- Turn the sleeve inside out and align the seam edges above the clip—right sides together as usual. Sew the remainder of the seam from the clip to the end. Press the allowances on both parts of the seam open.
- You now have a seam that shows on the outside at the bottom, under the hem, and is on the inside for the rest of the sleeve. Complete the hem as you wish. I wouldn't use this technique on a fabric that ravels, but on a stable fabric it works great!

—*Irene Q*

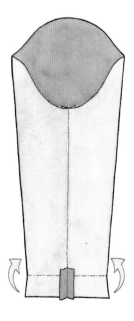
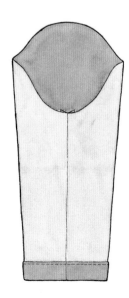

**853** I have a coverstitch machine, but sometimes it's just easier to use my twin needle. To prevent tunneling on knit tops, I serge or zigzag clear elastic (width of elastic = width of hem, if possible) to the wrong side of the hem, then turn and topstitch with the twin needle on the right side. The elastic provides the extra "beef" needed to prevent tunneling, plus it keeps the hem from getting too wavy or stretched out. The clear elastic doesn't seem to add any visible bulk on most knits. I also do this on my gym clothes, but I'll often use poly knit elastic as it's available in wider widths than clear elastic and is a better match for the thick, sturdy knits I use in my workout tops.

*—Jackie M*

**854** As with a lot of good tips, I made this discovery by accident. I was trying to hem a knit fabric with wide ribs and I couldn't get it to lie flat. So I aligned a length of blue painter's tape over the area to the immediate right of my stitching line and sewed the hem with a straight stitch. Perfect! The tape acts as a temporary stabilizer and provides a straight edge to guide your stitching. Of course, you will want to test your fabric to make sure the tape won't mar it. To avoid problems, I recommend sewing right after applying the tape and then removing the tape before you press the garment.

*—nanflan*

**855** The coverstitch hems on my stretchy knit t-shirts have been coming out really wavy. I decided to cut strips of water-soluble stabilizer and place under the fabric when sewing them. Then I throw the shirt in the washer and voilà! Great even hems.

*—Liane M*

**856** My sewing machine has a lot of problems making a decent, non-wavy twin-needle hem. I finally resolved this by using Wooly Nylon in the bobbin (threading it through the tension area, not bypassing it). I place torn strips of newspaper under the fabric, next to the feed dogs; then sew with matching poly thread in the twin needle. I tear away the newspaper after sewing. If the fabric is fragile, it's better to soak the hem before tearing away the wet newspaper.

*—Katharine in BXL*

**Deepika adds:** Tissue paper or a tear-away stabilizer might be easier to remove from the zigzag of the twin-needle bobbin than newspaper.

# Garment bits & pieces

*If you're looking for details that add a special touch or techniques that make assembly faster or easier, browse the creative odds and ends gathered here.*

## SEVEN COOL DETAIL HOW-TOS

**857** **Removable cowl.** I've developed a really easy way to make a detachable collar for a pullover top. I use it for cowls and even to add a turtleneck to a crew-neck shirt. The collar connects with tiny elastic loops to small buttons sewn inside the neck edge. I really enjoy doubling my options like this—I get a lot of extra use out of my garment with just one little trick!

- You need five small, flat buttons for a cowl (eight for a turtleneck) and $1/8$" (3 mm) elastic (I prefer flat elastic, but oval could work).
- First finish the neckline of the garment as usual and make the cowl or turtleneck with finished edges as well.
- For a cowl, sew five buttons to the underside of the neck edge, placing one on each shoulder seam, one at the center back, and the remaining two spaced evenly on each side between the shoulder seams and the center back. I don't put any buttons in the front, since the cowl will drape nicely and there's no need to attach it there. For a turtleneck, sew three buttons evenly spaced along the front neckline too.
- Cut elastic to make a loop for each button. To determine the size, fit the loops to the buttons on the garment. Inside your collar, sew the elastic loops to the underside of the lower edge, along the hem, attaching them so that the neckline of your garment slips under the lower edge of the collar, with the loop reaching under the garment edge to the button. This gives you a smooth line where the cowl joins the garment.

*—Noile*

**858** **Bias cuff bands.** If you have a full sleeve that is supposed to be finished at the wrist with an elastic in a casing, consider gathering it onto a bias binding instead. I find this more comfortable and better looking, though admittedly not as tight. Cut the bias strip long enough to form a ring through which you can slip your hand, and wide enough to make a short cuff—say $3/4$" (1.9 cm) finished—I think anything very wide might be risky as the bias might eventually distort. Sew the ends of the strip together to make a ring. Gather the bottom of the sleeve; attach the ring to it as you would a binding.

*—Margaret*

**859** **Unsew as you grow.** Often the extra room in maternity clothes may seem too much at the beginning of a pregnancy. If you have a machine that sews a chain stitch, try this quick and easy way to eliminate that feeling yet still have the additional room: On the side seams only, make two separate rows of chain stitching at ½" (1.3 cm) intervals inside the "real" seamline. When the time comes where you need the extra room, just pull out the chain stitching, and give the hem a slight adjustment.

—*newlywedws*

**Deepika adds:** Taper the added seams into the original side seam below the armscye so you don't run into trouble with the fit of your sleeve or facing.

**860** **Durable knees for little ones** Knees seem to be one of the first things to wear through on a boy's garment. To add durability as well as rugged styling I like to add a layer to the knee of boys' pants. This is great for little ones scooting their trucks around on the floor:

- Cut a piece of the fashion fabric so that the length equals the width of the pant leg. I've found that 6" (15.2 cm) works well for the width (top-to-bottom dimension) of this piece, but you'll need to experiment with wider or narrower to match the proportion to your garment size.
- Press under the top and bottom edges of the piece and then center it at knee height across the pant leg. Trim the side edges even with the leg edges. Topstitch the piece in place. Then construct the pants as usual.
- Optional: You could place a piece of batting under the knee band if you wish to make a padded knee. You could also quilt in various design lines onto the band if desired.

—*CharityAK*

**861** **Turned-up slit cuffs.** I bought a shirt that has a cool treatment for those turned-up cuffs that have a slit, usually found on three-quarter-length sleeves. The cuffs are separate pieces sewn to the sleeve with a French seam. This solves the problem I have of slits that split and ravel as soon as I start to wear the shirt, no matter how carefully I do them. The shirt was done this way:

- Shorten the sleeves to finish about 1" (2.5 cm) longer than the point where you want the cuff to fold back (this includes seam allowance for attaching the cuff) and set them into the body.
- Cut two cuffs with rounded ends like a regular shirt cuff: for each cut two layers of fabric (and maybe a light interfacing), planning them to be exactly the length of the sleeve bottom or longer if you want the ends to overlap; add seam allowances, making the one at the edge to be sewn to the sleeve 1" (2.5 cm) deep.
- Sew the cuffs, leaving the sleeve edge open, and turn them right side out. Press. Topstitch each ¼" (6 mm) inside the finished edge.
- Put the cuff on the inside of the sleeve, with the cut edges aligned and the slit or overlap placed where you want it. Typically, the slit is about one-quarter of the sleeve circumference to the back of the sleeve seam. Make sure the cuffs overlap in opposite directions on the two sleeves. Sew with ¼" (6 mm) seam allowance. Fold the cuff to the right side of the sleeve and press; then sew again with ⅝" (1.6 cm) seam allowance. Fold the seam allowance inside the sleeve side and press. Topstitch ¼" (6 mm) from the seam.

—*Debbie Lancaster*

**862** **Modesty panel.** I was tired when cutting out a T-shirt and grabbed the pattern for the lower-cut view, which I didn't realize until trying it on. Oops! Fortunately I had a scrap that made a pretty contrast to the fabric, and cut a piece on the lengthwise grain, which I turned 90 degrees to fill in the lower neckline/upper bust area. I topstitched it to the finished edge of the neckline and voila! Modesty prevails! I may even make this "mistake" again and use a contrasting fabric for a layered look without the actual layers. A good save!

—*Oopsy-Daisy!*

**863** **Sharp Western yokes** For most western-style shirts the yoke is appliquéd to the shirt body and many pattern instructions say to "press under the seam allowances" on the decorative edges. This can be kinda tricky, especially if they're fancy. Instead, I use this technique, borrowed from appliqué quilters:

- Cut a lining for the yoke from something very thin—organza, batiste, or lightweight interfacing. Trim ¹/₁₆" (1.6 mm) from the fancy (lower) edge of each lining piece.
- Sew the front and back yokes together at shoulder seams; sew the yoke linings together at shoulder seams too. Sew the shirt fronts to the shirt back. Press all the seam allowances open.
- Place the yoke and the lining right sides together, with the fancy edges even. Sew along each fancy edge; leave the armhole and neckline edges unsewn.
- Trim the seam allowance at the points and turn the piece right side out. Press; the tiny bit of trimming done on the lining pieces should keep them from showing.
- Now simply lay the assembled yoke on top of the shirt, aligning the shoulder seams and the neck and armhole edges. Pin the yoke in place and topstitch.

—*Diana M*

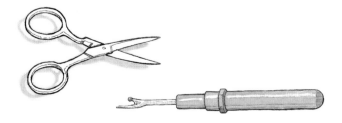

## PERFECT YOUR UNDERLINING TECHNIQUES

**864** I underlined a white silk charmeuse dress to eliminate seam allowance show-through and reduce wrinkling. Here's how I made sure the underlining would not become larger than the charmeuse due to the turn of the cloth at the seams:

- I cut the charmeuse and underlining from same pattern pieces.
- I laid the underlining on the wrong side of each corresponding charmeuse piece and pinned them together down the center, along the straight grain.
- Then, to adjust for the amount of space taken up by fabric's thickness when folded, I folded the piece in half over the pins. This forced the underlining to extend past the charmeuse at the edges.
- With the piece still folded, I hand basted the charmeuse to the underlining all around the perimeter.
- I trimmed the excess underlining after sewing the first step of my French seams (wrong sides together).

—*monahan*

**865** Here's a way to line, underline, and finish the edge of the seam allowance all at the same time. This is an easy and elegant way to finish any vertical seam in a garment. It eliminates the need for a lining, prevents seam allowance show-through on sheer fabrics, and gives a couture look to the inside of your garment. Plus it's not much more work than simply underlining (less, if you are planning to hand baste the layers together). It works on any vertical seam, as long as the seam is straight or only slightly contoured.

- When cutting your underlining, add ⁵⁄₈" (1.6 cm) to the allowances on the vertical seams; for instance, if you are using ⁵⁄₈" (1.6 cm) seam allowances cut them 1¼" (3.2 cm) wide.

- Place the underlining and fashion fabric right sides together. At each vertical edge, align and pin the layers together (the underlining will not lie flat as it is bigger than the fashion fabric). Sew the layers together at each vertical with a ¼" (6 mm) seam allowance.
- Turn the panels right sides out. Press the edges so the underlining wraps around the edge of the fashion fabric and lies flat, like a binding; this looks a bit like a Hong Kong Finish.
- Now you treat the two layers as one and complete your garment as usual. You can baste the upper edges together if necessary.

—*julieb*

Right sides together

Wrong sides together

## REPLACE FACINGS WITH BIAS STRIPS

**866** Instead of cutting and sewing facings for neck and armhole edges, use a bias strip of your fashion fabric, sewing it on and then turning it entirely to the inside of the garment along the seam. Because it's bias, the inside edge will stretch to lie flat as it follows the curve. Here's what to do:

- Trim the seam allowance on the garment edge to be ³⁄₈" (1 cm) wide.
- Cut the bias strip 1¼" (3.2 cm) wide and 2" (5.1 cm) longer than the edge to be faced. Press under ³⁄₈" (1 cm) along one long edge.
- With the right sides together, sew the opposite edge of the bias strip to the garment edge, stretching slightly on inside curves. (If you need to join the strip ends, stop and do so, then finish sewing it on.)

- Trim the seam allowance to be very narrow. Turn the garment inside out. Fold the bias to the inside on the seamline and press it, stretching the loose edge as you go.
- With the right side of the garment facing up in your machine, edgestitch or topstitch through all layers close to the seamed edge. Then stitch again at a distance that looks nice and secures the loose edge of the bias too. (Or use a twin needle or a decorative stitch to secure the facing in one pass.)
- I often apply this kind of facing to an armhole before sewing the garment side seam. Then I sew the side seam from hem to armhole, stitching through the facing.

—*katlewo3*

**867** Lately I have become frustrated with making facings on clothing—especially the facing at a skirt waist, which often won't stay in place unless sewn down and can be bulky. So I decided to replace the facing with purchased single-fold bias tape. I unfolded one edge of the bias tape, placed it wrong side up on the right side of the skirt, and stitched it on along the fold line. Once the stitching was completed, I turned the bias tape to the inside of the skirt, and stitched the opposite side down. This made the waist so much more comfortable.

—*newlywedws*

**868** Here's a way to ease a sleeve cap in one step: Holding your index finger against the back of the presser foot, sew ½" (1.3 cm) from the cut edge using a basting stitch. Sew for 2" to 3" (5.1 to 7.6 cm), lift your finger to release the stitched fabric, and repeat. If the cap is too tight when you're done, clip the thread in a couple of places so it releases. If it's still too loose, lift the bobbin thread with a pin and then pull it to tighten.

—*Jennifer shaw*

**869** I use Seams Great (lightweight nylon seam tape) for easing in the fullness in fitted sleeve caps. I place the sleeve cap wrong side up in my machine, lay the Seams Great over the seam allowance, and sew about ½" (1.3 cm) from the cut edge, pulling the Seams Great taut as I go. This causes a slight gathering that is usually just enough to work nicely into the armhole. I love this stuff and have been using it for years this way !!

—*anetjay*

**870** This is a tip that I received from Shannon Gifford in her "Stitch and Flip Jacket" class on PatternReview. com. I was having difficulty easing my sleeve cap evenly—little tucks were forming along seamline and I was getting frustrated. Here's what Shannon suggested: "Use three rows of basting. Stitch one row on the stitching line, the second row ⅛" (3 mm) to one side of the first line, and the third row ⅛" (3 mm) to the other side of the first line. Draw up the basting until the cap fits into the armscye. Then take the sleeve to the ironing board, and press the area that has been eased. Use lots of steam, and let the sleeve cap cool before stitching it into the armscye. After you stitch it into the armscye, remove the basting. There may still be some small dimples, but the sleeve head will fill those out and make them disappear." This procedure caused the seam line to curve appropriately and the sewing went much smoother—not perfect—but MUCH better!

—*CSM--Carla*

**Deepika adds:** Be sure to read Shannon's master class on page 152 of this book. And here's the URL for the class Carla took: http://sewing.patternreview.com/cgi-bin/ sewingclasses/class.pl?id=40

**871** To increase the strength of an armhole seam, many pattern instruction sheets tell you to sew again along the bottom of the armhole after you've set in a sleeve. Instead of trying to go back and sew again, try this: I start sewing on one side between the shoulder and the side seam, follow this all around and continue around to end up on the other side between the shoulder and side seam. This means you go all around the armhole and the under arm area is sewn twice.

—*Mary Stiefer*

**872** A professional seamstress gave me this tip a long time ago: Always make sure you are using your flat bed extension when setting in a sleeve in the traditional way. This helps to eliminate drag on the sleeve or garment. Of course, this is logical, but it is good to remember when we get going with a sewing project.

—*mamacita*

## *Nine tips for sewing a bias garment*

**LauraLo** *says, "I like bias-cut garments very much. I find them flattering for the figure and feminine. My first bias skirt, tried years ago, was a total wadder that left me so depressed I've only recently tried again." Here are handling tips she developed that help to tame the unstable pieces:*

**873** Especially when working with thin slippery fabrics, I use homemade starch to make the fabric as stiff as possible. It's very easy to work with it afterwards. Caution however, from my experience, starched fabrics tend to dry off grain and you have to straighten them when pressing, before cutting.

**874** Staystitch waistlines, necklines, and armholes immediately after cutting.

**875** Stabilize zip openings (I use premade fusible tape or strips of fusible knit). A good idea is to center the strips on the seamline and thus your zip won't "poke" (as happens on my bias RTW skirts).

**876** Stitch the darts (in thin fabrics) using the one-thread technique, which makes the point perfect (see els' tip on page 117 for how to do this).

**877** Normally the bias doesn't fray, so you could leave the seams unfinished. However, satin does fray quite a lot. I prefer to leave the seams unfinished and press them apart. When sewing satin, I serge the allowances together (the finishing needs to be elastic, to have some give, just like the stitching).

**878** Sew side seams using a stretch stitch (a narrow zigzag, 0.5 mm width and about 2.5 mm length) and gently stretch the seam while sewing.

**879** Mark the stitching lines, either with vanishing pencil, chalk or by thread-tracing. If you use your presser foot as a guide and stretch while sewing, the seam allowances will appear narrower; then when finished and the seam allowances relax, you will discover they are much wider (1" [2.5 cm] for instance instead of the ⅝" [1.5 cm] you thought). As a result, the garment will be narrower (especially after hanging) and cling too much to your body.

**880** Experiment with wider allowances. The excess often stretches when the garment hangs, reducing the amount to the standard that you're used to.

**881** Always hang the garment overnight. I usually hang it for 72 hours. You will find out that it gets longer and narrower and your initial hemline gets distorted: the skirt is longer in some places and shorter in others. After hanging, I correct the hemline, decide the length, and sew a narrow hem or I use my serger to do a rolled hem.

**Deepika adds:** Some people baste vertical seams (lightly, by hand or with pins) and hang the garment overnight, test and adjust the fit, and then sew permanently.

**882** If you have ever tried to cut out and sew a tiny item like a patch pocket or an appliqué you know that preserving the shape and not messing up the stitching line is nerve racking! Here's what I do—the result is no raw edges to turn, no little seam allowances to cut, no tiny corners to turn:

- Draw the shape outline (without seam allowance) onto the wrong side of the fabric but do not cut out! Place a backing fabric underneath, so the layers are right sides together, and pin.

- Sew completely around the shape on the marked line with a very small stitch, leaving NO opening for turning.
- Trim the fabric outside the stitched outline. Make a tiny slit in the backing, turn right side out, and finger-press or steam and, voilà, instant appliqué or pocket.
- If you use iron-on interfacing for a backing, be sure to put the glue side against the feed dogs. Once slit and turned, carefully finger-press and then press with an iron: the glue from the interfacing will adhere to the top fabric.

—*Janie Viers*

**883** I always struggle to get patch pockets correctly positioned. And I'm lazy, so hand basting is not high on my list. Instead I use fusible thread to help: First I press under the raw edges of the pocket. With the fusible thread in the bobbin and the pocket right side up, I stitch around the edge using a long stitch. Neatness doesn't count so this is perfect for me! Then I position the pocket on the garment and fuse it in place. Once the pocket is adhered, I pull out the basting thread on the right side and permanently sew the pocket in place.

—*ValerieJ*

**Deepika adds:** Use this for any patch pocket, appliqué, or similar embellishment.

**884** This is a way to avoid interfacing the top portion of a patch pocket (front bands on shirts are sometimes made this way too). Pocket patterns typically have a portion on the top that is folded over to form a facing and this section is also interfaced. Try this instead: On the pocket pattern, double the facing depth. Once you've cut out the pocket, fold the facing section in half to the wrong side to form the interfacing. Then construct the pocket as usual, folding the top section to the outside and stitching on the seamlines, then turning this back to the inside.

—*Irene Q*

## TAILORING HINTS

**886** To minimize bulk at the neck of a tailored jacket, press the allowances open on the neckline seams—the seams that join the upper collar to the facings and the under collar to the jacket body. Then, once the collar and jacket body are turned right side out, align the neck seams on the facings and body (the collar allowances will be inside the collar), lift the facings, and sew the facing and body neck allowances together—by hand or by machine with a zipper foot. Isn't it beautiful? Light and without bulk.

—*LauraLo*

**887** When making a tailored jacket, I prefer to make shaped sleeve heads instead of using a straight strip of soft fabric. I find a shaped piece gives more satisfactory results and supports the sleeve cap better. I use either Armo Fleece or HTC Fleece. Using the sleeve pattern, I cut a shaped piece that follows the contour of the sleeve cap and is approximately 2" (5.1 cm) deep. After setting in the sleeve, I hand sew the sleeve head to the seam allowance along the stitching line.

—*Sew4Fun*

**885** A quilting friend taught me this cool method for invisibly adding a hanging sleeve after the quilt is finished. You can add patch pockets with a variation of this method as well: First cut the sleeve the length and width you want it to be plus seam allowances; press under the seam allowances. Lay wrong sides together along the top edge of the quilt. Stitch the top edge very close to the top of quilt. Here's the neat trick: Lay the quilt right side up, with the sleeve at the left edge. Fold back the quilt just to the left of the loose edge of the sleeve. Now attach the quilt to the sleeve using the blind hem foot, just nipping into the backing with the point of the zigzag stitch. This seam doesn't show on the front and is secure enough to hold it securely.

—*Patti B*

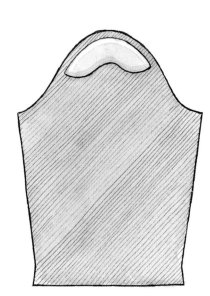

## TAILORED SLEEVE PLACKET

**888** A one-piece sleeve placket is easy to make this way. (If you don't have a pattern piece like the one shown, you can easily draft one.) Not only is this the best looking placket I ever have seen, it's also very strong and very easy once you know how to make it.

- Transfer the pattern lines to fusible interfacing, make sure to reverse the pattern for the second piece. Fuse it to the fabric and cut it out. Position the piece on the sleeve so that right side of the placket is against the wrong side of the sleeve.
- Sew along the outline of vent opening (the shaded column in the diagram) and cut it open with a V in the top, turn through the opening, and press the edge.

- Then press the back section of the placket toward the front and fold it on the dot-dash lines; secure it with a line of straight stitches, this should cover the "hole."
- Press the seam allowances on the front section (the point) to the wrong side, folding it on the dot-dash lines as you do this. It should now lie over the back placket. Move the back placket out of the way and secure the front one by stitching as indicated by the dotted lines.

—*Karin Mantefors*

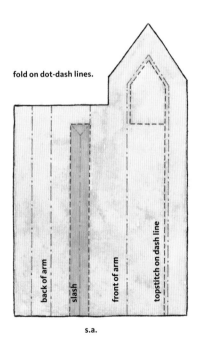

fold on dot-dash lines.

back of arm

slash

front of arm

topstitch on dash line

s.a.

## CUT THE BULK FROM PANTS

**889** We all have those little hills and valleys in the hip and thigh area. Here's a tip to smooth out the side seam silhouette on pants. Press the side seam allowances open. Cut a 1" (2.5 cm) strip of interfacing that's as long as the area from waist to knee. Fuse this strip to the open side allowance. Press on the outside for a smooth, sleek look.

—*BJ1400*

**890** Disclaimer at the start: I only do this for children's clothes. My sewing perfectionism won't let me do this for my own pants, since it's not very RTW. But I can deal with it on kids' clothes (especially if they're for MY kids): I press the center front and center back seam allowances to one side, and press both in the same direction. That is, if I press one to the left, then I press the other to the left. Then when I line up the crotch seams to sew the inseam, the allowances lie in opposite directions. This makes for less bulk, which makes it easier to sew over the join without having a machine hesitate and make non-uniform stitches (one of my pet peeves).

—*khurtdvm*

## GOOD FACINGS

**891** The facing can make or break a neckline, depending on how well it is done. Here are some steps I follow to get a nice, flat facing.

- Use a serger to clean finish the outside edge. This gives a much flatter finish than turning under and stitching.
- After sewing on the facing, trim the seam allowances, holding the scissors at a bit of an angle in order to "grade" them. This means that one allowance will be slightly narrower than the other.
- Clip all the curves close up to the stitching, cutting at an angle to the fabric grain. Don't be afraid to have too many clips; they will give you a smoother seam.
- Press the seam allowance toward the facing over a ham.
- Use a blind hem foot to understitch the allowance to the facing.
- When you turn the facing to the inside, press over the ham again, rolling the seam line slightly to the inside with your fingers.
- I often use something like Steam A Seam to tack down the facing in the front and back—test first to make sure it will not show or pull.

*—Nancywin*

**892** Here's a great way to finish the edge of a facing and add the interfacing at the same time. It works for both sew-in and fusible interfacings:

- First, seam together any facing pieces that will be sewn to each other (for instance, the shoulder seams of a neck facing) and do the same with the interfacing. Trim and press the facing, and finger press the interfacing.
- Place the facing and interfacing right sides together. Stitch along the edge that usually would be clean finished using ¼" (6 mm) seam allowance. Any where the facing would be turned under a full seam allowance, stitch using an allowance a tad less than usual. Do not stitch the bottom edge of a shirt center front facing—leave it free just as you would normally. Trim and clip.
- Turn the facing and interfacing wrong sides together. If the interfacing is fusible, fuse it in place. If not, press and baste along the open edge. Then attach the facing as usual. This produces a beautifully finished facing, no serging, turning under, or zigzagging needed.

*—Debbie Lancaster*

**893** How to finish the edge of a facing nicely has been bothering me for a while. I really like my garments to be as nice inside as out. My mother, who taught me to sew, simply folds the edge over once and hems, and that gave me this idea: I stay-stitch fairly close to the edge of the facing. Then I fold over the edge once along the stay stitching, press, and then do a simple decorative stitch along the edge. The folded edge is neat and very flat, and the density of the stitch pattern stops the fabric fraying. And the effect is so pretty!

*—Annelune*

## POCKETS ON PANTS

**894** This is a side-seam pocket technique that I saw in several patterns. It looks very ready-to-wear when finished and could be used for any pants pattern that has side-seam pockets or no pockets. Basically, the front pocket piece becomes a facing, with the seam offset from the side seamline just enough for you to later sew the side seam from the waist to hem without catching the faced edge:

- Interface the opening edge of the front pocket bag (the piece to be sewn to the pants front).
- Place this piece right sides together with the pants front, and sew a box-shaped seam as shown below; stitch the vertical portion just slightly to the garment side of the seamline. Clip to the corners, trim the allowance, and turn the pocket/facing to the wrong side and edge-stitch.

- Now sew the back pocket bag to the front one along the curved, inner edge and press the pocket toward the pants front. If you've done it right, you can stitch the pants front to pants back at the outseam along the regular seamline and just miss the faced opening. Since the top and bottom horizontal edges of the opening are faced, there is no chance of fraying (see below).

*—Lisa Laree*

**895** To help prevent the bias edge of a slant pocket from stretching, cut the pocket facing piece so that the grainline is running parallel to the slanted edge. Note that this won't work for pockets with curved opening edges—the opening must be fairly straight!

*—Lisa Laree*

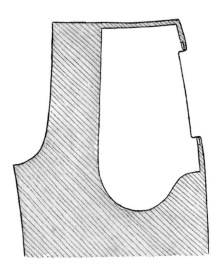

## NICE NECKBANDS

**896** After the neckband has been applied to a knit shirt, do one more step using a twin needle and Woolly Nylon thread in the bobbin: topstitch the neckband/shirt seam, keeping the seam centered between the needles. This is basically a faux coverstitch. It gives a very RTW look on the neckline and has the bonus of holding the band flatter too!

—*Lisa Laree*

**897** Here's an easy sequence for putting a neckband on a knit pullover: Put your shirt together at one shoulder (or if it has raglan sleeves, at three seams). While it is flat, attach the neckband and finish the seam. Then serge the remaining shoulder seam, continuing across the neckband ends. You can do cuffs the same way.

—*salruss*

## EASY BRA PADDING

**898** Fiberfill can be used in any soft-cup bra pattern to add some body and modesty. Use iron-on fiberfill, and cut the pieces using the cup pattern. Press on and use as the inner lining for the cup pieces. It's great stuff.

—*Dale C*

## Sew for your home too

*You can dress your home exactly the way you like if you sew your own soft furnishings. Here a few tips specific to pillows and drapes.*

## MAKE PILLOWS LIKE A PRO

**899** Recently, I made some large bolster pillow forms for my couch. If you use batting as a backing for your pillow forms it will keep them looking smooth, not lumpy. Just cut the batting the same size as each piece of pillow form fabric; then baste together. Sew and stuff the form. You can fill it with polyfill, batting bits, or shredded foam; whichever you use, the finished form will be smooth.

—*Dale C*

**900** If you are struggling to get a pillow form into its cover, just wrap it in plastic first: Recycle one of the many plastic bags we seem to accumulate, cutting it open so you have a long strip. Wrap this around the form with the loose ends in hand. Then slip the form into the cover. To remove the plastic, take hold of one of the loose ends and pull out the plastic. You may have to reach into the cover and slide the free end down toward the bottom of the form to get it started.

—*PattiAnnSG*

## LAYER DRAPERY PANELS WITH EASE

**906** I was making ten panels of drapes lined with cotton sateen lining, working on the floor because they were large, and having trouble getting the lining smoothly positioned on each panel prior to sewing. Then I remembered reading the trick to put a plastic bag around a pillow form before inserting it into a pillow casing. The eureka moment: plastic makes fabric scoot! So I laid a sheet of thin plastic painter's tarp on top of the drapery fabric and trimmed it slightly smaller than the panel. When I placed the lining on top, a minimal amount of pushing got the alignment correct because the plastic kept the lining from sticking to the drapery fabric. Then I pinned the lining to the drapery fabric and gently pulled out the plastic. A headache solved.

—*utz*

### ✎ *Five tips for perfect pillows*

**Anncie** *says, "I do lots of custom interiors and everyone wants pillows and more pillows. Here's what I do for a great-looking pillow:"*

**901** When you sew your pillow square make sure you reinforce your corners; I restitch the corners when I'm done.

**902** Don't pivot at the corners. Sew all the way off the fabric, cut your threads, and sew the next side. When done, clip your corners just above the meeting threads and trim a bit off each side at the corner so it looks like a point. Press all seams open before turning! This eliminates creased sides and ensures the tips of the pillow are nice and pointy.

**903** If using a pillow form, trifold your fabric and make a cover or add a zipper opening. Make your pillow measurement about ¼" (6 mm) smaller on all sides. Now the form will fit tightly and your pillow will look smooth even when "abused".

**904** For those of you who like to use stuffing, separate the fill first, stuff the corners and then stuff the middle. I use a wooden spoon from the kitchen. The spoon keeps your hands out of the hole and keeps you from stretching the opening

**905** Close the opening using a fusible web tape. This finish looks seamless and nobody can tell where you closed it.

# CHAPTER EIGHT

# Finishing

> " *I absolutely love love sewing!
> It's more than a hobby, it's more than a
> passion, it is a genuine addiction that keeps
> me some evenings for hours in front of
> the sewing machine, bringing my husband
> to despair.* "
>
> —LauraLo

# Topstitching chat

*Topstitching gives a crisp decorative finish to seams and edges. It seems such a no-brainer, but these tips for how to keep the fabric from jamming, turning corners, and using the right thread make it truly trouble-free.*

## KEEP THE FABRIC FEEDING SMOOTHLY UNDER THE FOOT

**907** To keep a collar point or similar element from getting hung up when you pivot while topstitching, try this technique:

- Keep a hand-sewing needle threaded with a doubled thread about 6" (15.2 cm) long by the sewing machine (don't knot the thread).
- As you approach the corner when stitching, run the hand needle through the very tip of the corner, pull the thread about halfway through, and just leave it there.

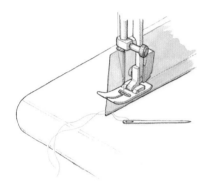

- When you are ready to pivot at the corner, grab both sets of thread tails (the needle end and the free end) and tug them gently to put some tension on the point; this will keep it moving through the machine.
- Once the presser foot is well past the corner, the needle and thread can just be pulled out and stuck back in the pincushion until you've another corner to topstitch.

—*Lisa Laree*

**908** When I topstitch corners with a twin needle, I stitch close up to the corner and then cut the threads leaving long tails. Then pulling a few inches of thread to leave thread tails at the start, I pivot the fabric and start stitching again close to the corner. When I finish stitching, I thread a needle with the long thread tails at the corner and complete the lines of stitches by hand, so they meet at the corner. (Sometimes I have to undo a stitch to finish the inside line.) Then I pull the thread tails to the wrong side and bury them between the layers.

—*JudyP*

**909** I have been machine-quilting a heavily padded fabric sandwich, and had problems with little tucks forming on the bottom layer—the layer closest to the feed dogs. Since I quilted the sandwich with the top layer down (with nice thread in the bobbin), I could not ignore the tucks. Rip, rip, and then hand quilt past the problem spot! When hand quilting, I draped the sandwich over my hand (with the top side up), and this helped ease the layers evenly. This gave me an idea: if I could machine stitch with the sandwich draped similarly, the tucks might be prevented. To accomplish this, I lift the front of the sandwich as high as I can to get a rounded shape as the fabric enters the feed dogs. It works even better than I imagined: no more tucks at all, and the finished quilting looks really smooth when I turn the piece right side up. I imagine that this method could be used for easing bottom layers in many situations, not just for quilting.

—*Asa Hagstrom*

## MASTERING TOPSTITCHING THREADS

**910** I like to topstitch jeans with heavy thread but my sewing machine doesn't like it. First I tried to put the heavy thread at the top and the bottom (in the bobbin). It didn't work very well, even if I tried to adjust the tensions, the stitches were uneven. Second, I tried to put the heavy thread at the top only and standard thread in the bobbin, but the heavy thread always jammed at on the wrong side and I still could not get the tension even. Finally, I tried the heavy thread in the bobbin only and standard thread in the top—and it works very well. Alleluia! So if you have problems with a special thread, try to put it in the bobbin.

—*Juli_et*

**911** Here's a way I add support to specialty threads such as metallics, shiny rayons, or variegated types that tend to break easily when used for decorative topstitching or embellishment.

- Make sure to use a topstitch or embroidery needle in the machine, as these have an elongated eye especially made for this purpose.
- Thread the machine with the specialty thread. Using a second spool pin at the top, run a thread of clear monofilament through the threading path too.
- Thread both the specialty thread and the monofilament through the needle together. This adds the support needed, you can't see the clear thread, and the fancy, yet temperamental, specialty thread gets structural support.

—*ShereeSews*

**912** I have always had trouble getting my topstitching for a pants fly to look right. So I tried using freezer paper as a template and found it works great! Just place the tissue pattern under a piece of freezer paper (with shiny side of freezer paper down) and trace the topstitching line. Cut the template out, position on the right side of the pants at the fly, and iron it in place with a warm dry iron. Then just stitch around the template. The template is repositionable if you don't get it lined up right the first time and it is reusable a number of times. Label it and keep with the pattern for the next time you need it. This idea could be used for other top-stitching areas if desired.

—*Jill Giard*

**913** I hate trying to eliminate that last tiny thread end that can ruin the look of topstitching at the center front or hem edge of garments. It's much easier to conceal if you start the topstitching about ³/₈" away from a finished edge with your machine set to backstitch. You'll stitch backwards to the edge of the garment, then forward to complete your line of topstitching; at the other end, you'll stitch to the edge, then backstitch. Trim the thread on the right side of the garment first, then give the wrong side thread a little tug before you trim it, so that the right side thread end is pulled to the inside.

—*Karla Kizer*

# Fastener chat

*If a zipper isn't called for, chances are you need buttons or snaps to hold your garment closed. Sewing them on is the easy part; spacing, marking, making buttonholes or loops, matching buttons to fabric, and affixing non-sew snaps take wits—handily supplied here by PatternReview.com members.*

## SMART IDEAS FOR NO-SEW SNAPS

**914** I've been squishing prongs on a lot of teeny-tiny purse snaps. I am always concerned that the pliers will scratch the metal face of the snap, so I used put a piece of thickish cloth between the snap and the pliers. Now, this obscured the snap and meant I worked blind and wasn't sure the snap was in the right place. It finally dawned on me to make a mitten for the pliers. I took some heavy, upholstery-weight faux suede, wrapped it around one jaw on the pliers, marked it with my marker and then sewed it. I can simply slip it onto the jaw whenever I need it.

—*MaryLynn in Long Beach*

**915** Anyone who puts in a lot of no-sew snap fasteners will no doubt want a snap-setting tool, but here's how to put them in if you don't have the tool. You need a firm surface with padding (washcloth on a table), a hammer, a pencil with a good eraser, a spool (the small Coats brand works for me), and some chalk. Mark your installation points on the underlap side of the placket as you would buttons (left front for a woman). Make sure that you understand which of the four parts of the snap goes where:

A. Decorative part with prongs, right side of the fabric, on the top layer of the placket or opening (where the button-holes would be).

B. Flat circle with a ring, underneath the decorative part.

C. Circle with the stud, right side of the fabric on the underside of the placket (where the button would be).

D. Open circle with prongs, underneath the stud part (next to the skin).
To install, begin with the stud half:

• Place piece D, with the prongs up, on your work surface; lay the fabric on it, and use the pencil eraser to firmly and smoothly push the prongs completely through the fabric.
• Center piece C, stud-side up, over the prongs, making sure you get ALL the prongs into the groove.
• Hold the spool on top of this, fitting the center hole over the little stud, and hammer firmly. Check for tightness; if you can get a thumbnail in between the snap and the fabric, hammer again!
• When all the studded halves are installed, put chalk on the studs. Very carefully, lay the other side of the

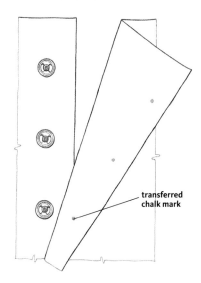

**transferred chalk mark**

placket on top and press your finger over the studs to chalk-mark where the decorative half of the snap goes.
• Repeat the process to install the decorative, socket half of the snap (pieces B and A). If you are using a pearl snap, the padded surface is very important, that pretty surface can crack!

—*Diana M*

## DRESSED UP BUTTONHOLES

**916** I have taken to making bound buttonholes, which look like miniature welted pockets, and to my eye, don't have the "made at home" look of machine zigzagged buttonholes. There are directions for making them in most basic sewing books and you can find them online too. I like my welts on the bias because they have better recovery and there is no need to match stripes or plaids that way. You don't always have to use the same fabric as the garment; I have seen contrasting bound buttonholes made of velvet and boy, did they look exquisite. If you've not made these, don't worry about messing up; practice on scraps.

*—Seamingly Simple*

**917** When I completed my latest jacket, I wasn't happy with the buttonholes. So I figured that I'd just hide them! I used ¼" (6 mm)-wide ribbon to create little mitered frames, and I hand stitched one around each buttonhole. I sewed the miters, trimmed the seams, and sealed the edges with Fray Check.

*—salruss*

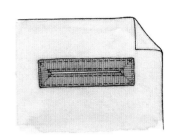

## MARK BUTTONHOLES WITH EASE

**918** I hate measuring button and buttonhole placement and have nearly quit doing it. Here's what I do instead—this is one of those things that's a lot easier to do than describe:

- Complete the top except for buttons/buttonholes and try it on. Using straight pins, pin the center front closed at the neck and at the fullest part of your bust (the top is likely to gap if there's no button there). With other straight pins, mark those locations on the right front and remove the pins holding the top closed.
- If you have a long, loose fitting top that only needs four buttons, fold the right front down at the bust-level pin; the place on the center front that now lies under the neckline pin is the location for button #3; place a pin there. Now, fold the shirt down from the level of button #3; the place under the bust-level pin is the location for the bottom button. You now have four evenly spaced button locations marked and you never picked up a measuring tool!
- If you need more closely spaced buttons, fold the top so that the neckline pin meets the bust-level pin and put a mark at the fold (dividing distance between the two original marks). Now, fold the top at the bust-level pin mark the front opposite the neckline and second pins. You can keep folding and pinning button placement until you get as many as you need and they will all be the same distance apart.

*—Lisa Laree*

**919** By chance, I experimented and found a good way to keep my buttonholes straight. I just finished a jacket made from silk tweed. Because of the various colors in the fabrics, marking the line with chalk was not possible. It dawned on me that I could baste the center line with long stitches in a bright thread color. The basting stitches give a strong guide to follow and don't rub off from handling. It is simple to pull them out when slashing the buttonhole. This technique could be used for any buttonhole, not just on hard to mark fabrics.

*—Kellie R.*

**920** When I need to adjust and transfer evenly spaced markings for buttonholes, I use elastic as a guide. I lay the elastic (relaxed, not stretched) on my pattern tissue and mark the buttonhole placement onto it. Then I lay the marked elastic on my fabric and transfer the marks. If I need the buttonholes spread further apart, I just stretch the elastic and the interval automatically adjusts. I pin the elastic in place at the top and bottom buttonhole positions and then mark all the in between positions alongside the stretched elastic. This obviously works only to transfer same-size or larger-spaced marks.

*—tweedcurtain*

## CUT THEM SAFELY; DON'T LET THEM FRAY

**921** Sew your buttonholes over a piece of fusible web placed, but not fused, on top of the fabric. After sewing, pull off the extra web and then fuse the stitched outline. Let cool and then cut open buttonhole. The web adds strength and minimizes any raveling.

*—comocosews*

**922** After you have sewn your buttonholes and before you cut them, put a small drop of Fray Check on a small piece of wax paper or something similar. Dip the tip of a pin into the Fray Check and dab it on the buttonhole between the stitching lines. Let it dry for 5 minutes. Then cut the opening. The inside is nice and neat and does not fray.

*—Sew it seams*

**923** I once cut right through the end of a buttonhole while trying to open it with a seam ripper. Since it was on a hand-embroidered blouse I had made for my daughter, I was visibly upset. Some people place pins across the ends of the buttonhole to preclude this problem, but since I don't like the idea of dulling my seam ripper by running it into a pin, I came up with this alternative: Starting at the middle of the buttonhole I poke the point of my seam ripper down through the cloth and bring it up just before the bar tack at the end. That way when I make the cut, I know that I won't go through the bar tack. I then turn the work around and cut from the center to the other end of the buttonhole in the same way.

*—Brine*

## THIS & THAT ABOUT BUTTONS

**924** If you are not sure which size button you need for your blouse or jacket, or if you want to use a different size than the pattern suggests, you can use this rule of thumb: The diameter of the button should be the same or slightly more than the distance from the center front to the garment edge—this means that when buttoned, the width of the placket visible next to the button is half of or slightly less than the button diameter. If you are making horizontal buttonholes, make sure they do not extend into the garment a distance greater than the width from center front to the edge—if you do, there will be flesh or your underwear visible behind them because the underlap won't be wide enough behind them.

—*els*

**925** To protect your buttons for dry cleaning or the washing machine, cover them with shields of Velcro tape. For each button, cut a length of Velcro (both the hook and loop halves) about 1" (2.5 cm) longer than the button diameter. Cut a slit that extends from one end a bit more than halfway across the hook half of the tape. Slip this piece under your button, and cover the button with the soft, loop half, pressing the tape halves together at the extending edges.

—*els*

**926** I always know where to find a replacement button if I have initially sewn an extra discreetly inside the garment. This saves money (especially if you have to buy a whole card) and time (especially if you are like me and have 2 million buttons floating around everywhere from jewelry box to baby food jars in the utility room).

—*Janie Viers*

## BUTTON SEWING KNOW-HOW

**928** I usually sew my buttons on by machine, with a zigzag stitch and the feed dog down. Once in a while there seems to be a thread that, if pulled, makes all of your stitches come undone. So now, after sewing on the buttons, I put a drop or two of Fray Check on the thread (on the inside of the garment) and—so far—this has worked to keep the threads from unravelling.

—*Mary Stiefer*

**929** Here's an easy way to hold a button in position so you can sew it on by hand or machine: Mark button placement with anything of your choice except a water erasable pen. Moisten (very slightly) a small scrap of water-soluble stabilizer and put it over your "button mark." Then moisten the back of the button very slightly and put it on the mark, on top of the stabilizer—the button will stay in place. Once you've sewn it on, spritz with some water to dissolve the stablizer. No struggles.

—*Judy Wentz*

**930** To sew on buttons quickly, thread your needle with more than one strand of thread (up to four or so), double and knot, and sew your button with one or two stitches. For really closely spaced buttons, don't even cut the thread, just move on to the next button, stitch, knot, and move on.

—*Debbie Lancaster*

**931** A common way to hold a sew-through button above the garment while you stitch it in place—so a thread shank forms—is to place a toothpick or something like it under the button. This doesn't work very well for me because the toothpick always seems to move away while I'm trying to hold it in place and stitch at the same time. Using a straight pin underneath does not usually give me enough height for a shank. Today I discovered that if I place the thick end of a sewing machine needle under my button with the pointed end secured into the fabric just beyond the button, I get the perfect size thread shank and the needle stays put until I remove it.

—*Sew it seams*

## HELP FOR BUTTON-COVERING BLUES

**927** I have been working on a blouse made of very slippery fabric and needed nine buttons. I wanted covered buttons but was not having much success making them until I came up with the following process. Once I got the hang of this, it was so relaxing to make these, I did a few extra buttons, in case I lose some after the blouse is made.

- After cutting the fabric for each button, fuse a small piece of Wonder Tape (paper-backed narrow fusible web) to the center of the wrong side of each piece. Remove the paper backing. Center the fabric on the button form, pressing into place with your fingers.
- Insert the fabric and button form together into the mold. Use a blunt object (like the eraser end of a pencil) to tuck the fabric onto the points of the form. Then snap the back cover into place and remove the button from the mold.

—*Lucy in Virginia*

## BUTTONHOLES FOR KNITS

**932** Vertical buttonholes are the best choice for knits fabrics, as they will stretch less than horizontal ones. I don't know about you, but once I finish the buttonhole portion of a project I feel like I can breathe a sigh of relief—the rest of the project should be pretty easy from there.

—*Sarah J Doyle*

**933** Buttonholes in knit fabrics used to give me the heebie-jeebies. Then I accidentally came across this technique: Cut a separate interfacing pattern for right and left fronts. Assuming your garment laps right over left, cut the left front interfacing as usual, to the fold line. Cut the right interfacing so it extends beyond the fold line and ¼" (6 mm) or more past center front—this provides double the stability under the buttonholes. Fuse the interfacing and then sew the buttonholes as usual. I dreaded those buttonholes, but the first time I did this they surprised me—they came out perfect with my plain ol' Kenmore. In fact, I was using a thermal knit and the placket was just about the only part of the garment that was NOT stretched out!

—*kv*

## BUTTON LOOP KNOW-HOW

**934** If you find that thread button loops tend to tangle, pull out, and twist too much, here's a suggestion for an alternative. You have to plan ahead, because these have to be added during construction: Hold two long strands of elastic thread side-by-side, thread through the hole in your presser foot (use a cording foot if you have one), and set the machine to a zigzag stitch just wide enough to cover the threads. Zigzag them together using a piece of Solvy (not necessary, but easier) under them. Don't make the zigzag too dense, as you want them to stretch over the button. If you use Solvy, rinse off and let the joined elastic dry. Cut into lengths measured to fit when slightly stretched over your button. Fold into loops and insert in the seam when you attach the facing (orient with tails in the seam allowance); I usually go over the area with the loops with a very small stitch to help prevent them from pulling out.

*—Sewshable1*

**935** I just made a pattern that features thread loops and buttons for closures at the neck and wrist. I generally make loops with several lengths of thread rather than something like buttonhole twist, since I never have anything like that around: Thread a needle with about four lengths of thread. Make them perhaps 18" (45.7 cm) long when doubled. Knot, insert the needle from wrong side to right side of the garment, loop around a short pencil or something approximately the button diameter, then pull back through

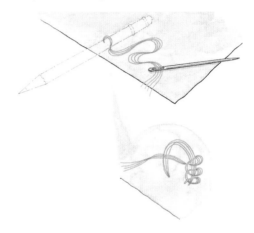

the fabric. Move the needle perhaps 1/8" (3 mm) to one side, and bring it to the right side again, pulling it all the way through. Pass the needle through the thread loop, and then between the thread loop and the length of thread coming out of the fabric. Gently pull the wrapped thread taut while positioning it close to the fabric on the loop. Repeat. When the loop is entirely covered, insert the needle to the wrong side again and knot the thread.

*—Debbie Lancaster*

## CLASSY SNAP CLOSURES

**936** Snaps are not often called for in pattern instructions, and not used too often in ready-to-wear anymore, but there is nothing that will ensure the exact placement of an edge or closure like a snap. Covering a snap makes it much less obvious—almost invisible; I find covered snaps are a lovely detail that is very simple to add to a garment. They make a very good hidden closure behind buttons that are too large for practical use. Lining fabric is often used as a cover, and a thin fabric is best. (If you suspect your fabric may be too thick, put a piece of it between the snap halves and try to snap them. If they won't stay shut reliably, try a thinner fabric.) Here's how I make them:

- Cut a circle of the covering fabric you want to use. Poke the stud of the snap through the center of the circle. You may have to push aside the threads with an awl or large needle, or the stud may just go through on its own.
- Wrap the fabric to the back of the snap and sew a few stitches by hand to hold it in place. Then position the snap on the

wrong side of the overlap portion of your garment and stitch in place. You may stitch through the snap holes and the covering fabric, or just through the fabric; I usually try to sew through the holes.
- Cover the socket half of the snap the same way; you do not have to make a hole in this fabric circle. Position and sew this half to the underlap portion of your garment, opposite the stud half.

*—Liana*

**937** When I wish to keep two edges abutted rather than overlapped, I find it very handy to employ a hinged snap closure—for which one half is attached through one hole only so it can swing across the opening to lap onto the other half. I recently used two of these to fasten a close-fitting standing collar on a knit top. Here's how to do it:

- Sew the socket half of the snap right at the edge of one side of your opening (on the inside of the garment). You want to get as close as you can to the edge without having the snap extend and show from the outside.

- Sew the stud half of the snap through one hole only to the other side of the opening (also on the inside of the garment), positioning it so it extends past the edge and lines up with the socket half as shown. Stitch securely since you're only going to have one point of attachment on this half and the thread forms a hinge by which the stud half can rotate onto the socket half. (It's possible to fasten the snap and still be able to take a first stitch through the stud half only, allowing you to achieve perfect placement.)

*—Liana*

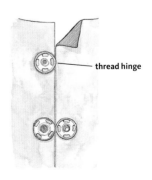

thread hinge

**938** **Turn them over.** I like to sew summer shirts for my husband, but he's very particular about buttons. Sometimes the only ones I can find to match the fabric are too shiny or not quite the right color. I've found that turning buttons over to their wrong side (which is generally the flattest side) and sanding with a bit of fine sandpaper or emery board makes them perfect for DH's shirts. Even the color changes slightly once the shine is gone. The buttons for the shirt I'm working on now aren't shiny, but I will turn them over so their flat side faces up because they just look better that way. So consider that when it comes to buttons, there is no right or wrong side, just the side that looks best.

—*dreamsofthetime*

**939** **Dye them.** I recently needed some rather odd colored teal buttons for a shirt, and could not find the appropriate shade at the fabric store. I remembered I had a zillion buttons at home so I bought some teal Rit dye and decided to experiment. Directions:

- Select different types of buttons to dye. I chose white fabric covered buttons and plastic buttons: gray and two different types of tortoiseshell/mottled brown. (I needed a grayish teal so I chose to dye brown and gray plastic.)
- Put 1 to 2 tablespoons (15 to 30 mL) of dye powder in a small food storage bag. Add about 1 cup (250 mL) of hot water and swish until the dye is dissolved.
- Add the buttons and swish them around for about 5 minutes, or until they look a bit darker than you want. Rinse the buttons in a strainer in the sink until the water runs clear. If they are not dark enough you can put them back in the dye. Wash and dry the buttons in a mesh laundry bag. One of the button types (one of the mottled brown), turned out to be a perfect match for my fabric. The other plastic types turned out well also and I will save them for another time when I need teal buttons. The white fabric covered buttons washed out when in the washing machine—I think the fabric must be polyester.

—*Mandolin82*

**940** **Nail-polish them.** Can't find the button or buttons to go with what you are sewing? Find the size you need and paint with nail polish to match or contrast. Let dry overnight for a really good bond. If the buttons are the sculptured kind, highlight the different areas with different colors of nail polish. Nail polish is relatively inexpensive and comes in every color imaginable. I've used this on many buttons over the years and they never chip or fade.

—*NanciPink*

**941** **Sponge-paint them.** I was in a pickle because I couldn't find the perfect-colored button to match my blue topstitching on a suit I just made. So I bought cheap, plain white buttons and acrylic paint the same color blue as the topstitching thread. I gave the buttons three coats of paint, which turned out to be too intense for my cream-colored fabric, so I sponge-painted it with a creamy shade the same color as the fabric and the buttons have a marbled look now. If you plan to wash and dry buttons treated this way, it's probably smart to test wash them first (pop in a lingerie bag), but I used mine on something I don't expect to wear often, maybe two or at most three times a year, so it's not like it will get a lot of time in the washer and dryer.

—*ryan's mom*

**CLEVER BUTTON IDEAS**

**942** Need stunning buttons for a jacket? How about jeweled dress clips for a 30s style gown? Go shopping for a jeweled stretch bracelet—the kind with small ornaments strung on elastic. I got a fab example quite inexpensively; cut apart, it yielded seven large square ornaments and eight smaller ovals. I used three pieces for the "clasp" of a halter neck, and the others for a decoration at center back as well as buttons on the sleeves of a 30s evening gown. These bracelets offer a huge variety in texture and color and there are plenty of holes to sew through!

- For buttons: You'll have to create either a thread shank, or use the loop of a metal hook and eye and sew that to the filigree shape. I recommend that you make two sets of corresponding buttonholes in your garment front (on both the overlap and underlap), and sew the buttons onto a piece of ribbon; then button through both layers. I would NOT recommend washing or dry cleaning these!
- For ornaments: Sew on using only a few stitches so you can detach for cleaning, or sew onto the hook half of a piece of Velcro and sew the soft half onto your garment (or sew onto snaps).

—*KMangum*

**943** An easy and versatile way to create detachable buttons is to sew a small button to the back of the fashion button with a short thread link between them—like a cuff link. Then make two buttonholes, one in the appropriate place on the overlapping layer of the garment and one directly opposite it on the underlap (where the button would normally be sewn on). Button the smaller button through both layers, from overlap to underlap. This method has a couple of advantages:

- Because both buttonholes are the size of the small button you can accommodate large or irregular size buttons without making an unsightly buttonhole.
- Because the buttons are detachable you can change the look of a garment by changing one set of buttons for another.

—*Helen near Sydney*

**944** If you've ever admired the sleek look of a top European designer jacket with invisible magnetic closures and wanted to get that look, you have a couple of options. You can order high energy magnetic closures online or you can create your own sleek magnetic closures at considerably less expense. I use ProMAG's high energy Magnetic Neo-Buttons. Note that these are not the bulky magnetic purse closures used for handbags. They're flat, ½" (1.3 cm) diameter, and slightly thinner than a nickel and available from many crafts supply sources. Make sure you choose the type specifically marked "high energy" because weaker magnets will not be strong enough to keep your jacket closed. To create a magnetic closure, simply take a magnetic disc and sew a small pocket to contain it. Then sew the pocket to the wrong side of your jacket facing. The stitches will be visible from the right side of the facing, but the magnet will not be detectable from the right side of the jacket. You can cover the spot with a regular button if you wish.

—*nancy2001*

# Cool finishing touches

*Hanging loops, lingerie guards, belt loops, and the like: Here are hints for discreet little extras like that make a garment look better and last longer.*

## BELT LOOPS TO SHOW OFF OR NOT

**945** Here's a way to make belt loops that are completely sewn by machine with all raw edges enclosed neatly and attached without any visible bar tacks.

- First, to make the loop strip, fold under both edges of the strip, and then fold lengthwise almost in half, so one folded edge extends slightly beyond the other. Topstitch to secure the layers; then topstitch at the same distance from the other edge as shown.

- To attach the top end of the loop, place on the garment finished side up, with the cut end at the top mark and the loop hanging down. Sew close to the top end; then fold the strip up and sew again, enclosing the top end. Now fold the strip down; it should look like the top of the illustrated loop.

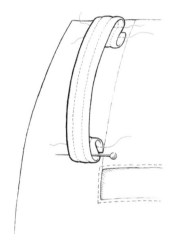

- To complete the loop, figure out how much room you need to accommodate the belt plus a little extra, and, with the cut end extending down, sew across the strip. Then cut off the excess close to the stitching. Now push the loop down, so it covers the cut end, and from the inside, stitch across it again, enclosing the end as shown.

—*Kay Y*

**946** I came up with the idea to make retractable belt loops because I couldn't decide if I liked a jacket belted or not. It's not fancy, but it works and the loops are hidden when not in use. You need embroidery thread in a color that blends with the garment fabric and a needle with eye large enough to fit two strands of the thread.

- Cut four strands of embroidery thread (two per belt loop). The length will depend on the thickness of the belt, but long enough to wrap loosely around the belt and also tie a knot in one end. Thread the needle with two strands.
- Find the waistline of the jacket at side seam and pass the needle from inside to outside and back inside—make the stitch small so it is less noticeable when retracted. Tie the four ends in a knot inside the jacket, leaving a large loop on the outside of the jacket (support with a dowel/glass/whatever that is the same diameter as the belt if it's easier). Repeat on the other side seam.
- If you don't want to wear the belt, pull the knot until the threads are flat against the jacket fabric on the outside. When you do want the belt, use a small crochet hook to pull both threads together so the loop hangs to the outside.

—*celeste*

## THIS & THAT FOR A BETTER FINISH

**947** Most of my skirts have inverted pleats at the back and in order to prevent the top of the pleat from coming undone I reinforce it with an arrowhead tack sewn by hand. This used to be standard practice many years ago (you can find directions in classic sewing books, embroidery books, and online) and somehow is not common anymore. But there is always a fair amount of strain at this point and the tack certainly does help. I use embroidery cotton.

—*regine*

**Deepika adds:** You can do this by machine too, either with a decorative stitch or an embroidery machine. It gives a great retro detail.

**948** I still use shoulder pads due to very sloping shoulders, but what I need are smaller than the Joan Crawford collection I've accumulated over the years. Shoulder pads are too expensive to buy in the quantity that I use. I found that I can alter many old pads for new garments by determining where the pads need to be trimmed to fit (around the curved edge, not the armscye edge), running a straight stitch along the trim line, and then zigzagging along the straight stitching before cutting off the excess shoulder pad. If the pads are just too big and thick to cut down, I stuff them in the toes of shoes—they do a good job of keeping the toes from caving in.

—*Joni2*

**949** Here's an easy tip to help keep those bra straps hidden when wearing tanks or sleeveless garments. Cut a strip of ¼" (6 mm)-wide ribbon (twill tape would do as well) long enough to span the shoulder seam. Secure one end at the armhole end of the shoulder seam; you can easily do this when you finish the edge, whether it's folded over and sewn or bias trimmed. (For a facing, fold under the ribbon end and hand-tack.) Fold under the other end and sew on one half of a snap. Then secure the other half of the snap to the shoulder seam allowances near the neckline. That should keep those straps in place. It also helps keep a wide neckline from slipping off your shoulders. Measure first of course, you don't want to make the ribbon too short.

—*Dale C*

**950** When I make lingerie guards to keep bra straps from showing, I put them ⅛" (3 mm) away from the neck edge—there's no chance the straps will peek out and it looks professional. I use teeny tiny snaps to close the ribbon loops even though they are a pain to sew on.

—*Deepika*

## HANG WITHOUT STRESS

**951** Hanger loops are essential to carry the weight and take the stress off the seams of garments made of delicate fabrics such as chiffon, all stretch knits, and also on strapless dresses or those with narrow straps. Here's the way I make them:
- For each, cut a ¼" (6 mm)-wide satin ribbon or twill tape strip about twice the armhole depth and attach one end at the junction of the underarm/sleeve/side seam. A few hand stitches taken with a needle that is double threaded is sufficient.

- To determine the length of the loops, put the dress on a hanger. Pass each ribbon up from the underarm seam around the hanger and back to the attachment point. Make it taut enough to carry all the weight of the dress, but long enough that the bodice shoulders will just rest on the hanger. Pin and then sew in place.

—*Marji*

**952** When I make hanger loops, I cut the ribbon ends on the bias to prevent fraying. Then I sew the loops so the ribbon ends point up—that encourages the loops to stay out of sight when you wear the dress. Some people attach hanger loops at the waist instead of the armhole.

—*Deepika*

# Label it!

*Labels serve several functions: they can identify the garment maker or wearer, record pattern info, or differentiate the back of your pants from the front. Whether you want them to add a creative flourish or be purely functional, you'll find clever ideas here.*

## LABELS ADD INFO AND PANACHE

**953** When I started sewing a lot of gifts for other people, I wanted to figure out a way to create labels. I could make handwritten labels, but my preference is to print them from a computer. That way the writing is legible, and I can include graphics and photographs. I prepare fabric with Bubble Jet Set, which is a chemical fluid that makes ink-jet printed images washable. You can buy it online and it comes with instructions. Basically, you soak your fabric in it, rinse, and let dry. Then you iron the fabric onto freezer paper so that it is stiff enough to go through your printer. One of the things I like about this method is that it doesn't change the hand of the fabric. Lots of people use this technique to print larger areas too, for example, for quiltmaking. The only serious limit is the size of the paper that your printer can take.

—*e_e_thomas*

**954** Recycling the labels from your old clothes (and maybe even your husband's and kids' clothes) can really jazz up your sewing projects. There are some great labels out there and not just on clothes—I even took the one off my new ironing board cover—so I suggest starting a collection. You can tuck them safely inside your garments where you'll enjoy them every time you put them on or go for a more avante garde look and sew them to the outside, at the hemline, into a seam. or even flight-attendant style on the lapel.

—*Helen near Sydney*

**955** I like putting my own label on the garments I make. I designed the label I wanted on my computer in a normal address label template. You can use any template size you want—mine is 2" × 1" (5.1 × 2.5 cm) and about 30 fit on a page. I print in REVERSE on iron-on transfer paper. (I usually do a test first on plain paper to make sure the size, font, etc., is correct and to be sure I've got the text reversed so it will read correctly once transferred; iron on paper is not cheap!) I used to use cotton fabric for the labels but they looked too homemade. Instead I now use 2" (5.1 cm)-wide white ribbon. Here's what I do:

- Cut a piece of ribbon about 2½" (6.4 cm) long. Fold it in half crosswise and press well.
- Cut out a label and iron it on with the bottom edge of the label at the fold of the ribbon.
- It's easy to customize the labels before I print them out: I make different tags for each of my children simply by typing the correct name into my basic graphic design.

—*ConnieBJ*

**Maria Hatfield says:** I like to make a simple label that identifies which pattern I've used to make each garment. I find it handy to have these marked tags when I'm trying to decide if I want to make a pattern again. Here are some examples of what I do:

**956** I just write the pattern name, number, and size on a piece of muslin with a permanent fabric marker and then sew it inside the garment.

**957** I sewed my label into the back seam below the waist on a pair of pull-on pants so I know which is the back and which the front.

**958** On shirts I put the label down towards the bottom of the side seam, only because I don't like tags at the back of my neck.

**959** My mom suggested I also sew a couple of buttons onto the tag in case I need them later.

 *Plain and fancy ways to ID the back*

*Follow the lead of some PatternReview.com members to end confusion as to which is back, which front, on pull-on and pullover garments.*

**960** **LiZ says:** When making clothes for children (especially elastic waist pants) I sew a marker at the center back waist so the child is easily able to work out which way to put the garment on and does not have to ask Mum. I just use a piece of cotton twill tape.

**961** **mamamaia suggests:** This is how I differentiate the front and back of pull-on pants for my children. I just sew a button at the center front—this keeps the elastic from turning too. I have so many single, plain, or unused buttons from two generations back; this is a good way to use them and the kids know the button always marks the front on any pants.

**962** **OP Gal has a delicate option:** I recently made a silk camisole to be worn as lingerie. Since it was very plain, it was difficult to tell the front from the back. I didn't want to insert a label as it would be scratchy. Instead I embroidered a couple of lazy daisy stitches on the binding at the center back. Now I can tell at a glance which is the back and which is the front.

# Rolled Hem Magic with a Serger

Shannon Gifford approaches sewing as a "sensible" undertaking and knows that once you understand the process, there's no real mystery to it. She loves seeing the light bulb go on in her student's heads when they realize that, yes, they can sew what they want, any time they want. Shannon believes that once you learn the specific skills needed to sew, you can sew anything. For example, she loves the rolled hem on her serger, and decided to show us how to master this stitch and use it to its max. Enjoy this class, and visit her Web site, sensiblesewing.com, to see her online offerings and newsletter.

*"When I bought my first serger so many years ago, the first feature I wanted to learn was the rolled hem. I used that stitch on every home décor item I made, but did not consider it for garments until much, much later! But the rolled hem is a model of versatility; it can clean-finish an edge, provide a decorative trim, and is strong enough to hold layers of light- or medium-weight fabric together. This jacket is proof that using a rolled hem can streamline garment construction while providing a beautiful, decorative accent—all seams, even the darts, were stitched with the fabric wrong sides together."*

# Plan ahead before starting

*Of course, "plan ahead" is standard advice, but it's especially important if you're about to construct a garment with a rolled hem stitch on your serger. The hem-seams will be visible, so you'll want to test your serger setup carefully and choose thread that complements your fabric. Select a garment pattern with simple lines that can be assembled with the serger—no deep curves or inside corners.*

## SET UP THE ROLLED HEM

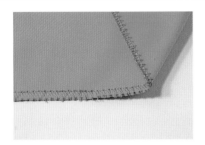  

1. Begin with a basic, 3-thread overlock stitch on your machine. Loosen the upper looper thread, and tighten the lower looper thread. The looser upper looper thread will wrap around the edge of the fabric, and be held in place with the tighter lower looper thread. The resulting stitch forces the fabric to curl, or roll, slightly toward the underside of the work.

2. The second adjustment is to the stitch length. A beautiful rolled hem should provide a clean coverage of thread, with no fabric visible between the stitches. I call the top of the work the "public" side, which you want to be the most prominent on your garment.

3. Using the rolled hem as a construction stitch requires one final setting adjustment. Widen the stitch to your preferred width for the fabric you have chosen. Test a double layer of fabric to be certain the width is correct for your fabric; the stitch should hold the fabric firmly together. The thinner your fabric, the narrower your stitch can be. Conversely, a thicker fabric will require a wider stitch.

## PLAN YOUR GARMENT

Choose a pattern with clean, simple lines. Deep, dramatic curves are best avoided for this technique. Eliminate any facings and hem allowances, as we will be using one layer of fabric throughout. For your first project, choose a one-piece sleeve, so it can be set in "flat."

Thread choices for serger rolled hems are wide and varied. For your lower looper and needle threads, a standard serger thread is fine. The upper looper thread will be the most visible thread in the mix; you may choose a matching color or a contrast, based on the effect you wish to achieve. Woolly Nylon is often recommended for good thread coverage, but do not overlook other options. If your serger can handle it, you might enjoy experimenting with narrow yarns or ultra-thin ribbons.

If you wish the serging to be on the outside of your garment, you'll sew with the pieces wrong sides together. Remember the rolled hem doesn't look the same on both sides, so to ensure that the seams appear

*My current favorite threads for rolled hems are rayon embroidery threads, and I love the effect of a variegated colorway!*

their best, it will be necessary to think about the orientation of each seam in the machine before you sew. For instance, for a side seam, sew with the front garment piece on top. In that manner, the public side of the rolled hem will be visible from the front of the garment. (For invisible stitching, place the pieces right sides together as usual.)

### The serger rolled hem

Serger rolled hem stitches are a close relative to the 3-thread balanced overlock stitch that is standard on every home serger. The primary difference between the standard overlock and the rolled hem is twofold: the tension and the stitch length. Your machine manual may provide some guidance regarding the best settings for a basic rolled hem. Some machines require a specific rolled hem attachment or foot. Other machines can be set up for the rolled hem with a unique threading sequence. It may be necessary to disengage the knife, as well. Check your manual as you set up your serger for rolled hem construction as explained above.

# Mastering the construction

*The stitching process is straightforward; place the fabric layers together, and run the fabric through the serger. Stitch slowly, holding the fabric so it feeds evenly through the machine. After stitching each seam, press it so that the public side of the rolled hem is most visible.*

## DARTS

1. Stitch darts first. I like to machine baste the darts together first, and trim the seam to an even ¼" (6 mm) width. Stitch a chain of thread a few inches long before inserting the fabric under the presser foot; then stitch the dart exactly on the basted line.

2. Stitch off the end of the dart tip to leave another chain of thread.

3. Insert the thread chain in the eye of a needle, and thread the tail through the last few stitches of the dart. Then trim off the excess, and place a drop of seam sealant on the point of the dart.

## BASIC SEAMS

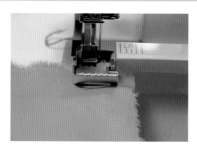

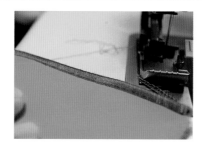

1. Straight seams are the easiest to sew on a serger. Position your fabric pieces wrong sides together, and line up the raw edge with the stitch width indicator on your machine. This will be a series of lines to the right of your needles. Be sure you know which line corresponds to your chosen seam allowance! Stitch the seam, holding the fabric taut and smooth as you sew.

2. For a princess seam, first machine baste the pieces together to ensure they are properly eased. Press the seam to eliminate any puckers, and then serge the rolled hem over the basting stitches. Position your work so the center front section is on top, so the public side of the rolled hem will be visible. Be sure to press the seam in the direction it will eventually lie.

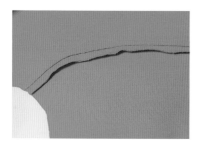

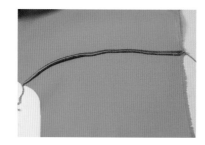

3. After stitching each seam, rub the last inch of the seam with seam sealant and allow it to dry for a few minutes. Then trim the serger threads close to the fabric edge. This will allow you to cross one seam with another, cutting off the seam allowance with the serger, without damaging the previous work.

## SLEEVES

1. Machine-baste the sleeve cap to the armscye, and press the basted seam to remove any wrinkles. Then serge the rolled hem over the basting stitches, placing the armscye on top and the sleeve on the bottom. Press the rolled hem seam toward the sleeve. Finish the bottom hem of the sleeve with a line of rolled hem stitching, and seal the ends.

2. Stitch the side seam and underarm seam in one pass of the serger; seal the threads at the hem edge of the garment body, but use a needle to work the sleeve hem threads into the end of the sleeve seam.

## FINISH THE PERIMETER

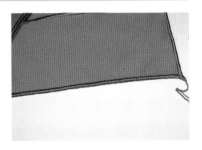

1. After the pieces of the garment are securely attached to one another, it's time to apply the final row of rolled hem around the edges. If you have a curved neckline or hem edge, make a single row of standard machine stitching exactly on the seamline to act as stay stitching. This will prevent the fabric from stretching as you roll the edges with your serger.

2. Serge a rolled hem along the neckline edge first, stitching from center front to center front. Seal the ends of the stitching with seam sealant, and trim the threads.

3. Begin each center front hem by first stitching a chain of thread, just as you did for the darts. Serge a rolled hem along the entire center front edge, and stitch a chain of thread at the end of the seam. Seal the two ends of the seam, and trim the threads.

4. Last serge a rolled hem the bottom of the garment, using a chain of thread at the beginning and the end, just as you did for the centers front.

# CHAPTER NINE

# Embellishments

"I started sewing for economical reasons and over time, it became a passion. Now I sew for pleasure and I enjoy it so much. Most of all I find it to be very relaxing; it makes me forget the rest of the world. And I love to have clothes that are original and elegant—I enjoy being different!"

—Mahler

# Trim it!

*We all love gorgeous fabric, but why stop there when there are ribbons, feathers, beads, and brads that beckon? They all promise pretty, practical, or sophisticated finishing touches that will make a garment truly one-of-a-kind.*

## COOL TRIM IDEAS

**963** Here's an easy way to make a fabric rose quickly and neatly.

- First cut a bias strip twice as wide as the depth you want the 'petals' to be, and about five or six times as long as the width (make some test roses to get the length right). Taper each end to a point, cutting from both edges to the middle.
- Fold the strip in half right side out. Serge the loose edges together, leaving a long thread chain tail when you finish.
- Thread the thread tail into a large-eye, blunt embroidery needle and run it through the stitches all the way back to the other end of the strip. Gently pull the thread tail through to gather the strip into a loose ruffle (the rose will be a better shape if the gathers are not tight). Tie the thread tail you threaded through to the one at the beginning and trim them off.
- Take a needle threaded with matching thread and attach it to one end of the stitching; this becomes the center of the rose. Now start rolling the strip up, stitching each round to the center as you go. When you finish, you have a rose that is already neatened at the bottom.

—*gabrielle stanley*

**964** I have seen mentioned on a couple of forums the possibility of making your own feet for handbags, but no one knew quite how. I decided to take up the challenge: I went to the scrapbooking aisle in a crafts store and checked out the brads. I found some that were approximately ½" (1.3 cm) across with very slender tiny prongs—ideal! They came in black, brass, silver, and copper colors, in packs of five. I bought a pack, went home, and after measuring, poked a hole for each foot in the bag bottom with a seam ripper, just a tiny hole. I inserted the legs of the brad, spread them apart, pushed down on them hard and voilà, had my bag feet. (This is all before attaching the lining.) I tapped my bag on the counter and the legs hit before the cloth so it worked. Back to the scrapbooking aisle!

—*solosmocker*

**965** I've been making some summer dresses out of very inexpensive fabric. I made some beads to coordinate by fusing a scrap to tissue paper and then cutting long, skinny triangles (like making paper beads). Starting at the wide end, I rolled each over a toothpick and glued the point to the roll. After the glue dried I used two coats of varnish to finish. I strung these on a cord with silver beads between. I work part-time as a bartender and customers commented that my necklace went so well with my dress—they were amazed when I said I made it and the dress!!

—*Victoria Sturdevant*

**CharityAK says:** It is a cardinal rule of sewing that the selvages are to be cut away and never included in a seam allowance. However, all rules are meant to be broken at times and this is one of them. While most selvages are ugly, every once in awhile a fabric will have an interesting selvage that could be incorporated into the design and become an important fashion element. So next time you're doing your layouts, take a look at those selvages and ask yourself: what if? Here are some examples:

**966** Such was the case of on a child's denim skirt I recently made, where the tan fringe selvage was so cool I decided to use it as is at the lower edge, instead of making a hem.

**967** I have seen tweeds with interesting selvages and these would look great on sleeve edges, hemlines, with reversed facings, on collars, on exposed lapped seams at yokes, on pocket flaps, etc.

**968** I have also seen some intriguing ready-to-wear jackets where the selvage was used creatively: on one as ties for a front closure and on the other as a drawstring in a waist casing. Both were deconstructed, urban-flavored designs and the concept totally worked.

**969** When sewing my wedding dress I came up with a good way to affix trim over a seam. My dress had 12 panels with each vertical seam highlighted with black satin bias. I tried at first to pin the bias in place and sew it, but after sewing the first vertical seam and trying to sew the second, I saw there were a lot of drag-lines (the bias was pulling to the right) and channeling. It was awful! Since then, every time I apply trim, ribbon and especially satin bias, I affix the respective trim with Steam A Seam before stitching. This keeps it nicely in place and also helps me get nice topstitching.

—*LauraLo*

**970** I recently trimmed the under bust seam on a knit top with a piece of organza ribbon that I had embellished with one of my machine's decorative stitches. Now, there was a problem doing this because the top does stretch (quite a lot) and the ribbon not at all. So how did I do it? First, I decided to put the ribbon only on the front of the top. I guess I could have put it on the entire circumference, but decided that I would like it better to still have all the stretch across the back. That way, if I misjudged and made the ribbon too tight I would still have plenty of stretch for pulling the top over my head. Then I worked as follows:

• I measured my under-bust line (since I wanted the ribbon ends to go into the side seams of my top, I wore a fitted T-shirt so I could measure between its side seams) and then cut the ribbon to the correct length plus seam allowances.

• I assembled the bodice front and then folded both the under-bust seamline and the ribbon into quarters, pinning together at the quarter points. You'll get a lot of ripples in the ribbon at this stage, but don't worry, it's normal.

• You can pin the ribbon at closer intervals to the bodice, but as I had backed the ribbon with Steam A Seam before embellishing it, I was able to fuse it to the bodice seamline while stretching the knit to fit the ribbon. I then sewed the ribbon onto the top, using a zigzag stitch 1 mm wide and 2.5 mm long.

—*LauraLo*

## Steps to success with feather fringe

**MagpieJan** *says Dancing in a feather dress is a joy. They may be a little over-the-top, but there's something very pretty and feminine about them too! So I'd like to share some of the things I learned while sewing many layers of ostrich feather fringe to a silk dress.*

**971** Feather fringe is sold in different fullnesses, depending on how many layers of feathers are attached. "1-ply" is a single layer, "2-ply" is two, and so on.

**972** Most often the fringe is attached to a round cord or string. Occasionally the feathers are attached to bias tape or ribbon, which is easier to work with, but is less common and the colors are limited. I was unsuccessful in figuring out how to attach the fringe to a bias tape myself. It just didn't look even. And if I tried to cut the cord off, the feathers would invariably slip out and fall out of the stitching.

**973** I sewed the fringe in layers on my dress. My 2-ply fringe was prettier than the 1-ply, and the cord was better quality too. So I made sure the 2-ply fringe was the top layer.

**974** The overcasting stitch by which I attached the cord of the 2-ply gave a finish that was nice enough to leave in full view.

**975** Feathers are very easily dyed. I did some tests with an acid dye. Acid dye baths are mixed with vinegar and salt, so they are very easy. Follow the instructions with the dye, but I found you don't need to cook them on the stove or even use super-hot water. Hot tap water worked fine on the feathers. When dyeing, always do a test to make sure you like the way the cord takes the dye too.

**976** The cord is somewhat rigid and therefore difficult to sew to long, flowing stretches of fabric. I found that if the garment was stretched too much while being sewn, the cord acts almost like you're sewing a hoop into a skirt—it introduces buckles and weird scallops.

**977** Feeding the fringe and fabric under the needle very smoothly is key: I found basting actually prevented this, so I marked placement lines and simply fed the fringe in as I sewed along the line.

**978** The feathers hang from the cord at a slight angle, from left to right and I found sewing with the "grain" worked best.

**979** Experiment with your foot and stitch so that you don't need to pull or push your trim under the needle. For my 2-ply fringe I used an embroidery foot and a long overcast stitch. For the 1-ply I used my zipper foot and a long straight stitch right next to the cord. It's best to test a fairly long section so you can get an idea what the fringe will do over long distances.

**980** Feathers are more robust than I thought. The ones I used were easily washed in water with laundry detergent, and I even needed to clean mine with grease-removers like DozAll/Gal Friday and they were fine. You want to be gentle so as not to break the shafts or pull them off the cord, so do this by hand. When drying the feathers, fluff them with a hair dryer on low and ruffle them gently with your fingers. They may look like a hopeless, sodden mess when you take them out of the water, but they will look good as new in the end.

**981** If you'd like to add an upscale touch to your zip-up jackets, trim the zipper tapes with ribbon the way active wear companies like Nike and Patagonia do. But the grosgrain ribbon they use is hard to work with, and it's difficult to get a perfect, consistent edge. A great alternative is packaged double-fold bias tape. The ¼" (6 mm) width of this inexpensive and widely available tape is the perfect size for outerwear zippers. And it's extremely easy to get foolproof results when you stitch the tape to your zipper before you sew it into your jacket: Simply wrap the bias tape snugly around the edge of the zipper tape and sew ⅛" (3 mm) from the edge of the bias. Use your finger to ensure the tape is snugly folded around the zipper tape edge as you sew.

—*nancy2001*

**Deepika adds:** To add a whimsical touch to your jacket, make your own bias trim from a funky print.

**982** It can be time consuming to sew on ribbon simply because you must stitch down both sides. A faster way to accomplish this is to use a twin needle. As long as the ribbon is a little wider than the twin needle spacing, this works great and will cut your sewing time in half.

—*newlywedws*

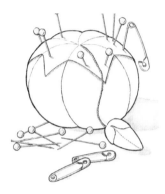

**983** I was doing a bead embellishment. After playing around with the placement and for the umpteenth time bumping into the table and watching the arranged beads roll away, I used my digital camera to snap a photo of my composition. Better to rely on the camera's memory than mine, especially working late at night!

—*Oopsy-Daisy!*

**984** I use fusible crystals for embellishment a lot and, although they usually stay through many washings, sometimes they come off right away—it depends on the fabric. Loosely woven fabrics or stress on the garment can be a problem. Now I add a tiny drop of Fray Check before fusing the crystals to the fabric and find that they stay on much better and even withstand my little grandson's occasional attempts to pick them off.

—*granny geek*

# Add embroidery or appliqué!

*Thread and fabric itself can be the materials of terrific embellishments. Here are creative ideas and practical advice for embroidery and appliqué.*

## MAKE MACHINE EMBROIDERY GO SMOOTHLY

**985** If you are hooping lightweight fabric or stabilizer, it can be difficult to get the hoop to GRIP the fabric firmly. Cut some strips of rubber grip mat (drawer liner) and insert them between the stabilizer and the top (inner) hoop—things will stay much firmer. The grip mat is inexpensive and readily available in home and hardware stores.

—*Shazza B*

**Dale C says:** I recently started using my mom's embroidery machine and here are a few things I've learned—they make embroidering a lot more fun.

**986** Line up your threads in order. That way you won't get confused as to which color comes next.

**987** Make a thread sleeve or net for each cone. Late one night, my son ripped the one thread net that the machine came with. I did NOT want to take a drive to the store, so I made a bunch using some slippery Lycra fabric. I simply cut a strip the height of the thread cone and cut and sewed it into little tubes. The sleeve should be loose so as not to create any extra tension on the thread. Having sleeves for each color is a lot better than changing the net each time you switch cones.

**988** Clip the threads between each color change, otherwise you'll have a mess.

**989** Have lots of bobbins prepared and pre-wound. Now I know why they sell bobbins pre-wound with white thread. I always thought it was rather silly, but now that I'm making lots of machine-embroidered items, I see the light.

**990** When I was about to do the decorative topstitching on the back pockets of my jeans (you know—the swirly stitching across the pockets that you do before you put the pockets on) I realized I was never going to get two pockets the same. I had carefully transferred the pattern with chalk, but the lines were just too coarse to be identical guides. (I even considered digitizing the dreaded "swirl" and stitching it with my embroidery machine—how two little scribbles can bug you!) However my solution was very simple: I traced the pocket pattern, including the swirl, twice onto tracing paper with a fine pen. Then I pinned a tracing to the right side of each pocket and topstitched the design through the paper. Just peel the paper off and you've got two identical pockets with ready-to-wear detail.

—*Agnes*

**991** I've been making my own embroidered ribbon because I like the custom finish it gives to the clothes I make. This is a very easy and quick way to make a simple basic garment quite unique. What I do:

- Take a piece of pre-folded satin bias or organza ribbon (bias is easier to "mold" with steam to match a neckline or a flared skirt).
- If using bias tape, unfold and press it, but not very hard, you still want those fold lines to show. Fuse Steam A Seam fusible web to the wrong side of the tape, then refold the tape and fuse closed. (Careful, use a Teflon sheet, you don't want fusible residue on your iron.) The Steam A Seam not only finishes the tape, but acts as a stabilizer.
- If using ribbon, fuse Steam A Seam to the wrong side; it will stabilize it for embroidery and then affix it to your garment when you're ready to sew it on.
- Experiment to sew decorative stitches along the tape or ribbon length. I've tried several that I like and used both variegated metallic thread and silk thread in the color of the ribbon. The results are very nice; I like best the variegated metallic thread version.

—*LauraLo*

## MOTIFS TO CUT, PRINT, OR PAD-AND-STITCH

**992** For a fun embellishment consider making dimensional cutouts from your garment fabric's motifs. This works best with medium-scale prints with designs that are intact and easily cut around, such as a simple flower. To make these I work as follows:

- Decide which motif would be used.
- Rough cut around it leaving about ½" (1.3 cm) margin.
- Fuse this rough cutout to paper-backed fusible webbing. Peel off the backing and then fuse the piece to buckram or very heavy interfacing.
- Fuse the buckram side to another piece of fusible webbing. Peel off the back and then fuse to fashion fabric again (needn't be a motif) to cover the back.
- Now cut out the motif along its design lines and use as an embellishment as desired.

—*CharityAK*

**993** Small photo portraits on kids' clothes are a nice ready-to-wear detail that can work as a logo. I use Photoshop Elements, Microsoft Word, an inkjet printer, and June Tailor Print and Press (a printable fabric sheet with an iron on adhesive backing) to make photo appliqués for my kids' clothes. Here's how:

- Take a picture with good details in the face and import it into a picture editing program.
- Using the cookie cutter tool (or shapes), select the face. Then change the color to grayscale. I chose a circle shape to frame their faces.
- Fiddle with the constrast slider buttons OR use filters like "stamp" or "cutout" to artistically blur the image.
- Change the colors by clicking "adjust color" (doing this produces gradations of blue, red, purple, etc).
- To conserve the printable fabric, cut a piece 3" × 5" (7.6 × 12.7 cm)—index card size.
- In a word processing program, make a 3" × 5" (7.6 × 12.7 cm) table with four cells and no borders.
- Import your image into each cell.
- Print the table onto the fabric; cut into four pieces, fuse each to a garment, and stitch around the edges. Or use all four images together as a large appliqué.

—*lisaquilts*

**994** A friend showed me this way to copy a motif from an embroidered fabric in order to use it as a quilting motif. This can be nice if you'd like to repeat the motif on a plain fabric to accent a garment made mostly of the embroidered one—I was adding a collar to a top made of embroidered linen.

- First, using the side of a pencil, I did a rubbing of the embroidered motif to transfer it to tissue paper.
- I dropped the feed dogs and with an unthreaded machine sewed the design lines of the tracing, thus punching holes in the tissue.
- Made a "pouncer" of a loosely woven knit scrap with Chalkoner refill powder, held closed with a rubber band.
- Laid my perforated pattern over the right side of the plain fabric and pounced so the powder transferred through the perforations.
- Padded the collar with a scrap of quilt batting and then stitched free-motion using monofilament thread.

—*Londa Rohlfing*

# Add texture!

*PatternReview.com members share some cool ideas for adding texture all over or to edges with tucks, subtle fabric manipulation, and embossing.*

## EMBOSSING SAVVY

**995** Embossing is a fun technique that can add texture to a garment. It's simple and can be done with items you already have on hand. Here's what you need to know in order to plan your project:

- The garment will have to be dry-cleaned. Washing and drying the garment will destroy the embossed motif.
- You will want to emboss the pieces BEFORE garment construction. You will need to think through where you wish the embellishment detail to occur. Along a hem? On a pocket? As a border down a front closure? Consider seam allowances, facings, and such when planning the placement of embossed motifs.

- The embossing works best on a napped fabric. However, I also had some wonderful results on a piece of black wool that had no nap. My best results occurred on wool, terry, textured knit, corduroy, velvet, panne velvet, and moleskin. I found that too much pile was not successful. So—you will want to do samples before embossing any of your garment pieces.
- Select your resist. A resist is a textured item that has a raised design that can be pressed into fabric. It needs to be able to resist heat. I found that rubber stamps can work if the heat is not too high or too sustained. Cookie cooling racks, trims, lace, hardware pieces, drapery hooks, even seashells could produce interesting results.

And here's how to emboss:

- Place your resist textured-side up on a hard, pressing surface. Then place your fabric napped side (right side) down over the resist.
- Spray the back of the fabric with water. It shouldn't be soaking wet, but more than a light misting.
- Press the fabric onto the resist with an iron on medium heat for about 20 seconds. The amount of heat and duration of heat will vary according to resist and fabric. Do samples to see what works. That's all there is to it!
- Optional idea: You can also paint your resist with fabric paints embossing to add color to your design.

*—CharityAK*

## TUCKS WITH PANACHE

**996** I created twisted tucks on the front of a vest made of an ethnic ikat fabric—these are closely spaced tucks that are pressed and stitched first to one side, then to the other, to created a wavy texture. My vest closed with toggle loops and bone buttons and it really turned out neat. A good way to learn this traditional technique is to use a plaid with a regular repeat. The plaid's horizontal and vertical lines make wonderful stitching guides and eliminate the need for marking:

- Fold and sew narrow tucks evenly spaced across the width of your fabric. The tucks take up a great deal of fabric, so you will need to start with a much wider piece than the pattern piece actually requires. Different sizes of tucks produce different results, as does the amount of spacing between them. You may want to experiment until you get the effect desired. I used ¼" (6 mm) tucks spaced ³/₈" (1 cm) apart.
- Press the stitched tucks in one direction—all to the right, or all to the left.
- Sew across the fabric, perpendicular to the tucks, stitching about 1" (2.5 cm) from one end of the tucks.

- Sew across the tucks again at regular intervals (try 4" to 6" [10.2 to 15.2 cm]), until you reach the other end.
- Now, in between the lines of stitching just made, press all the tucks in the opposite direction. Stitch across the

tucks again at the same interval, but this time halfway between every two previous lines of stitching. You can see the effect in the illustration.
- Cut your pattern piece from your tucked fabric.

*—CharityAK*

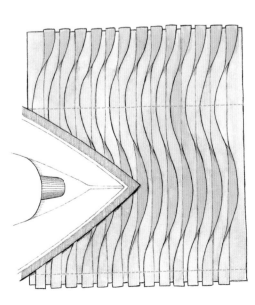

**997** Shark's teeth embellishments are rows of small adjacent fabric triangles that make a nice border treatment. They look a bit like quilter's prairie points, but they're made from a tuck in your fabric, not formed from separate pieces that must be individually sewn to your garment. They're especially effective if you make multiple tucks so you have several rows of shark's teeth, as shown below. You can experiment with the proportions, but here's the basic process for making them:

- Create a series of tucks ¾" (1.9 cm) deep and ¾" (1.9 cm) apart (so that when pressed to one side, the fold of one tuck just meets the stitching of the next tuck). How many tucks to do depends upon your design; the illustration shows three tucks. Press the tucks in the direction you want the teeth to point.

- Cut across the tucks at 1½" (3.8 cm) intervals (this is twice the depth of the tuck), cutting from the fold up to, but not past, the seamline. Offset the slashes on alternate tucks so that the cuts on one row meet the middle of the tooth space on the next.
- Fold the cut edges of each tooth under at a 45-degree angle, so they meet the seamline. Press neatly as you go.
- To secure the folds, sew across the top of the teeth right next to each tuck seam with a wide zigzag stitch. You can sew through the tuck only, or stitch the tuck down onto the garment, as you prefer.

—*CharityAK*

**998** The Threads magazine Web site has an twin-needle reference chart you can download to learn how to use a twin needle to create various texture and surface designs. Go to threadsmagazine.com and search for "twin needle reference chart."

— *els*

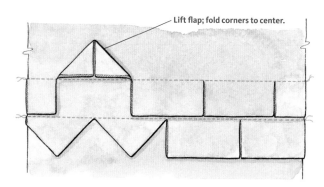

Lift flap; fold corners to center.

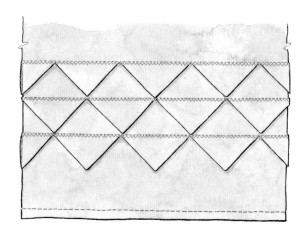

## Add a scalloped neckline trim

*Two PatternReview.com members have discovered clever ways to add a shell-like scalloped binding to a neckline or other edge. One is subtle, the other more dimensional.*

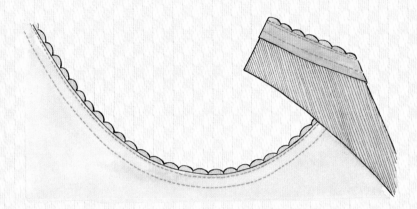

**999** **Sherril Miller adds a narrow, delicate shell.** Here is an easy to do trim to sew to the neckline of any T-shirt. You need a strip of knit fabric 1½" (3.8 cm) wide folded in half lengthwise, right side out. In your sewing machine, you need to have matching thread. Set the machine for the shell stitch, which looks something like the blind hem stitch except that is in reverse. (Instead of the needle moving to the left to make the prick stitch on the hem, the shell stitch moves to the right one stitch to make the shell.) Here's the technique:

- Stitch along the folded edge of your fabric strip, making sure that you get the prick stitch to land just off the fold. This will stretch your fabric out a bit, which is normal. (After testing the stitch, you may have to tighten your thread tension.) Then with your serger, serge the open edges together to finish the trim edge.

- Sew up one of the garment shoulders, leaving the other one unsewn. Apply the shell-edge trim to the neckline, right sides together, stretching it a bit as you sew it on. Make sure you sew just inside the straight stitch on the shell stitching. That way, those stitches won't show on the outside of your garment.

- Then fold the trim up, into the neck area, and press. With a twin needle, cover stitch, or tiny zigzag stitches, topstitch the seam allowances onto the shirt. Sew up the shoulder seam and you're done.

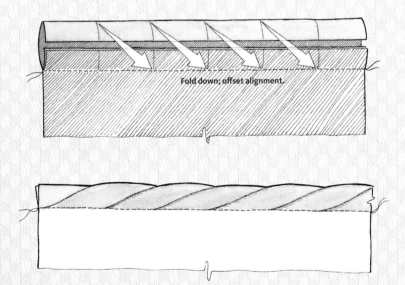

Fold down; offset alignment.

**1000** **Liana makes a twisted binding.** Here's a way to make a decorative binding that appears twisted—like a soft rope—that looks pretty at a neckline. It is very cute with a contrast binding: Make a binding strip, and mark straight across it on the wrong side every inch (or so, test to see what you like). Stitch one edge of the binding to garment, right sides together as usual. Wrap the binding over the garment edge, and instead of aligning the two ends of each marked line, shift them over by one, matching the end of the line on the loose edge of the binding with the next line on the attached edge.

# Elegant Bead Embroidery

Anna Mazur is passionate about embellishment. Ask her for an idea, or even ask what she's working on, and she'll give you a long list of options and descriptions of her many works in progress. If you're lucky enough to meet her face to face, you're in for a treat. She'll pull one wonderful item after another from her tote bag. Appliqué, beads, and elegant trims are what make sewing exciting for her. PatternReview.com members know Anna from her online chats and her enthusiastic participation in weekend get-togethers. Contact Anna at MazCouture@aol.com.

> *"I made this skirt for a special event and wanted every detail to complement the sheer overlay, which was a purchase I couldn't resist: I took one look at the embellished floral fabric and knew I had to have it. I sewed ribbons to the under layer to make the lattice background for the sheer. To give the skirt an elegant finish, I bead-embroidered the waistband with a dense lattice pattern. It's not a big area, so this detail was manageable and so worth it!"*

# Bead-embroider a motif

*Bead embroidery is easy. There are only five basic techniques, but with them you can make the simplest item special. You don't need to start a design from scratch. Instead, you can enhance a motif that's already in your fabric. There's no need to transfer a design to your fabric! In this master class, I'll show you how to use those five basic techniques to embellish a printed motif, an embroidered motif, and an appliqué.*

## Start with an Appliqué

First, yes, you have to appliqué motifs onto your background, but it doesn't take long to do it. I use a bonding material to "baste" the shapes and then permanently secure them with an open, multi-step machine-zigzag stitch. For the example shown, I simply scattered tiny beads over these motifs and sewed them on individually. For the stems, I used machine satin stitch to outline curvy shapes and then sewed shells inside the outlines. For fun, there is a bead and shell pendant. Try this technique on a pocket, collar, neckline, or hem.

*These floral appliqués (easy to apply by machine) look fancy with a scattering of beads stitched onto selected petals.*

## SEWING BEADS INDIVIDUALLY

By sewing on beads one at a time you can add subtle highlights and create interesting delicate effects and light textures. You can easily incorporate beads in a variety of shapes and sizes.

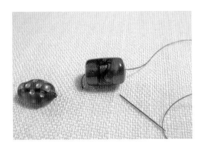

1. Pick up a bead on the needle and let it slide down the thread onto the fabric. Lay the bead on its side with the hole parallel to the surface; orient the bead to point in the desired direction. Insert the needle back through the fabric right next to the free end of the bead.

2. Pull the thread all the way through so the bead lies snug—but not so tight that the fabric puckers—and repeat the process as you wish. If you like, instead of laying the bead on its side, orient the hole straight up, slide a smaller bead onto the thread and then pass the needle back through the first bead, pulling the small bead snug against the larger one.

## Beading tips

- There are several types of beading thread, both waxed and not waxed, and which to use depends a lot on personal preference and the particular beads you're working with. Both beading needles and thread come in various sizes—you want to make sure your choice for both will pass through the hole of the bead you're using. Ask a salesperson for advice if you're unsure.

- No matter which bead embroidery technique you use, work with a single strand of thread, knotting one end. To begin, always bring the needle up from the wrong side of the fabric. To finish, knot the thread on the wrong side again and cut off the excess.

## Start with a Print

Choose a printed fabric with a clear motif that can be enhanced with different beaded treatments. I've highlighted various parts of this stylized floral print with couched strung beads and satin-stitched beads: It's beginning to sparkle; I might add more beads to some of the leaves or the red flowers. The fabric you begin with will affect the kind of garment or accessory you make, but I like this approach for a bag, belt, or jacket front or to highlight an interestingly shaped pocket, yoke, or similar detail.

*A printed motif sparkles when accented with glass bead embroidery.*

## BEADING SATIN STITCH

By securing several beads in one stitch, and arranging these beaded stitches next to one another or in radiating patterns, you can create a satin-stitch effect.

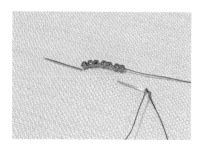

1. Pick up several beads on the needle and let them slide down the thread onto the fabric. Lay the group of beads on its side with their holes parallel to the fabric and their ends flush against each other. Orient the stitch in the desired direction.

2. Insert the needle back into the fabric right where you want the loose end of the stitch to be secured. To start the next stitch, float the thread under the fabric and bring the needle up again next to the beginning of the first stitch and half a bead width away—this creates space for the beads on the second stitch.

3. Repeat this process as many times as you like.

4. Vary the orientation of the stitches to create different effects. Groups of perpendicular stitches form a basket-weave effect. Stitches placed on an angle are good for leaves.

## BEADING A LONG STRAIGHT LINE

This process is really the same as sewing a backstitch, but you incorporate beads as you go. I've separated the beads slightly for photography, so you can see the thread, but you want their ends to be touching.

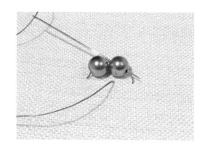

1. Pick up two beads on the needle and let them slide down the thread onto the fabric. Lay them on their sides, with the holes parallel to the fabric and their ends flush against each other. Orient the stitch in the desired direction.

2. Insert the needle back into the fabric right where you want the loose end of

the stitch to be secured. Bring it up again between the beads. Pass it through the second bead again.

3. Pick up two more beads and repeat the process. Keep the line of beads straight. When you make the next backstitch, bring the needle up between the third and fourth beads.

4. Here you can see the result when many beads are affixed end-to-end by this backstitch process.

## Start with Thread Embroidery

I like to begin with a fabric that's embroidered in a color that matches the background or is just a shade different. In this example, Jennifer Haseman of jsterndesigns.com used a purchased digital design to machine embroider the motif that I used as a base for the beads. You could also start with an embroidered linen fabric or accessory, or an embroidered ready-to-wear item—a sweater would be a lovely choice. This motif gave me a great start; satin-stitched beads follow the shape of the flirty peplum, individual beads accent the bodice and skirt, and I added little pendants for earrings.

*I took a literal approach to embellishing this thread embroidery, using the beads as they might be used on a real dress of this style.*

## BEADING A SMALL PENDANT

It's easy to create small dangling bead pendants. Use them to accent a neckline, a shaped pocket, or a decorative motif.

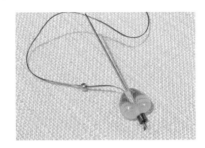 

1. Choose three beads for your pendant and arrange them in sequence; the bottom bead is called the stopper. Insert the needle through them so that the stopper is the last one you pick up. Let them slide down the thread onto the fabric.

2. Bypass the stopper and insert the needle back through the two other beads, in reverse order.

3. Insert the needle back through the fabric and pull the thread taut until the stopper is flush with the middle bead. Lay the pendant against the fabric before you secure the thread on the wrong side—you don't want it so tight it sticks straight out, it should dangle.

4. Now that you've made one pendant, put your imagination to work: You're not limited to three beads and the variations possible are nearly endless.

## COUCHING BEADS IN A CURVE

To apply beads in a curved pattern, you use two threaded needles—one for stringing the beads and one for attaching the string of beads to the fabric.

1. String as many beads as needed (or as manageable) on the first needle and let them slide down the thread onto the fabric. Temporarily secure the needle in the fabric so that the beads won't fall off while you work. Arrange the first few beads to follow the desired curve.

2. Bring the second needle up through the fabric three or four beads away from the first bead. Take a stitch over the first thread, between two beads.

3. Pull the second needle through to the wrong side so the thread is taut. Bring it out again several beads farther along and take another stitch between two beads. Continue in this way until the string of beads is secured in the desired pattern. You can add more beads to the first thread as you go.

4. Finish off by inserting both needles to the wrong side at the same point; pull the threads through and knot to secure.

5. You can make the curve as tight or loose as you like. If you make a spiral, be sure to start at the center and work out.

# Appendix

## PatternReview.com Useful URLs

*Go online to check out PatternReview.com. Here are some especially cool features (links are case sensitive):*

**PatternReview.com mobile site (only for Friends of PR members)**

http://mobile.patternreview.com

**Find your perfect sewing machine in the Sewing Machine Central**

www.patternreview.com/SewingMachine

**Deepika's Fabric Organizer Form**

www.patternreview.com/downloads/FabricOrganizer.pdf

**PR Member Sewing Spaces Photos**

www.patternreview.com/sewingspaces

**PR Member Favorite Snoop Shopping Web sites**

www.patternreview.com/snoopshopping

**PR Fitting Forum**

sewing.patternreview.com/SewingDiscussions/forum/35

### Classes, Chats & Articles

**Faux Fur Class**

www.patternreview.com/class/93

**Better Photos of Your Work**

http://sewing.patternreview.com/article/022308

**No Time to Sew**

http://sewing.patternreview.com/article/110202

**Helpful Pressing Techniques**

http://sewing.patternreview.com/article/011803

**Sarah Veblen Class: Understanding Knit Fabrics**

www.patternreview.com/class/58

**Stitch 'n' Flip Jacket Class**

www.patternreview.com/class/40

**All About Buttons and Buttonholes**

www.patternreview.com/class/92

**Knots and Frogs**

www.patternreview.com/class/95

**Embellishments and Trims Workshop**

www.patternreview.com/class/49

**Four-part Guide to Cover Stitch Hems**
Part 1 [Buying Your Coverpro ]

http://sewing.patternreview.com/SewingDiscussions/topic/41698

Part 2 [Supplies, Feet, Binders ]

http://sewing.patternreview.com/SewingDiscussions/topic/41699

Part 3 [Learning to Use Your Coverpro ]

http://sewing.patternreview.com/SewingDiscussions/topic/41700

Part 4 [Sewing Tips & Sample Projects ]

http://sewing.patternreview.com/SewingDiscussions/topic/41701

**David Coffin Chat: Construction Techniques in Men's and Women's Clothing**

www.patternreview.com/chat/dpc_part_1

# Index